Praise for **Stupid to the Last Drop**

NATIONAL BESTSELLER

WINNER OF THE NATIONAL BUSINESS BOOK AWARD

"For the . . . dozen or so Albertans who believe the energy industry and its friends in the Alberta government are neither all good nor all bad and who believe the same of ardent death-to-civilization environmentalists—you need to read this book. It could not have come out at a more opportune time. Marsden takes the worries of ordinary citizens and voices them. He pulls together all the disparate concerns into a readable whole . . . None of us can feel smug. The sensible use of non-renewable resources is all our duty, regardless of our association with the energy business." —*Calgary Herald*

"Marsden tells his story with a judicious mixture of personal stories and technical details of oil and gas extraction." —*Edmonton Journal*

"Marsden brings a fresh pair of discerning eyes to an unusual series of nation-changing events. He confidently reports how an entire province is destroying itself, and then asks why no one in Canada 'seems to care.'. . . The biggest stupidities that Marsden discovers could and probably should shock any Canadian. . . . He has walked into a provincial boom-town, populated largely by arrogant and greedy males (Hells Angels with suits), and not flinched. Good on you, partner." —*The Globe and Mail*

"An engaging and entertaining read . . . Marsden mingles amusing anecdotes with some hefty science. A worthwhile read [that] will likely generate a fair bit of discussion about the industry." —*National Post*

"This is a gripping and horrifying account of how the province of Alberta and the U.S. are ripping up tens of thousands of square kilometres of vital natural habitat to extract bitumen from the 'oil sands' in one of the most murderously polluting processes available to human beings." —*New Statesman*

Also by William Marsden

Angels of Death: Inside the Bikers' Empire of Crime
    (with Julian Sher)

The Road to Hell: How the Biker Gangs Are Conquering Canada
    (with Julian Sher)

STUPID TO THE LAST DROP

HOW ALBERTA IS BRINGING ENVIRONMENTAL ARMAGEDDON TO CANADA (AND DOESN'T SEEM TO CARE)

WILLIAM MARSDEN

VINTAGE CANADA

To Janet, Caroline and Katharine

VINTAGE CANADA EDITION, 2008

Published in Canada by Vintage Canada, a division of Random House of Canada Limited, Toronto, in 2008. Originally published in hardcover in Canada by Alfred A. Knopf Canada, a division of Random House of Canada Limited, Toronto, in 2007. Distributed by Random House of Canada Limited, Toronto.

Vintage Canada and colophon are registered trademarks of Random House of Canada Limited.

www.randomhouse.ca

Photograph on page 17 courtesy of the Natland family. Photographs on page 21 courtesy of Campbell River Museum. Photograph on page 48 courtesy of Marion King Hubbert Papers, American Heritage Center, University of Wyoming. Photographs on pages 173, 185 and 222 by Rita Leistner. All other photographs by William Marsden.

Library and Archives Canada Cataloguing in Publication

Marsden, William

Stupid to the last drop : how Alberta is bringing environmental Armageddon to Canada (and doesn't seem to care) / William Marsden.

Includes index.

ISBN 978-0-676-97914-5

1. Petroleum industry and trade—Environmental aspects—Alberta.
2. Petroleum industry and trade—Economic aspects—Alberta.
3. Alberta—Economic conditions—1991–   . I. Title.

TD195.P4M38 2008   333.8'23214097123   C2008-900329-2

Text design: Jennifer Lum

This book was produced using ancient-forest friendly papers.
Printed and bound in Canada

2 4 6 8 9 7 5 3 1

We are reasonable people all, and we have nice conversations, very profound conversations, but nothing happens. And I think that nothing happens because the overwhelming majority of us did not enjoy that preadolescent identification with nature . . . It is simply academic talk . . . What enables natural communities, I mean multi-species communities, to function is the fact that they have a shared awareness of themselves as a community, which we have not lost because it lives in us. But we have deliberately shelved it and filed it away in the interest of the human enterprise of the consumption of what we call resources and what I call nature.

—*John Livingston, naturalist*

CONTENTS

WE HAVE THE TECHNOLOGY

IN WHICH AN AMERICAN DISCOVERS HOW TO BLAST HIS WAY TO PARADISE

Manley L. Natland was sitting alone in the southern desert of Saudi Arabia when an extraordinary idea popped into his head.

It was the end of a long day, and Natland was watching the sun set. Wrapped in thought and a Bedouin turban, the American geologist contemplated the climax to nature's magic hour. "It looked like a huge orange-red fireball sinking gradually into the earth," Natland later wrote in his diary. His mind wandered, and the display of the sun's explosion of light caused his thoughts to take a sinister and disturbing turn along the following lines: sun, heat, 15 million degrees Celsius, energy, *thermonuclear weapons*. And then the idea struck.

Why not nuke Alberta?

It was an odd, disjointed thought process. Yet there was an unmistakable logic to it. Natland at that moment was sitting on the biggest oil reserves on the planet. It was 1956 and the world was in fact swimming in oil. In Saudi Arabia alone, Natland's employer, the Richfield Oil Company of California, had all the oil they could ever dream of. All you had to do was sink a pipe; nature would do the rest. Yet Natland had become obsessed with a scientific challenge central to a place more than seven thousand kilometres away, in a remote area of Canada few people had even heard of: Alberta's vast oil sands in the Athabasca basin. This was a place where you didn't even have to look for the oil—you just reached down and picked up a handful of dirt and it was right there, black and tar-like, clinging to the grains of sand. But it was a treasure chest for which nobody had the key. For half a century a small group of scientists had tried to find a method of extracting the oil at a cheap price. Now Natland joined in the hunt. His solution was by far the most creative—and the most radical.

Natland came down from the mountain and began to record his epiphany. He pulled his ever-present notebook out of his pocket and quickly set to work outlining the basics of his nuclear brainwave. He figured a 9-kiloton bomb, what he referred to as a "thermal device," would do the trick. Hiroshima's "Little Boy," dropped on Japan only eleven years earlier, had a yield equivalent to 13 kilotons of TNT; "Fat Boy," which was dropped on Nagasaki, yielded about 20 kilotons. So a 9-kiloton bomb, he thought, would be a good start. Bigger bombs could be employed later. Natland imagined bombs as big as 100 kilotons. The size would depend on the proximity of towns and cities, and the effects of the bomb's resultant seismic shocks on human structures. But for now, 9 kilotons would be good enough.

Natland drew up a plan of action. Bombs would be inserted into boreholes 1,300 feet (396 metres) deep and about 100 feet (30 metres) into what geologists call the Beaverhill Lake Formation of silty limestone, which runs to depths of 600 metres beneath the Athabasca oil sands. The bombs' massive shock energy as well as the extreme heat would crush and melt the limestone rock, creating a giant underground cavity about 230 feet (71 metres) in diameter, into which, he predicted, several million cubic feet of oil sands would collapse. Natland was confident that the intense thermal heat plus the high-pressure shock waves would literally boil the oil out of the sands and greatly reduce its viscosity, allowing it to migrate into pools.

Natland figured that each cavern could hold about two million barrels of oil, which is almost equivalent to Alberta's current daily production. With an estimated two trillion barrels deep underground and unreachable by known mining technologies, that would come to one million nuclear bombs blowing up the underbelly of Alberta, a horizontal cutout of which would ultimately resemble the world's largest honeycomb. Of course, there was always the danger that down the road the honeycomb would collapse and Alberta would cave in. One minute you're home on the range without a care in the world and the next you're dropping 600 metres into a radioactive cavity.

But Natland didn't want to think about that. In fact, the whole idea seemed so good to him that he quickly sketched out a rough pictogram of how it would work.

One possible glitch was the issue of radioactivity. Natland considered the problem but quickly dismissed it, predicting the radioactivity would be contained within the cavity, trapped inside the molten rock. Therefore, the oil itself would not be contaminated. Nor would the radioactivity escape into the atmosphere. Or so he thought. "The vitreous nature of the slag will reduce the possibility of introducing objectionable levels of radioactivity into the oil," he later wrote. He went on to describe what he thought would happen after the bomb was triggered:

> A few millionths of a second after detonation, temperatures rise exponentially to millions of degrees, vapourizing and melting the surrounding rock and the superheated gases at pressures of several million atmospheres radially expand to create a cavity. After a time ranging from a few seconds to a few minutes, the roof of the cavity formed by the nine-kiloton explosion is expected to collapse from the weight of the overburden. When this occurs several million cubic feet of oil sand will fall into the cavity where the oil will be heated sufficiently to be recovered by conventional methods.

In other words, the underground explosion would produce temperatures and pressures several million times greater than we normally experience on earth, vapourizing, melting and crushing rock to create the cavity and release the precious oil. An oil recovery well would then be drilled and pumps would bring the crude to the surface. Just like a conventional well.

Natland had no illusions about his nuclear solution; there would be a lot of convincing to do, a lot of strategic planning ahead of him. But even Natland was to be surprised at how quickly the idea caught fire. In fact, among its biggest fans would be Albertans themselves. In those heady days of nuclear enthusiasms, it seemed everybody wanted to nuke Alberta.

◆

Some might dismiss Natland's atomic revelation as that of a mad scientist. Yet his oil sands solution became a serious enterprise undertaken by otherwise sane men. The project employed the expertise of hundreds of scientists, including geologists like Natland, physicists and chemists, plus engineers, politicians and businessmen in both Canada and the United States. For anybody studying its genesis, the idea soon acquires symbolic and metaphoric proportions.

Even in the 1950s, oilmen appreciated the size of the oil sands. They take up about one-fifth of the province—148,000 square kilometres. That's bigger than New Brunswick and Prince Edward Island put together. It's the size of Florida.

To be prepared to blow up a geological structure of such magnitude simply to extract oil requires breathtaking single-mindedness. Some might even call it psychopathic. But the point is that, in a sort of manic determination to exploit its resources, Alberta showed that it was ready to sacrifice itself.

As is still the case today.

PART I

TECHNOLOGY AND
MUTUAL DESTRUCTION

CHAPTER 1

HIGHWAY TO HEAVEN

IN WHICH WE HEAD NORTH ON A THURSDAY
DESPITE WARNINGS FROM DR. O
AND DO BATTLE WITH AN OIL SANDS DUMPER

Dr. John O'Connor, the coroner for Fort McMurray, had warned me:

"Never drive Highway 63 south or north on Thursday . . . Or south or north on Sunday or Monday."

"Why's that?"

"Shift changes at the oil sands. The traffic is crazy. Your heart is in your mouth."

Then he told me about the last accident he investigated: it's winter and dark. A logging truck swerves to avoid a pickup parked on the shoulder but with one wheel still on the road, its driver fast asleep. Logs fly off the flatbed, piercing the windshield of an oncoming van. Two workers dead, one screaming for an hour before his heart finally gave out.

It's Thursday morning. I put the car in gear and head north out of Edmonton.

Some Albertans think Highway 63 is a conspiracy. They think the government has intentionally made this 400-kilometre asphalt track narrow and dangerous, with few gas stations or stopovers. It's the only road north into Fort McMurray and the oil sands. The government wants to discourage Canadians from visiting the sands, the conspiracy theorists suggest. Out of sight, out of mind. What you don't know won't hurt you. Maybe the theorists are right. Or maybe it was just a total lack of planning, as Ralph Klein said, that turned the highway to heaven into a death trap.

Highway 63 is the feed line to Alberta's golden goose. Along this conveyor belt streams an endless flow of heavy machinery weighing up to 145 tons [132 metric tons]. This includes drilling rigs, prefabricated steel sections of refineries, ore crushers, oil extractors and sulphur plants, as well as building materials, food and other essentials and non-essentials. They all move north with the grinding determination of a combustion-driven consumer society. Convoys of tankers, container trucks and flatbeds, which often take up both lanes with their towering, super-wide loads, clog the thin two-lane highway. An ode to perpetual motion.

Every Thursday it becomes a workers' run. They speed south towards Edmonton when their twelve-hour, six-day shift ends and they're free to head back for a week at home, spending their money in shopping malls. Too many little white roadside crosses with fresh or plastic flowers mark the spot where the unlucky few didn't make it, where their boom-time rhythm of work and sleep and fast money abruptly ended. Roadside real estate comes at a heavy price up here.

Disregarding O'Connor's advice, I leave Edmonton at nine-thirty on a frosty Thursday morning in October. I'm expecting a long drive. I've been told to give it at least five hours. Highway 2 takes me past Edmonton's broadening urban sprawl, where the automobile remains king and global warming is still treated as a joke. Edmonton's huge steaming refineries can be seen on the western horizon. I pass the strip malls full of Safeways, Arby's, McDonald's and Tim Hortons and the automobile concessions with their shiny new pickup trucks all lined up ready for business.

The breakout into the country happens abruptly about twenty minutes up the highway. The urban landscape suddenly becomes a patchwork of greens and golden browns with cut hay and rolled-up bales. This is what Albertans refer to as "parkland," a rolling landscape of ranchland and aspen groves. It is tidy, precise rural countryside that acts as a transition into the more northerly boreal forest where I'm headed.

At Morinville, the highway narrows to two lanes and continues north towards Athabasca. The sky is grey but not threatening, and the rented white Toyota is humming. The radio is tuned to CBC and a reporter is interviewing American border guards in Montana who have taken to horseback patrols to stop enemy aliens and terrorists from invading the United States. It's too stupid to think about, so I randomly scan over to a country music station, because that's about all there is and Kenny Chesney's singing "She thinks my tractor's sexy." Country music sets you free. It should be a good drive up.

This section of the highway is straight and clear, and as I close in on Athabasca there's a billboard advertising a whisky store ten kilometres down the road, which is something to look forward to.

After about an hour I pull into Athabasca and the Husky store, where I fill the tank at eighty-three cents a litre, which is pretty good. I have to make sure I have enough gas to make it to Fort McMurray. I buy a giant takeaway cup of Kicking Horse black coffee, their Kickass blend. I take a sip. Disappointment. It's weak.

"There's not much kick to this Kickass," I say, trying to be funny.

The cashier, whose moon face is pursed and suspicious, refuses to play along. She just stares up at me from behind the counter with a blank, unfriendly look and I can feel her wondering: "What are you thinking?" We have one of those awkward moments between strangers when neither one really knows what's going on.

"You want another?" she finally asks.

I tell her thanks but no, grab my change, take my coffee and hustle out of there.

Across the street is Athabasca landing, where the Athabasca River begins its swing north to Fort McMurray. This is where, in 1913, a federal geologist named Sidney Ells and his crew of "breeds and Indians," as he called them, loaded up scows for his trip down-river to Fort McMurray. His mission was to bring samples of the tar sands back to Ottawa to experiment on how best to extract the oil—triggering a technology quest that still goes on today.

The Athabasca is unique in Alberta: it's the only major river that hasn't been dammed up. All of its 1,232 kilometres, from the Columbia icefields of Jasper National Park to Lake Athabasca on the northeastern corner of Alberta, is free-flowing except for the fact that five pulp mills and five oil sands projects—with about twenty more in the works—take millions of litres out of it every year. The pulp mills put it back, but the oil sands operations don't; the water is too toxic. It's the river that makes the oil sands possible. It's the oil sands that are destroying the river.

The Athabasca River is two hundred metres wide at the landing. The water is clear and the bottom rocky. A sign on the opposite bank exhorts people to keep Alberta green and warns about forest fires. A large white cross stands nearby.

Athabasca is a crossroads to the former Hudson's Bay Company forts of northern Alberta. West is the Lesser Slave Lake. East and then north is Fort McMurray. I head up Highway 63, switch the radio back to CBC, where they are talking about oil prices—a constant theme in this province—and how lucky Alberta is to have an abundance of energy resources. "A lot of people would like to be in our position," one commentator says. "Alberta has such a positive resource in terms of all the massive amounts of oil we've got in the oil sands, then all the natural gas and all this stuff, and then with other countries that are energy starved and, you know, we have a thousand years' supply of coal as well—they think we're truly blessed."

They start talking about dwindling water resources—another constant theme in Alberta—and I switch the channel to a news item about how cutting down the forests of Indonesia is putting more greenhouse gases into the air than are produced by

German industry. Then there's news of a British government study warning that global warming will cost trillions of dollars unless we act now to save the planet. I push the scanner button back to country, and Alberta's own Carolyn Dawn Johnson is begging me to take her fast or slow. Just don't leave her with a broken heart.

Two hours of driving and the highway enters the boreal forest. The birches are naked. The tamaracks have turned amber yellow. The spruce and balsam look tired and wizened, like old men searching for something to lean on. That's the way of the boreal forest, struggling in the cold and dark of winter among peat bogs, wetlands, lakes, fens and rivers, stretching from Alaska to Newfoundland, as much the earth's lungs as the Amazon forest. It's the mantle over Canada's shoulders, the last largely untouched forest area. But here in Alberta they are quickly doing something about that. Clear-cut swaths and burnt forests with an eerie mist flowing through the tall, blackened trunks break the monotony of Highway 63.

Halfway to Fort McMurray and the oncoming traffic is beginning to pick up. But I still don't find it crazy. Then I catch up to slow-moving convoys of pickup trucks with flashing lights surrounding a line of flatbeds. One is ferrying a massive new yellow dumper to be fitted onto the back of an oil sands dump truck. The trucks themselves are so big they bring them up in pieces. On the highway the dumper looks monstrous, stretching across both lanes, and that's with the flatbed hugging the shoulder. Oncoming traffic has to ride the opposite shoulder to avoid it.

After about fifteen minutes we come to a passing lane. The convoy moves to the right, but there's still not enough room to pass safely. This was probably what the coroner was talking about. One by one drivers wait for an opportunity before racing out into the oncoming lane, which is chancy because there's a lot of oncoming traffic. When my turn comes, I gun the little Toyota. With the four-cylinder engine whining at maximum rev, I rush past the convoy. That's when I see the rising roof of an approaching pickup and understand Dr. O'Connor's apprehension. The pickup swerves onto the shoulder and I'm forced to veer to the right, passing just slightly under the dumper where it overhangs the lane. And I'm hoping to God that my rental doesn't strike the dumper's underside.

I hunch down in sudden instinctive anticipation of my roof caving in. But nothing happens. The dumper's overhang is avoided and I'm okay. It's a lucky move. Close calls like this one are what those tiny white roadside crosses are made of.

Within 150 kilometres of Fort McMurray, I begin to look for signs of Pony Creek and Chard. This was where Manley Natland wanted to plant his atomic bomb. They should be to the east of me. But there's nothing. No road sign points to either place. Just dense forest. It seems Natland was right to pick this place; it was nowhere—at least for a man from Los Angeles. Chard is a railway siding named after railway employee Alfred Chard. Several Cree families lived—and still live—in the area. The mere thought of Natland and his Pony Creek experiment reminds me that I'm driving over undeveloped oil sand. In fact, the surrounding lands have already been staked out and leased. Soon this vast forest will be toast. If all goes as planned.

I've been five hours on the road, and without much warning Highway 63 suddenly morphs into a four-lane freeway that descends into the Athabasca River valley and right through the heart of Fort McMurray.

I've made it to the oil capital of the world—the new Saudi Arabia.

CHAPTER 2

MANLEY NATLAND'S FANTASY

IN WHICH WE PROBE THE ATOM, BUY A BOMB
AND TAKE A QUICK SIDE TRIP
TO BLOW UP SEYMOUR NARROWS INTO A BEAUTIFUL BOUQUET

For Manley Natland, Pony Creek was comfortably and safely nowhere—little more than an addendum to a railway siding. The creek was located 8.7 kilometres northwest of Chard, Alberta, which in turn was just 103 kilometres south of Fort McMurray and 305 kilometres north of Edmonton. Nobody except a priest, who had recently replaced his dog team with a motorized sled from Bombardier, and some Cree hunters and trappers lived anywhere near it. It was a wonder that it had a name at all.

Natland had flown up several times in 1957 in Richfield Oil Company's twin-engine Beechcraft to scout out the terrain. "The area has no surface culture," he reported back to his Richfield bosses, discounting the Native population as well as the natural environment where they lived. That could all go. "Nobody gave them any thought," Tom Wright, Richfield's northern district exploration geologist, recalls. Which is why nuking Pony Creek to get at the oil sands was considered no big deal. With no cultural structures, seismic damage would be of a "low order of magnitude" limited to "one half mile from the shot point." Since you can't destroy what isn't there, Pony Creek seemed ideal.

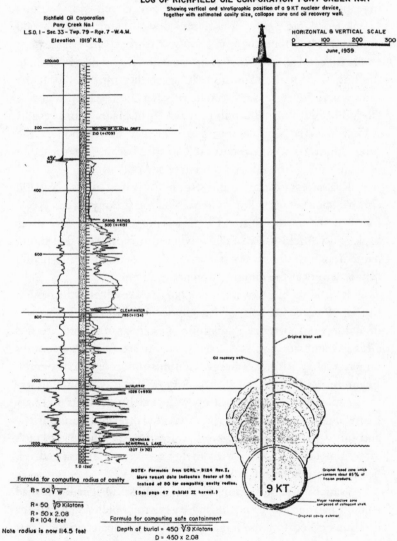

Natland's drawing for the nuke oil sands project

Richfield had purchased leases on about two million acres of land in the area with several other oil companies. Wright was sent up to Chard to drill test holes. He spent two winters sinking about fifteen holes—known as Pony Creek No. 1, Pony Creek No. 2, etc.—at various depths down to approximately 600 metres into the limestone. His job was to chart the exact extent of the oil sands in that region in order for Richfield to calculate the best site for the explosion. "One of the things I did at the time was to increase our estimate of what the reserves might be from 300 billion to 900 billion [barrels] in place," Tom recalls. "What was recoverable wasn't particularly understood at the time. None of it was recoverable really, because there hadn't been any successful efforts to recover the oil."

Reassured by the results from Tom's test wells, Natland chose a spot between Pony Creek No. 1 and Pony Creek No. 2 for his first nuclear test site. He drew a map just so the executives back at Richfield Oil could see where nowhere was. He didn't name it; he just drew a big star with "Proposed test site" typed in capital letters at the end of a thin arrowed line.

Richfield Oil gave Natland's plan to nuke Alberta the benign title of "Project Oil Sands." Luckily for Natland, the University of California Lawrence Radiation Laboratory in Livermore was already conducting tests for the peaceful use of nuclear bombs under a U.S. Atomic Energy Commission research program. Begun in 1958, it was called Project Plowshare. The thinking was to use nuclear bombs to blast open the earth for canals and harbours, change directions of rivers, create lakes, and mine surface and subsurface ore bodies as well as fossil fuels. Under Natland's direction, the oil sands, with their vast wealth of trapped oil, became a prime target.

Natland was not a physicist or chemist. Originally he had studied paleontology, specializing in microscopic, single-cell sea creatures called foraminifera. It was a field of paleontology that excited oil companies because they believed that if you could locate the fossilized animals from prehistoric times, you would find oil. First Shell Oil and then Richfield hired him to start up their

Natland in Saudi Arabia

paleontology departments. Ironically, Natland's academic research had proven that the fossil theory was not necessarily true. Yet his work with the oil companies paid off. His combined skills as a geologist and paleontologist helped Shell and Richfield Oil find hundreds of millions of barrels of oil as well as some sizable gas wells. In 1954 Richfield added Canada to his responsibilities, which was why he became attracted to the oil sands—and nuclear weapons.

He didn't know much about atomic weapons, but he was a scientist with an eager mind and so he set out to learn as much as he could about the nuclear option. "I remember he had reams of physics books on nuclear bombs and he was studying to find out about yield and heat and what would be sufficient to crack oil," his son Martin recalls. "He was a very innovative person, full of good ideas."

These were giddy times for nuclear researchers. There were no test-ban treaties. Research money flowed in from the American military. The field was wide open and largely unexplored.

In 1952 America had exploded its first thermonuclear device, code-named "Mike," blowing up a good part of the Pacific atoll Enewetak. Considered a great success, Mike taught scientists that the nuclear fusion of a hydrogen bomb was cleaner and packed a more powerful explosive yield per kilogram than the first atom bombs. Actually, scientists didn't think Fat Man and Little Boy had been all that dirty given the fact that both Nagasaki and Hiroshima were being rebuilt and people were still living there. Radiation had abated. True, Japanese citizens had died by the tens of thousands and in the following years many more would die of agonizing burns and radiation poisoning; but what mattered was that the world's only ground zeros were up and running.

Then, in 1956, the Americans conducted a fresh series of thermonuclear tests on a second-generation bomb design. Code-named Operation Redwing, it consisted of five explosions set off between June 2 and July 8 on the Pacific atolls of Enewetak and Bikini. The newly designed bombs were between 8 kilotons and 1.85 megatons. One of the observers, Dr. James McRae, president of the nuclear research lab at Sandia National Laboratory in California and a leader of Project Plowshare, was so impressed with Redwing's results that when he returned to his lab he asked Luke Vortman of the Weapons Effects Department to check out a project up in British Columbia where, he thought, a nuclear bomb could play a major role.

The targets were two massive rocks located just below the surface of Seymour Narrows, an ocean river of dangerous and deceptive water near the town of Campbell River, B.C. Locals called these twin peaks Ripple Rock. They had been a navigational nightmare for ships heading north through the Discovery Islands towards Alaska, and were blamed for sinking more than 120 ships since 1875, resulting in the deaths of at least 114 people. Some ships had literally been pulled under by the whirlpools that were known to churn the powerful sea currents near the rock. Captain George Vancouver, who first charted the narrows, had called it "one of the vilest stretches of water in the world." But for Dr. James McRae it presented an opportunity.

The Canadian government had decided to blow up Ripple Rock and had spent $3.1 million tunnelling under Seymour Narrows and up through the rock's twin peaks. The idea was to pack the tunnels with enough explosives to blast the rocks to oblivion. McRae had another idea.

A gentle, unassuming man with wire-rimmed glasses, hair greased back in the neatly compact style of the fifties, McRae thought a thermonuclear bomb would do the trick more efficiently and cheaply. At the same time, it would help scientists gather important information about radiation and seismic damage. Scientists and engineers were still not absolutely sure whether underground explosions might trigger massive tidal waves or tremors and even earthquakes that could—if you wanted to let your mind wander— topple California into the sea. That wouldn't be good. So McRae sent up his colleague Luke Vortman to convince the Canadians that nuking Ripple Rock would be a good idea.

The Canadians were interested. But, unfortunately for McRae, they had a problem: they had already contracted the ammonium nitrate explosives. McCrae was a bit disappointed, but there was at least one consolation: the amount of conventional explosives was so huge—the biggest non-nuclear explosion in the history of mankind—that it could easily simulate a nuclear blast.

So, on April 5, 1958, as American scientists watched, Canadian engineers packed the tunnels with 1,270 tons of Nitramex 2H explosives while police evacuated nearby towns. Except for a few low-hanging clouds, the day was clear, and the tidal waters were unusually still. Nature seemed braced for something terrible. Canadians across the country tuned their black and white TVs to the spectacle, dubbed an "engineering marvel." CBC reporters Bill Herbert and Ted Reynolds, secure in a wooden bunker about half a mile away, delivered the play-by-play.

> TED: You can see our camera and out on its snout that great long snorkel that sticks out there is a 25-inch lens and that will pretty well put Ripple Rock right smack in the middle of your living room when it goes up or out or sideways or whatever it's going to do in two minutes and 15 seconds from right now.

BILL: How about the countdown, Ted?

TED: Well, the countdown, Bill, will be your baby and you will start that with one minute to go until blast time and then Bill will count down starting at 30 seconds. He'll give you down 30, 25 and count it down stopping when there are five seconds remaining until the time from the blast. Then we will open our mouths, which is the approved thing to do we have been told . . . We will have our helmets on, we will have our mouths wide open and we will just stand here and watch like you're going to do."

BILL: "I don't know about you, Ted, but I'm really intense right now."

As promised, Bill began his countdown at the 30-second mark, stopping at five seconds so he could open his mouth. Rockets carrying a payload of scientific monitoring equipment shot into the air rising more than 4,000 metres. At zero hour, Dr. Victor Dolmage, of Dolmage and Mason Consulting Engineers, pushed the plunger.

A split-second pause.

And then, at 9:31:02 a.m., the earth shivered underfoot, the ocean heaved and as Bill and Ted and all the other journalists and scientists in the bunker stood with their mouths wide open in case the pressure blew out their eardrums, Ripple Rock shot 305 metres out of the sea's ruptured belly. The awesome blast, whose roar was somewhat muffled by the quiet waters of Seymour Narrows, pierced the air with 635,028 metric tons of rock and water and clouds of gas. The whole spectacle lasted about 50 seconds. And when it was all over and Bill had announced in his most dramatic vocals that "that was the end of Ripple Rock," the American nuclear scientists were left dumbstruck that such a huge explosion could be so well contained without seismic damage. Aside from a small tidal wave that quickly petered out, nature had easily absorbed the shock. Fish kill was minimal, and five orcas, a school of porpoises, two sea lions and one fur seal in

The destruction of Ripple Rock

the area before the explosion all survived. This nuclear simulation went a long way towards proving that the nuclear alternative was indeed a go. It was cheaper and more efficient, and California hadn't fallen into the sea. Clearly, there could be a big future in nuking Alberta.

Buoyed by the successes of Enewetak, Bikini and Ripple Rock, Natland proceeded full steam ahead on Project Oil

Sands. Initial tests on the effects of radiation on the oil sands looked good. Scientists irradiated six samples of oil sands for up to two weeks in a reactor in Oak Ridge, Tennessee. Seven and a half days later, the samples showed about the same amount of radiation as the face of a wristwatch. Northern Alberta might take on an unnaturally green glow, but at least, the scientists claimed, nobody would die. So that too was promising.

Natland also received one other bit of encouragement. One year before Ripple Rock lost its twin peaks, the U.S. Atomic Energy Commission and scientists from the Livermore laboratory had exploded the first underground nuclear blast, called the Rainier Shot, at a nuclear test site in Nevada, just north of Las Vegas. As nuclear physicist Edward Teller, who helped develop the atom bomb in the Manhattan Project and was among the most enthusiastic supporters of Project Plowshare, later described it, the "1.7 kiloton explosion shattered approximately 200,000 tons [181,436 metric tons] of rock and . . . it is clear that under some conditions very great holes can be punched into geological formations." He also noted that "most radiation from a nuclear blast can be contained underground." Rainier created a giant underground cavern that scientists were able to enter through the expanded 2.4-metre-diameter drill hole.

With Ripple Rock and the Rainier test yielding positive results, on May 9, 1958, Richfield Oil executives went to Washington to propose Natland's Project Oil Sands. All they needed from the U.S. government was a hydrogen bomb. They met with Willard F. Libby, commissioner of the United States Atomic Energy Commission (USAEC), and his aides as well as scientists at the Livermore nuclear research centre, including Project Plowshare founder Edward Teller. Libby and the scientists immediately liked the idea. A cheap method of releasing the oil from the sands would mean a secure energy supply for the American military and industry for centuries to come. At a hearing of the Atomic Energy Committee on March 22, 1960, Project Oil Sands got the stamp of approval from the U.S. Congress.

At the same time as the committee hearings were under way, Natland and other Richfield officials were talking secretly with the Canadians. On June 5, 1958, in Edmonton they met with H.H. Somerville, Alberta's deputy minister of mines and minerals. They quickly obtained his support. Premier E.C. Manning and his executive council also liked the idea. The prospect of turning the oil sands into a viable commercial operation was too enticing to worry about the environmental effects, such as possible radiation leakage, accidental bomb detonation or what was called "tired mountain syndrome"—the possibility that the earth could simply collapse under the strain of repeated subsurface nuclear explosions. Richfield executives also met with federal government officials who, with the participation of Albertan officials, established a technical committee to study how the whole thing could be carried out.

While Richfield was lobbying various governments, U.S. scientists had conducted a second underground test in Nevada on October 30, 1958, detonating a twenty-kiloton bomb called Blanca. What was not immediately disclosed at the time was that the radioactive containment was "unsuccessful and resulted in a surface venting of radioactive material," according to a 1989 report to the U.S. Congress entitled "The Containment of Underground Nuclear Explosions." The Canadians were not told about this.

Canada's technical committee's first meeting was fittingly held at the Nevada nuclear test site. Members were "conducted through the labyrinth of tunnels driven through the cavity areas created by Rainier (1.7 kiloton) and Blanca (20 kiloton) underground nuclear explosions," Natland later recalled.

The U.S. government agreed to supply the bomb, which would be 34 inches in diameter—small enough to fit down the 38-inch-diameter borehole. A specially designed stem plug would be rammed down the borehole to stop the bomb's blast yield and radiation from escaping. Or so everybody thought.

The United States Atomic Energy Commission initially intended to ship the bomb by railway to Chard. Then they decided it would be cheaper and faster to fly it into an airstrip that Richfield had built near Chard. The bomb would then be trucked 9.6 kilometres along a dirt track cut through the forest to the Pony Creek test site. The bomb was packed into a steel, shockproof casing. "With the possible exception of a major accident like an aircraft crash, no accidental explosion can occur during handling and transportation," Richfield claimed. Natland reassured the Canadians: "Safety measures will be taken to assure that no nuclear explosion is possible except at the bottom of the hole." The U.S. government charged Richfield Oil $350,000 for the bomb, including delivery.

By July 1959, the Canadian and Albertan governments were ready to give final approval for Project Oil Sands. It seemed that it was time to nuke Alberta.

CHAPTER 3

EARLY SIGNS OF MADNESS

IIN WHICH ONTARIO DISCOVERS OIL, TWO WARS ARE FOUGHT,
SCIENTIFIC NOTES ARE PURLOINED
AND MANKIND FINDS A CURE FOR THE OIL SANDS

AMERICAN HISTORIANS CLAIM THAT THE AGE OF OIL BEGAN IN 1859 in Titusville, Pennsylvania. They say a New York lawyer named George Bissell started it. The story goes that Bissell hired Colonel Edwin L. Drake to drill—or more appropriately dig—for oil in this backcountry region of Pennsylvania known for oil springs that bubbled crude into small pools. These historians maintain that on August 27, 1859, Drake drilled the world's first oil well and in so doing took the first step in transforming the world into a "symphony of motion."

The American claim is myth. Drake was a year too late.

The truth lies right where Charlie Fairbank and I are standing: in the oil gum beds of Oil Springs, southwestern Ontario. It was here that in the summer of 1858, before Drake had even arrived in Pennsylvania, James Miller Williams, a Hamilton carriage maker, struck oil. And it was here that Charlie's great-grandfather, John Henry Fairbank, became one of the world's first oil barons.

In the 1850s, this section of Lambton County was undeveloped bush, swampy land with the tiny village of Bear Creek at its centre. But it was already known for an unusual oil gum that slowly oozed up through the ground, hardening into an asphalt-like substance that could be boiled down and used for roads, roofs and medicines. In 1851, Charles Nelson Tripp of Woodstock, Ontario, bought land in the area and formed with his brother the first oil company in North America. The International Mining and Manufacturing Company made asphalt from the gum beds of Enniskillen Township. The venture initially looked promising. In 1855 the company secured contracts to send seven shiploads of asphalt to pave the streets of Paris, France. Transportation, however, proved an insurmountable problem and the company floundered. And that is when James Miller Williams came on the scene and found an opportunity at just the right time.

The world was running out of its standard illuminant, whale oil. Over-hunting had reduced the populations of sperm and right whales to the point of extinction. Consequently, whale oil prices had soared to the equivalent of US$1,680 a barrel (in 2007 dollars). At the same time, in 1846, a Nova Scotia geologist and inventor named Abraham Gesner developed a method of refining coal and oil into "kerosene," which gave off a clean, brilliant light. Gesner's Kerosene Gaslight Company became the world's first refinery. Kerosene not only supplied light, it also saved the whales.

James Miller Williams figured that if he could find a steady supply of oil, he could make a fortune selling kerosene to light the homes of North America and Europe. When Tripp's company failed, Williams bought up his eight hundred acres and started digging and drilling for oil. His first well came in during the summer of 1858 at a depth of only fifteen metres. Williams stored the crude in whisky barrels. By the end of the year he was selling kerosene through his own refinery. In 1860 he created the world's first integrated oil company, the Canada Oil Company.

Williams's discovery sparked the world's first oil boom. Nearby wetlands were drained. Forests of black ash were cut down to make derricks. It wasn't long before a five-square-kilometre industrial landscape of about 1,600 oil rigs sprang up around the tiny village of Black Creek, which was soon renamed

Oil Springs because property owners thought they would sell more land at higher prices if the name had the word "oil" in it.

The boom in Lambton County lasted three decades. It gave birth to towns such as Petrolia, enriched thousands of oil patch investors, helped turn Sarnia into Canada's refinery capital—at one point there were about a hundred refineries in the area—and led to the creation of dozens of oil companies, including Imperial Oil. It also produced the first major oil spill, contaminating Black Creek and shutting down shipping in Lake St. Clair. This was the foundation of Canada's oil and gas industry.

But the man who became the oil king of Ontario was not Williams but Charlie Fairbank's great-grandfather, John Henry Fairbank. J.H. Fairbank was a surveyor who arrived in Oil Springs in 1861. He bought a quarter section of land and struck oil on his first dig. By the 1870s he had become the richest oil baron in Canada, subsequently starting businesses in oil well supplies as well as hardware and banking that helped develop two other major oil fields in the region.

Oil Springs, Ontario: One of the world's first oil wells

Oil Springs and Petrolia, which is a few kilometres north on Oil Heritage Road, produced many of the early technological drilling innovations that drove the fledgling industry. This area also produced hundreds of oil drillers who would pioneer oil fields in the Middle East, South America, Asia, Australia—and western Canada.

"We are the start of the modern oil industry in this field," Charlie says, leaning against the rocker arm of an old wooden oil jack, which to this day still pumps oil.

◆

As early as 1742, Indians were boiling the Athabasca oil sands to extract fuel for heat and to seal the seams of their canoes. A Connecticut Yankee named Peter Pond explored the area in 1778 and wrote about the "springs of bitumen which flow along the ground" where the Clearwater and Athabasca rivers meet—site of the future Fort McMurray. Ten years later, when explorer Alexander Mackenzie set off on his exploration of the Mackenzie River as a possible shipping passage to the Pacific, he wrote in his diary of miles upon miles of black sands along the Athabasca with "bituminous fountains into which a pole of 20 feet long may be inserted without the least resistance." Then, at the height of the Ontario oil boom, in 1875, Ottawa sent a survey crew to chart the Athabasca oil sands. The surveyors recorded how in the hot summer sun, the oil seeped out of the seams of black bituminous sand that ran along the bluffs of the Athabasca River near the tiny trading post of Fort McMurray. Ottawa followed up the survey in the 1890s by sending drilling expeditions to the oil sands. The government reasoned that Alberta's oil sands were probably similar to the gum beds and oil springs of Lambton County and of Pennsylvania; if there was oil oozing to the surface, there had to be oil wells underneath.

But nobody understood the unique geology of the oil sands, where liquid hydrocarbons, over millions of years, had soaked into Alberta's huge sandstone basin, transforming the fluid into the tar-like substance that became the oil sands. So even though two separate expeditions uncovered traces of gas, oil wells were never found. Ottawa turned to private companies, selling them cheap oil leases and hoping they would find oil. They fared no better. (They didn't, however, come out empty-handed: they scammed a lot of investors along the way, laying the groundwork for a long history of fraud in the Canadian resource industry.)

At the time, the oil sands were part of the Northwest Territories; Alberta didn't exist. Eager to exploit the resources, settlers lobbied hard for provincial status, and in 1905 the province of Alberta was created. But much to the settlers' fury, they didn't gain control over the resources. Both Ontario and Quebec had insisted that since the people of eastern Canada had bought the land from the Hudson's Bay Company, surveyed its territory, invested in the region, lured settlers, drew up its boundaries and basically put Alberta on its feet, the province's resources should remain in Ottawa's hands so all Canadians could benefit. The oil sands were regarded as a potential jackpot, and easterners figured they deserved a payback.

Since private companies had been unable to find wells under the oil sands, Ottawa's Mining Branch turned its attention to the possibility of extracting the oil contained in the sands themselves. Sidney Ells, an eager and determined federal mining engineer and surveyor, was the first scientist to confront the problem. At Ells's insistence, his bosses sent him in 1913 on Canada's first research expedition into the Athabasca tar sands regions. This was no small venture. There were no roads or railways into the area, so the government had to finance an extensive expedition lugging tons of heavy equipment to Athabasca Landing—the spot where I bought my Kickass coffee—at the southernmost point of the Athabasca River and 128 kilometres due north of Edmonton. Ells and his crew then poled a large fifteen-metre scow downriver to Fort McMurray. His survey included sampling and pinpoint-ing the richest oil sands areas in the north. He returned upriver to Athabasca Landing in late fall with several scows loaded with ten tons of oil sands. His "crew of Breeds and Indians" harnessed to tracking lines "fought their way grimly along the shores, often through tangled overhanging brush, knee-deep mud and waist-deep water," he later wrote. "The ceaseless torture of myriads of flies from daylight till dark, the harassing and heavy work which only the strongest men could long endure made tracking one of the most brutal forms of labor." The "first important shipment of sample of bituminous sand from McMurray" took twenty-three days, journeying up the fourteen sets of rapids to Athabasca Landing. The work crippled three men while others simply deserted. But Ells returned to Ottawa with enough samples to allow him to conduct a string of promising experiments.

The oil sands pose several basic problems. The oil, which when extracted is as thick as cold molasses, is attached to each grain of sand by a thin film of water. Oil sands contain about 10 to 12 percent bitumen; the rest is clay, sand, water, heavy metals and other minerals. The problem is how to extract the bitumen, and how to do it cheaply enough to make it profitable.

Ells correctly surmised that heat was an obvious solution. Hot water and steam would leach the oil from the sands. But the First World War interrupted his research. Ells shipped off in 1917 to join the Canadian Expeditionary Force in Europe, leaving behind his research papers under the title *Notes on Certain Aspects of the Proposed Commercial Development of the Deposits of Bituminous Sands in the Province of Alberta.*

His absence opened the door to a cruel intrigue that soured relations between Alberta and Ottawa for years to come. It was a simple act of academic pilfering: while Ells was fighting in Europe, an ambitious chemist named Dr. Karl Adolph Clark purloined his work. Son of a linguist and Germanophile who taught at McMaster University, Clark worked for the federal Mines Branch in Ottawa, where he had been doing his own experiments on extracting oil from the sands Ells had brought back. Clark had tried using chemical solvents, but they didn't work. According to Clark, in 1917 he was given the task of organizing Ells's notes. The notes showing that hot water and steam were the best extractors launched Clark in a whole new direction of research and on a lifelong quest to extract oil from the sands for commercial production.

Clark's oil sands career started on a larcenous note when he declared to his bosses that Ells's work was a "hopeless mess." Clark and two other researchers then took Ells's ideas and used them as the basis for their own 5,000-word research paper. Clark sent it off to the University of Alberta, whose president, Dr. Henry Marshall Tory, was determined to make the university a technology centre for development of Alberta's resources. Impressed, Tory hired Clark and set him to work on the technical problems of extracting oil from the sands. Research money flowed his way.

Far from having produced a "hopeless mess," Ells was remarkably prolific and well organized, and his work was detailed. Before he went to war, he had published in January 1914 a 110-page report on his expedition to Fort McMurray and his work using heat to extract the oil. It was a meticulous, clearly written paper that not only described exactly where the richest veins of oil sand could be located—the exact areas where Canada's two largest oil sands companies, Syncrude and Suncor, now mine—but also detailed their chemical and molecular content as well as the various degrees of heat required to extract the oil. The report contained photographs of the oil sands region, including the Athabasca bluffs and Steepbank River sands, as well as detailed descriptions of how best to mine the oil. Ells was keen to restart his research as soon as the war ended.

When he returned to his desk in Ottawa in 1919, however, he found that his work had been usurped and the perpetrator had disappeared west to Alberta. Bitterness against Clark and Tory for belittling his work and then purloining it to launch their own careers would fester for decades. Ells went back to work for the federal government, hoping to get back into the game. But he was no longer welcome at the table.

◆

Ells's research became Clark's springboard. He quickly developed a method of using hot water to separate the oil. He built a sort of washing machine where he mixed the oil sands with hot water and steam, turning the resultant solution into a froth that drained into separation tanks, where he skimmed off the oil. By the early 1920s he was confidently claiming that hot water extraction was the answer to the oil sands challenge. But one problem remained: bitumen's density meant that even after separation it tended to sink, which made it difficult to scoop out without remixing it with water and sand.

Financed with both federal and Alberta money, over the next thirty years Clark perfected his work. He built three pilot plants and eventually succeeded in developing the technology upon which today's oil sands extraction is built.

After years of negotiations, Ottawa finally agreed to transfer mineral rights to Alberta in 1930. However, at the last minute the federal government held back a relatively small area of 5,100 square kilometres that included what Ells had assessed as the richest, most accessible part of the Athabasca oil sands. Despite the fact that the oil sands stretched over 140,000 square kilometres, Alberta's politicians were furious that Ottawa had hived off a slice for itself. But Ottawa reasoned that Alberta, which was a poor province about to get even poorer with the Great Depression and droughts of the 1930s, didn't have the resources to exploit the oil sands. And Ottawa still wanted payback from a province it had created.

So Ottawa continued to pour money into the sands and gave an American engineer, Max Ball, and his Abasands Oil Limited the right to develop a commercial oil sands plant near Fort McMurray. As the Depression deepened and the droughts worsened, Alberta was basically bankrupt. Thousands of Albertans moved east and Ontario residents sent donations to help Alberta families who remained. Research into the oil sands ground to a halt. Abasands suffered. By the beginning of the Second World War it was producing only seventeen thousand barrels of oil a year.

The war reignited Ottawa's interest in the oil sands. The demand for fuel was soaring. The federal government plowed millions into Abasands, hoping to increase its production. But, preoccupied with the unprecedented demands of fighting a total war in Europe and the Pacific, Ottawa didn't keep its eye on the ball, and the Abasands project was ultimately a failure. Alberta relished the spectacle.

By the end of the war, Alberta's oil and gas prospects looked dim. The oil fields of Turner Valley, which were discovered in the 1920s, were already declining. Canada still imported 90 percent of its oil, mostly from the United States. And there was so much surplus gas that Alberta couldn't give it away. By the middle of 1946, Imperial Oil had spent $23 million drilling 133 dry wells in a row and was ready to give up. As oil was where the money lay, the oil sands were increasingly a desperate hope for a bleeding province.

Resentment towards Ottawa for retaining control of a relatively small section of the Athabasca oil sands grew. In a letter to a friend on July 20, 1946, Clark described Alberta's paranoia over Ottawa and its "real motive force" behind supporting a postwar oil sands project as "the political one since our government pleases to regard the Ottawa government as the lowest thing on earth, incapable of doing anything right but capable of the lowest forms of political dirt such as deliberately sabotaging the chances of development of Alberta's great tar sand resource." He went on to say that the "last crack will not stick unless Alberta can produce a successful tar sand plant where Ottawa failed." Alberta decided to go ahead with its own oil sands project.

Clark enjoyed playing the Alberta card to extract money for his oil sands research. He griped that Ottawa hadn't given unqualified support to oil sands development even though at the time it simply was not economically viable given the low cost of oil and the flood of postwar conventional oil wells that constantly came on stream. Then, in January 1947, Imperial Oil finally struck oil just south of Edmonton at Leduc. Subsequent drilling that year showed the field contained about 390 million barrels of oil, more than doubling Canada's reserves. Leduc held a special significance: it proved that oil could be found deep down in the province's Devonian reef. The discovery opened whole new drilling opportunities. Alberta's producing oil wells soon jumped to 7,400 from a mere 523. When Leduc was followed ten years later by the Swan Hills oil discovery north of Edmonton, Alberta found itself with more oil than it could sell—which didn't bode well for development of the oil sands.

After the war, Ottawa finally acceded to Alberta's demands and transferred full mineral rights to the oil sands to the province. Because of a surplus of conventional oil, however, development of the sands stalled. Clark's proven technology still awaited large-scale commercial development. Help eventually came from America.

Sun Oil of Philadelphia was anxious to proceed with its Great Canadian Oil Sands Company that wasn't Canadian at all. Equally eager to get started was a rival company called Syncrude, which was also foreign owned, consisting of a consortium of primarily American companies—Cities Service, Imperial Oil, Royalite and Atlantic Richfield. However, Alberta's premier, Ernest Manning, was leery about creating further competition for conventional oil suppliers. But when studies in the 1960s predicted that the world would soon need billions more barrels of oil to meet growing demand, Alberta finally gave the two companies approval.

Sun Oil and Syncrude prepared to dig up Alberta.

Meanwhile, Manley Natland's Atlantic Richfield Oil still dreamed of an easier path—nuking it.

CHAPTER 4

BREAKING ALBERTA'S ATOM

IN WHICH THE SOVIETS AND AMERICANS TEST METHODS
OF BLOWING UP ALBERTA
AND THE UNITED STATES OBTAINS THE PATENT

THE USSR TOOK THE LEAD. THEY HAD BEEN GEARING UP FOR more than a decade.

As early as 1949, Andrei Yanuarievich Vishinsky, the Soviet Union's chief jurist, show-trial judge and foreign minister, told the United Nations that his country was dedicated to the peaceful use of atomic bombs: "Right now we are utilizing atomic energy for our economic needs in our own economic interest. We are raising mountains; we are irrigating deserts; we are cutting through the jungle and the tundra; we are spreading life, happiness, prosperity, and welfare in places wherein the human footsteps have not been seen for a thousand years." Of course, the Soviets weren't doing any of this. But they certainly intended to.

Unrestrained by any environmental or even human concerns, the Soviet Union in the 1960s eagerly pushed forward with its peaceful nuclear explosions (PNEs). Under a secret project called Program No. 7—Nuclear Explosions for the National Economy, between 1965 and 1989 Soviet scientists set off 128 PNEs, including 12 for oil stimulation, 3 for cavity technology development and 25 for cavities for underground storage. The explosions produced some exciting results.

The Soviet experiments were top secret, but after 1990 their secrets emerged and in 1996 Milo D. Nordyke, of the Lawrence Livermore National Laboratory in California, gathered enough information to write an extensive report on Program No. 7 for the U.S. Department of Energy. With depleting energy stocks in the U.S.A., the Department of Energy wanted to explore methods that would enhance oil and gas extraction from both old and new wells. Canada's oil sands were an important target and back on the long-term agenda. Which was why one experiment, carried out in March and June of 1965 in the Grachevka oil field in the Ural Mountains north of the Caspian Sea, was of particular interest. While not identical to the oil sands, Grachevka had a similar heavy, bituminous oil.

Program No. 7 scientists on March 30, 1965, exploded two 2.3-kiloton nuclear bombs set two hundred metres apart at depths of 1,375 and 1,341 metres. They were embedded deep within a layer of bitumen 25 to 50 metres thick. In other words, these PNEs were almost a mirror image of Natland's plans for Project Oil Sands, except that Natland had proposed a much bigger bomb. But that issue was soon satisfied. Two months later, the Soviets exploded a third bomb 350 metres west of one of the two smaller PNEs. This bomb, at 7.6 kilotons, was more than three times the tonnage of the two earlier ones. So the combined explosions of all three test bombs more than met Natland's vision.

The Soviet experiment did the trick. It created the predicted cavities into which oil flowed. Oil production in surrounding wells increased considerably. "Results available to date indicate that the stimulation will increase the ultimate recovery from the formation by 40 to 50 per cent," Nordyke wrote in his report. What's more, the radiation levels were small and the explosions had no noticeable seismic effect. In fact, they didn't even register on American Cold War monitors.

These PNEs were followed four years later by two more 7.6-kiloton explosions in the Osinskii deposit southwest of Perm, also in the Urals. A similar increase in oil production was noted. In other words, it seemed that oil really was draining into the cavities just as Natland had predicted. Unfortunately, when the Russians drilled into the new cavity, radiated water, which was pumped to the surface, contaminated the area. The Russians now claim the contamination is at acceptable levels—simply "background contamination." But the Russian media has reported just the opposite. One Russian academic has stated that by 1978 PNEs in Perm had contaminated about sixty-five oil wells and threatened to contaminate the Votkinsk water reservoir, the Kama River and even the Volga River basin. Today, the oil from some wells is so radioactive that local refineries won't accept it.

This was not something Natland had predicted. Nor was it borne out by the initial radiation tests on oil sand samples, which showed the sand's radiation level to be the equivalent of the green illuminated face of a wristwatch. But results in the laboratory are not always duplicated in nature.

The contamination didn't stop the Russians. They carried out three more test projects on oil and gas fields right up to 1990. They all showed increases in gas and oil production of 40 to 80 percent, according to Nordyke. Then the USSR's nuclear program collapsed into the rubble of Soviet Communism.

The Americans were as eager as the Russians to go full throttle on PNEs. Like the Soviets, they showed little concern for the environmental impact of their nuclear tests.

Led by nuclear physicist Edward Teller, Atomic Energy Commission scientists kicked off their testing on December 10, 1961, with the Gnome Project. This was an explosion of a three-kiloton bomb set 365 metres underground in a salt deposit near Carlsbad, New Mexico. The explosion created a giant cavity measuring 28,316 cubic metres. The goal was to assess if the explosion would release hot vapour from the salt that could be used to drive turbines and generate electricity. The experiment produced 150 tons [136 metric tons] of water boiled out of the salt, but the saline content was enough to corrode the pipes of any power plant. So, in that sense, the experiment failed.

But there was a bright side. The explosion created the predicted underground cavern and hot vapour. Radioactivity, however, escaped from the explosion via two shafts and then quickly dispersed over New Mexico. Teller was not alarmed; he saw the positive side. "Due to these developments, we have gained the important knowledge that gaseous radioactivity produced in nuclear explosions underground can be readily and almost quantitatively recovered." He added that "production of such radioactive materials might at some time become of economic importance."

Teller of Project Plowshare was still keen on his "dream" of using nuclear bombs to extract oil from the tar sands. "Heating of the material by the nuclear explosion should suffice to transform the material into a liquid state that can be pumped to the surface," he wrote in a 1963 AEC report at the Lawrence Radiation Laboratory at the University of California Livermore. "Using the nuclear car to move the fossil horse is in the long run a promising one." But he felt a nuclear solution for the oil sands was premature for the 1960s. This had nothing to do with issues of radiation or environmental damage; he believed the Gnome explosion proved the radioactivity could be contained. Instead, he wrote that, given the abundance of cheap oil, "that particular project (nuking the oil sands) seems to lie in the indefinite future."

Alaska was drawing attention of oil companies away from Alberta's oil sands. New oil fields had just been discovered in Prudhoe Bay on the north shore. At the same time, a temporary glitch in the nuclear planning occurred when Prime Minister John Diefenbaker's government rejected American pressure to arm the Bomarc missile with nuclear warheads and imposed a ban on nuclear testing on Canadian soil. This decision was quickly reversed in 1963 by the new Liberal government, but Richfield had by that time already left for Alaska, putting Project Oil Sands on hold. "Everybody was pretty enthusiastic [about Project Oil Sands] and it looked like it was going to happen, and then we ran into this crunch," Tom Wright, the Richfield geologist who sank the test holes for Project Oil Sands, recalls. "So they had to decide which way to spend their money. They chose Alaska. Prudhoe Bay turned out to be very successful."

Still, Teller continued with his experiments. He undertook four major "stimulation" projects for oil and natural gas recovery. The basic theory was similar to Natland's ideas for nuking the oil sands: blast a cavity deep inside the earth, and oil and natural gas, which otherwise would be trapped in small, unprofitable quantities between rocks, would migrate to the larger cavity, creating one big money-making well.

The first shot was fired east of Farmington, New Mexico, and was code-named Gasbuggy. Today the test site is a broad empty grassland and minor tourist attraction. A slab of concrete seals the well hole. A plaque set into the concrete marks ground zero with a caution:

> A 29 KILOTON NUCLEAR EXPLOSIVE WAS
> DETONATED AT A DEPTH OF 4,227 FEET BELOW
> THIS SURFACE LOCATION ON DECEMBER 10, 1967.
> NO EXCAVATION, DRILLING, AND/OR REMOVAL OF
> MATERIALS TO A TRUE VERTICAL DEPTH OF 1,500
> FEET IS PERMITTED WITHIN A RADIUS OF 100
> FEET OF THIS SURFACE LOCATION.

The experiment was considered a success and, like the Soviet tests, improved gas productivity.

Two more gas well explosions followed. On September 10, 1969, scientists from the U.S. Atomic Energy Commission ignited a forty-kiloton nuclear device near Rifle, Colorado. A few protesters showed up. Among them was a local beekeeper named Chester Mcqueary. He secretly penetrated the no-go zone with fellow protester Margaret Puls. They waited to experience first-hand the nuclear blast. "As the countdown reached zero we lay on the ground, afraid and wondering what would happen," Chester later wrote. "Then a mighty WHUMP! and a long rumble moved through the earth, lifting us eight inches or more in the air. We felt aftershocks as we lay there looking at each other, grateful that we were still breathing and all in one piece."

Again, the experiment was a success: it created a gas well. The only problem was, the gas was radioactive. But that didn't deter AEC scientists, who basically believed that small amounts of radiation were not dangerous.

In 1973 in western Colorado, scientists triggered three 30-kiloton bombs simultaneously in the same underground shaft. They hoped the three explosions would create three "chimneys" that would collapse into one huge chimney full of natural gas. But the collapse never happened and all they got for their trouble were three separate contaminated gas wells.

Throughout it all, the Americans had their eyes on Alberta's oil sands, and in 1973 they made their move to patent the nuclear oil sands technology. The first patent they sought was in Canada.

The U.S. government, represented by the Secretary of the Navy, applied for and, on September 4, 1973, received from the Canadian Intellectual Property Office patent number CA 933087 for a "Nuclear Explosive Method for Stimulating Hydrocarbon Production from Petroliferous Formations [oil sands]." The named inventor was none other than Milo D. Nordyke of California's Lawrence Livermore National Laboratory. But he doesn't own the patent. As stated in capital letters on the patent document, it is owned by "THE GOVERNMENT OF THE UNITED STATES OF AMERICA AS REPRESENTED BY THE SECRETARY OF THE NAVY." It was, as Teller said, a technology for the future.

If ever Alberta green-lights its own nuking, the Americans will hold the patent.

◆

Tom Wright, who worked on Richfield's Project Oil Sands for about eight years, recalls that Natland's nuclear solution started out as an academic exercise. "It was questionable about whether or not it might make sense to actually do it. And then, when we pressed on, it just became a more and more doable thing. And then people began to kind of catch fire on the idea and it seemed to make a lot of sense. So I think in a way it was almost a surprise when it became a real possibility. And it was really quite interesting. You were going to harness all this energy and use it to useful purposes. We were pretty optimistic. I guess, when you look back on it, I wonder if I wasn't somewhat naive to think we could use nuclear energy and treat it so lightly."

Wright left Richfield soon after the project ended and moved to Salt Spring Island, British Columbia, where he became a teacher. "I was having a bit of a philosophical difference with the oil patch in general. Just largely to do with the treatment of the Native people and so forth and the environment up there. I was uncomfortable about that."

As for Natland, he retired in the mid-1970s to Laguna Beach, California. His nuclear fantasy soon became a distant memory. He started a business selling fossil rock, a kind of pre-historic marble-like stone embedded with shells, corals and snails. He discovered the fossil rock next to his office in downtown Los Angeles. Richfield Oil, which by that time had become Atlantic Richfield and then ARCO Corp., was digging a foundation for its new Los Angeles headquarters when workers uncovered the fossil rock bed. Richfield viewed it as debris and just wanted to get rid of it. Natland saw it as a remarkable find and had the company truck it to a storage site he rented for the purpose. He sorted out the best pieces and sent about five hundred tons of it to Italy, where it was cut and polished into tables, statuary, kitchen tops and ashtrays. It became known as Natlandite, and in 1981 Los Angeles named it the city's official rock.

Natland died in 1991 of complications of Alzheimer's disease.

PART II

THE POLITICS AND
BUSINESS OF OIL

♦

CHAPTER 5

WASHINGTON'S DOOMSDAY POLITICS

IN WHICH THE AMERICANS DISCOVER THE OIL SANDS, CONTEMPLATE THE INVASION OF CANADA AND DISCOVER IT'S NOT NECESSARY

ON SUNDAY, JANUARY 22, 2006, AT 7 P.M. EST, AMERICA discovered the oil sands. Bob Simon of CBS's *60 Minutes* was their man on the scene:

> There's an oil boom going on right now. Not in Saudi Arabia or Kuwait or any of those places, but six hundred miles north of Montana. In Alberta, Canada, in a town called Fort McMurray where, in the dead of winter, the temperature sometimes zooms up to zero. The oilmen up there aren't digging holes in the sand and hoping for a spout. They're digging up dirt—dirt that is saturated with oil. They're called oil sands, and if you've never heard of them then you're in for a big surprise because the reserves are so vast in the province of Alberta that they will help solve America's energy needs for the next century.

There followed haunting shots of a dark, deeply cold and deeply remote strip mine where "vehicles that look like prehistoric

beasts move across an arctic wasteland." Simon, the latest geographically challenged American journalist, was standing on the
oil sands, a thousand kilometres *south* of the Arctic. "There is so
much to scoop," Simon informed his audience. "So much money
to be made."

He continued, zeroing in on the size of the oil sands:

> BOB SIMON: The estimate of how many more barrels
> of oil are buried deeper underground is staggering.
> CUT TO CLIVE MATHER, Shell Canada chief: We
> know there's much, much more there. The total
> estimates could be two trillion or even higher. This
> is a very, very big resource.
> BOB SIMON: Rick George, the Colorado-born
> CEO of Suncor Energy, took *60 Minutes* into his
> strip mine for a tour. He says the mine will be in
> operation for about twenty-five years.

Then Simon posed the big question:

> BOB SIMON: The oil sands look like a very rich, pli-
> able kind of topsoil. Why doesn't oil come out
> when squeezed?
> RICK GEORGE: Well, because it's not warm enough. If
> you add this to hot water you'll start the separation
> process and you'll see the oil come to the top of the
> water and you'll see sand drop to the bottom.

Finally, Simon's zinger:

> BOB SIMON: It may look like topsoil but all it grows
> is money.

That impressed America—knowing you just had to add hot
water. Massive amounts of oil in a safe, friendly democracy that's
right next door. Even more reassuring was that America already

has a man up there—Rick George—who's running the show. Canada was not only throwing America a lifeline, it was also letting Americans captain the lifeboat. The show lit up the Internet energy chat lines with gleeful banter zeroing in on geopolitical forces and how America can grab the oil sands.

Posted by Yankee on Sunday January 22, 2006, at 8:36 PM EST:

China is in a desperate competition with the US for these resources.

Posted by thelastsasquatch on Sunday January 22, 2006, at 9:41 PM EST:

When I signed up for my Phd, I tried to get into the Dept for Study of US Invasion Tactics for Canadian Provinces, but the program was full, so I don't know. But if you look at the bigger picture, Canada has trees, and natural gas, and water and tar sands. The US has people and art, and bombs. I guess one could plausibly make that conclusion (that eventually America will invade Canada).

Posted by Jack Greene on Sunday January 22, 2006, at 9:51 PM EST:

The American people would not go for it. We will go through a great deal of economic adjustment instead of doing something incredibly mean spirited and greedy.

Posted by thelastsasquatch on Sunday January 22, 2006, at 10:06 PM EST:

We ARE mean spirited and greedy. So are Canadians and so are Chinese . . . Some societies are LESS mean and LESS greedy than others but evolution has made us resource acquisition machines. I do not dispute reciprocal altruism and genuine sacrifice for one's tribe, but let's face it—increased energy per capita has made everyone pretty much June and Ward Cleavers. Decreased energy per capita . . . we'll be fighting like cats in a sack.

Posted by XAXAT on Sunday January 22, 2006, at 9:43 PM EST:

Imagine the Canadians sitting quietly by . . . Everyone from the Cheney-ites on down consider it all to be a Mad Max future.

Posted by PhilRelig on Sunday January 22, 2006, at 11:17 PM EST:

I remember that some months back there were many voices in Canada . . . who issued strong protests about certain aggressive steps the US was pressing for with regard to [military] integration. I guess my question is this: What role, if any, are ruling elements in the US envisioning for this military integration as a possible means for facilitating an eventual takeover of Canada?

♦

Long before the oil and gas wells dry up and the tar sands are gone, a line will be drawn. It will descend gradually over a graph that charts world oil reserves, consumption and time. It will look a bit like a bell curve, with the odd hiccup here and there. As the years pass and the last drops of oil are used up, the line will descend towards the inevitable zero. The question is, when will this downward slope begin? And what will happen when it does?

Some geologists say we have already peaked. Others say the peak is about ten years away. Still others, such as those at ExxonMobil, say oil production will continue to rise at least through to 2030. And finally, the Cambridge Energy Research Associates, a leading worldwide energy consulting company, in 2005 predicted we will hit the peak in 2030 or 2040 but it will turn into an "undulating plateau that will continue for several decades." Whether it comes two years, five years, ten years or even thirty years down the road, it hardly matters. The point is: we're almost there. And as resources dry up and we inevitably roll over the top, the descent will be rocky and uncomfortable.

Each new year will bring a greater chance of chaos as oil and gas prices rise and nations begin to fight over what's left. Economies will slow and then collapse; refineries will become fortresses; armies will march, nation against nation, neighbour against neighbour, as we fight over every last puddle of fossil fuel. As we enter the downward curve on the oil reserve chart, the conflict will intensify. If only we had listened to M. King Hubbert.

◆

Dr. Marion King Hubbert was the first man to contemplate the end of the world as we know it. A stubborn, clear-eyed scientist, he thought it vitally important to pinpoint our day of reckoning so mankind could prepare for a new reality. Born in 1903 in San Saba, a tiny rural community in the middle of Texas, he studied geology, physics and mathematics at the University of Chicago, where he earned a reputation for being outspoken and fearless.

Coming from Texas, he had the oil business in his blood. At various points in his career he was Shell Oil's chief geophysicist;

Dr. Marion King Hubbert

he worked for the United States Geological Survey; and he taught at Stanford, Berkeley and Columbia Universities.

His expertise in physics led him to explore how liquids move through porous rocks, allowing him to understand better how much recoverable oil and gas existed in the world. After the Second World War, when energy consumption rose dramatically, he began making mathematical calculations on when mankind will run out of fossil fuels.

Hubbert understood that we are living an anomaly. If mankind has been on the earth in one shape or form for about a million years, then the hydrocarbon age is a blip. In a roundabout sort of way, you could say that the fossil fuels we use today are a product of 500 million years of geological time. It would take the earth a lot longer than any single lifetime to add another drop of oil to these accumulated reserves. As Hubbert observed:

> When these fuels are burned, their precious energy, after undergoing a sequence of degradations, finally leaves the earth as spent, long-wavelength, low-temperature radiation. Hence, we deal with an essentially fixed storehouse of energy which we are drawing upon at a phenomenal rate . . . The release of this energy is a unidirectional and irreversible process. It can only happen once, and the historical events associated with this release are necessarily without precedent and are intrinsically incapable of repetition.

In other words, in the history of the world the hydrocarbon age is one of a kind. A blink of an eye. Been and gone in a second of geological time.

Yet that blink has completely transformed our civilization into one of perpetual motion. As the only beast on earth that employs external energy sources to support and improve its lifestyle, we've developed a vast array of machines that have given us the power to reshape the globe. We've turned our environment into a tamed and quasi-managed garden of concrete and planted vegetation. We've penetrated its darkest corners with vast networks of roads and highways. We've industrialized its agriculture and engineered and re-engineered its watersheds. In the process, our population has exploded beyond anything imaginable a century ago. We've also polluted practically every square metre of the earth and obliterated thousands of species of plants and animals. God, appearing in the shape of an oil well, has indeed given us dominion over the earth.

This sudden explosion of activity was made possible by and is reflected in our energy consumption. Energy consumption can be measured in kilogram calories, the energy needed to increase the temperature of one kilogram of water one degree Celsius. Before oil was first transformed into a commercial product in 1858 in Oil Springs, Ontario, human beings used about 300 kilocalories a day in coal. By 1900, the average kilocalorie consumption had shot up to 9,880. By 1940, it was 22,100. That's a world average; in industrial areas such as the United States, the per capita energy consumption was much higher. By 1940, Americans were consuming about 129,000 kilocalories a day.

It was this sudden spike in energy consumption that alarmed Hubbert. He realized that what happens after we reach peak consumption will reflect how well we manage the inevitable transition from the hydrocarbon age to a new and as yet undefined reality. "It is upon our ability to evolve a culture more in conformity with the limitations imposed upon us by the basic properties of matter and energy that the future of our civilization largely depends," he wrote in 1949. So, he reasoned, we better start planning now.

By 1956, Hubbert had done the doomsday math. He devised a formula that could be applied to pretty well any finite resource. Presented graphically, the formula acquires the shape of a bell curve that starts with zero (the point when oil was first commercially produced) and ends in zero (the point when we run out). What he came up with was first referred to jokingly by his colleagues as Hubbert's Pimple. Now it's more commonly called Hubbert's Peak. Or simply Peak Oil.

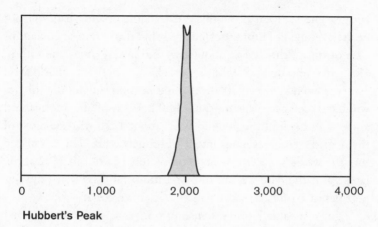

Hubbert's Peak

The formula plotted time, population and consumption growth against world oil reserves. Using the most recent geological surveys, he took the amount of fossil-fuel-bearing sedimentary rock that exists in the earth and calculated the percentage of recoverable fossil fuels it could be expected to contain. He came up with some stunningly accurate conclusions. He estimated the United States had at the most 200 billion barrels of recoverable oil under its territory. He noted that from 1859, when the United States produced its first barrel of oil from the Drake Well, until 1955 cumulative production totalled 53 billion barrels of oil. The first half of this amount was consumed between 1859 and 1939; the rest was consumed during the remaining sixteen years. By his calculation, at this accelerated rate of consumption, America's oil reserves would peak between 1966 and 1971. To be even more precise, he pinpointed 1970 as the rollover date and predicted the country would completely run out of oil in 2050. As events played out, Hubbert's calculation was nearly spot-on. By the end of 1970, America's reserves had peaked.

Hubbert also applied his formula to the crude oil reserves for the entire world. Again using the latest available estimates based on extensive geological mapping of the world's sedimentary basins, Hubbert claimed the world reserves were 1.25 trillion barrels of oil. (He did not include Canada's oil sands in his calculations because, he said, an economical extraction process had still not been developed.) Hubbert calculated that if the rate of consumption of oil maximized at about two and a half times the rate in 1956 (or about 12.5 billion barrels a year), the world's oil reserves would peak in 2000. "A child born in the middle thirties will have seen the consumption of 80 percent of all American oil and gas in his lifetime; a child born about 1970 will see most of the world's reserves consumed," Hubbert said. He calculated that the world's reserves would completely run out in 2102 at the latest. But the date we run out isn't important; by that time our petroleum-based economy will already have collapsed.

In fact, the world's consumption rate far exceeds what Hubbert calculated. The world is consuming about 30 billion barrels of oil a year. This is almost two and a half times the peak consumption rate Hubbert predicted sixty years ago. And consumption is still rising.

"It does pose as a national problem of primary importance, the necessity both with regard to requirements for domestic purposes and those for national defense, of gradually having to compensate for an increasing disparity between the nation's demands for these fuels and its ability to produce them," Hubbert wrote.

But nobody was listening.

The American government's initial reaction to Hubbert's predictions was to ignore them and embark on a billion-dollar program to build interstate highways. This was understandable. At the time, Americans were awash in oil and remained the world's largest exporter. The United States was Saudi Arabia. It produced almost half of the world's oil and natural gas (a lot of which it wastefully flared off as worthless). After the Second World War, the growth of America's economy seemed unstoppable and its oil and gas reserves limitless. What's more, the U.S. Geological Survey was estimating reserves were three times Hubbert's numbers. The country felt there was enough fuel to drive the economy for centuries to come. Nobody wanted to hear about running out of oil. Hubbert was just a nut.

Then the 1973 oil crisis hit—and hit hard.

◆

A crisis had been simmering for years, but once again nobody wanted to address it.

For decades, more than two-thirds of oil industry profits had gone to the oil companies, the so-called Seven Sisters: Standard Oil of New Jersey (now ExxonMobil), Royal Dutch Shell, BP (originally Anglo-Persian Oil Company), Standard Oil of New York (became Mobil before merging with Exxon), Texaco (now Chevron), Standard Oil of California (later Mobil and now ExxonMobil) and Gulf Oil (since split up between Chevron and BP). Oil-producing countries were incapable of breaking what was essentially a cartel that had vertical control of the petroleum business. This was particularly galling in the Middle East, where American and British companies ran the show like colonial masters. Then, in the 1970s, the entire structure collapsed. Inflation in the United States had risen to more than 8 percent. In response, Washington imposed price controls and removed the U.S. dollar from the gold standard. The dollar immediately sank by 8 percent, which meant Arab countries were getting even less for their oil, plus they had to buy Western goods at inflated prices. Then the Yom Kippur War broke out between Israel and an Arab coalition of Syria and Egypt. When the Western countries supported Israel, the Organization of Arab Petroleum Exporting Countries (OAPEC) retaliated by imposing on Oct. 16, 1973, a preplanned embargo of various degrees of severity on Japan, Western Europe and the United States. The U.S. and Holland were hit the hardest for sending emergency military aid to Israel. At the same time, the Organization of Petroleum Exporting Countries (OPEC) seized control of the pricing systems from the Seven Sisters and almost immediately quadrupled oil prices.

The embargo's effect was an immediate wake-up call. Gasoline pumps dried up. Rationing was imposed. Americans, who consumed a whopping 33 percent of the world's oil despite having only 6 percent of its population, suddenly had a taste of life without oil—and they didn't like it.

The American government's first reaction was to plan an invasion. Soon after the embargo was imposed, U.S. Defense Secretary James Schlesinger told Lord Cromer, the British ambassador in Washington, that "it was no longer obvious to him that the United States could not use force." British cabinet documents released in 2004 show that America contemplated invading Saudi Arabia and Kuwait, seizing their oil fields and imposing what the Americans now call "regime changes" on the region. Concerns were raised in the British cabinet that an attack would inflame the Arab world and an occupying force might have to remain in place for ten years or more. The British government worried about what it called the "dark scenario": that the embargo would continue long enough to cause serious damage to Western economies, making a military intervention unavoidable.

But that never happened. On March 17, 1974, diplomacy won out and the embargo ended. The experience, however, had forced the United States to examine its own oil and gas reserves. The country suddenly had to face up to the cold hard fact that King Hubbert was right: American oil reserves had peaked in 1970, and the most powerful nation in the world now had to depend on other countries to fuel its military-industrial complex.

President Richard Nixon imposed a series of conservation measures. He reduced highway speeds, raised automobile fuel consumption standards, strengthened building codes for insulation and encouraged development of alternative sources of energy. A lengthy recession also contributed to reduced consumption. When Jimmy Carter became president, he told the nation in 1979 that securing America's long-term energy needs was the "moral equivalent of war."

> To give us energy security, I am asking for the most massive peacetime commitment of funds and resources in our nation's history to develop America's own alternative sources of fuel—from

coal, from oil shale, from plant products for gaso-
hol, from unconventional gas, from the sun. I'm
proposing a bold conservation program to involve
every state, county, and city and every average
American in our energy battle.

Carter's ambitious energy plan was never implemented.
Concerns about the end of oil drained away along with the
Carter presidency. In April 1980, oil reached an all-time high of
US$99.21 in inflation-adjusted dollars before beginning a free
fall. With new oil discoveries in the North Sea and elsewhere,
Arab producers lost their clout. Another era of cheap oil
inspired a new profligacy, banishing all thought of conservation
or developing alternative power sources. Again OPEC countries, desperate for cash, opened the pipelines. Prices crashed to
near-record lows. Gas-guzzling 2.7-ton sport-utility vehicles
ruled the road. The world began pumping more oil than it
could find—to the point where we are now pumping six barrels
for every new barrel discovered. "We have dug about five million wells worldwide," Senator Roscoe Bartlett, who chairs a
peak oil caucus committee, told the U.S. Congress in 2005.
"There is just no real expectation that there are going to be big
additional fields of oil found out there. This dropoff in discovery
is really in spite of very improved technology for finding oil." He
went on to note: "There never was a moment in time between
the big Alaska oil find and all of the discovery and pumping in
the Gulf, there never was a moment in time when it decreased
the fall [of oil reserves] in our country."

While economies surged, the embargo and subsequent
recession had left an ugly legacy. By flexing their muscles, Arab oil
countries suddenly became enemies of the West, demonized by an
occidental consumer culture accustomed to having its own way in
the shopping line. The Arabs could no longer be relied upon to
supply Western industrial needs with cheap power in return for
expensive Western goods. When oil prices returned to pre-1973
levels, Arab oil economies suffered and Arab youth unemployment

skyrocketed. With the Soviet invasion of Afghanistan in 1979, and Israel's continued, often brutal occupation of the West Bank and Gaza, Arab hatred of the West helped turn Islamic fundamentalists into terrorists. In response, a new militancy was developing among American conservatives, who believed energy problems could be solved at the point of a gun. Chief among the proponents of a more unilateral and militaristic America was Dick Cheney, a CEO of Halliburton Energy Services, one of the world's largest oil and gas service corporations. He was also a prominent member of a little-known government-appointed organization that reported directly to the United States cabinet called the National Petroleum Council (NPC).

◆

The NPC was the brainchild of President Harry Truman. He had been sufficiently concerned about tracking U.S. supplies that in 1946 he signed an executive order to create a council of petroleum executives and other interested parties that would advise the government on energy issues. According to its charter, it was to report annually to the Secretary of the Interior on supply issues. Instead, over time it became a powerful industry lobby group that campaigned against conservation measures and in favour of drilling rights on federal lands, weaker environmental laws, secrecy legislation and tax breaks. Funded by energy companies, the NPC fashions American energy policy according to the needs of the oil, gas, coal and nuclear industries.

After the energy crisis of the early 1970s, when Hubbert's predictions were proven correct, the U.S. government established the Department of Energy. Ever since, the NPC has reported directly to the energy secretary, who in turn reports to the president.

The NPC's current 189 members, who sit for two-year terms, come almost exclusively from the oil patch. Four members are Canadians whose companies are crucial to American oil and gas reserves: Harold N. Kvisle, president and chief executive officer of TransCanada Corporation, whose gas pipelines transport the majority of gas exported to the States; Patrick D. Daniel, president and CEO of Enbridge Inc., another major exporter to the U.S. through its 13,500 kilometres of oil and gas pipelines; Charles W. Fischer, president and CEO of Nexen Inc. of Calgary, owner of the Long Lake oil sands project south of Fort McMurray; and Randall K. Eresman, president and CEO of EnCana Corporation, the world's largest independent oil and gas producer. EnCana is investing, along with U.S. giant ConocoPhillips, $12.5 billion to ship 400,000 barrels of raw oil sands bitumen every day to new refineries in Texas and Illinois, where Canadian bitumen will be turned into value-added fuel and then sold back to Canadians at a premium. Ironically, EnCana was once the Alberta Energy Corp., which was owned 50 percent by the Alberta government before Ralph Klein sold it off in 1993. Now the same company is shipping raw Canadian bitumen, which is owned by the people of Alberta, plus jobs and profits south to the U.S.A.

In addition to controlling the NPC, energy companies in the United States spend millions each year lobbying the U.S. Congress. Between 1998 and 2004, the oil and gas industry spent more than $420 million lobbying Washington politicians and financing their campaigns. The largest contributions came from the world's biggest oil companies: ExxonMobil $51 million, ChevronTexaco $27 million, Marathon Oil $27 million, Royal Dutch Shell Group $25 million and British Petroleum (BP) $24 million. The Center for Public Integrity in Washington tracks special-interest lobbying groups. In a 2004 report, the Center said the NPC has been an "underground pipeline of political influence for the oil and gas industry in Washington for years." These lobbying efforts have effectively stopped the United States government from putting any check on energy consumption. The energy companies spend millions to keep the good times rolling.

CHAPTER 6

ROLL CALL

IN WHICH AMERICA SEEKS REFUGE IN ALBERTA FROM
GANGSTERS, THIEVES AND A SURLY VENEZUELAN

By 1999, even the oil industry couldn't ignore Hubbert's Peak. Dangerous trends were converging to create a nightmarish scenario for the United States and its 300 million consumers. Firstly, in many major oil regions, reserves were peaking. Refining capacity was struggling to meet rising demand, and production was strained to the breaking point. Secondly, to make matters worse, China and India were emerging as major competitors of the West for resources. Both countries were beginning the hunt to secure long-term supplies, and in so doing their national oil companies were directly challenging the hegemony of the United States. Finally, increasing amounts of the world's resources were in the hands of unfriendly and unstable states. In fact, a handful of unstable states, thuggish dictators, klepto-oligarchs and gangster democracies—such as Russia and most of central Asia and OPEC—controlled about 90 percent of the world's oil and gas reserves. A sort of cold war in resources was developing.

The election of George W. Bush brought a fresh urgency to the energy file. It was no surprise: the new administration had plenty of oil experience and knew the stakes. The president himself had been a wildcatter—a failed one, but a wildcatter nonetheless—and his new national security adviser, Condoleezza Rice, had been on the board of directors of Chevron Corporation, where she had a supertanker named after her. Another oil loyalist was Philip Cooney, chief of staff of the White House Council on Environmental Quality, who had been a lobbyist for the American Petroleum Institute. (He resigned in 2005 after it was revealed that he had doctored scientific reports on global warming to cast doubt on consensus findings that greenhouse gas emissions caused climate change. He went to work for ExxonMobil, a major supporter of those who disparage scientific studies on global warming.)

U.S. senators and congressmen were already addressing these issues when George Bush came to power. In 2000, former senator Sam Nunn co-chaired an energy panel with James Schlesinger, who at various times had served as secretary of energy and secretary of defence. The panel concluded that the U.S. military had to be equipped and expanded to secure world oil supplies; the armed forces were about to become a petroleum protection agency. At the same time, the NPC began preparing, at the request of the secretary of energy, a U.S. energy policy. Chairman of the committee overseeing the project was Dick Cheney.

Within ten days of taking office, President Bush put Vice President Cheney in charge of a cabinet committee that would prepare a report on America's energy policy for the twenty-first century. The basic concern was that America would need another six million barrels of oil a day by 2020 to meet rising demands. That is exactly what China consumes today—a figure that's expected to double by 2025, exceeding the present rate of consumption in the United States. The question was where to get all that oil. The other question was more geopolitical. The United States buys about $103 billion worth of oil and gas from countries "some of which use revenues to support terrorism and spread ideology hostile to the United States," as a U.S. government report states. The dilemma was clear: how to maintain the American economy while not jeopardizing American security by supporting terrorists and failed states.

Cheney acted with remarkable speed. Four months later, in May 2001, a report was released, based upon the information from the NPC policy development group. One fundamental recommendation was that the "President make energy security a priority of our trade and foreign policy." A second important aspect of the report targeted Canada's oil sands.

> Estimates of Canada's recoverable heavy oil sands reserves are substantial, and new technologies are being deployed to develop their potential . . . Their continued development can be a *pillar* [author's emphasis] of sustained North American energy and economic security.

The chapter is highlighted by a full-page picture of three workers in a freshly dug ditch welding a pipeline that will carry Canadian oil to U.S. customers. In the background, the Canadian and U.S. flags flutter over a pile of dirt. It was clear to Cheney's committee that Canada's oil sands would be one of several pivotal elements in the United States' new energy policy of creating a continental energy fortress.

Over the next five years, the geopolitics of oil changed even faster than Cheney could imagine. By 2002, China had surpassed Japan in oil consumption, becoming second only to the United States. At the same time, however, China's reserves of 18 billion barrels of oil were declining. Production at its largest oil fields in Daqing was down 3.5 percent in 2003 and 4.3 percent in 2004. Consequently, China cut its exports to its biggest client, Japan, in order to safeguard its own future. Were China to consume as much oil per capita as the Americans, it would require more energy than is now consumed by the entire world. In 1999, the Americans knew that China's need to secure long-term oil supplies would inevitably conflict with American interests. Africa, the Middle East (particularly America's arch-enemy Iran) and Alberta's oil sands have all become targets of the Chinese. As has the United States itself.

The state-run Chinese National Offshore Oil Corporation Ltd. (CNOOC) in 2005 outbid Chevron in an attempt to take over America's fifth-largest oil company, Unocal of California. But the deal never materialized; the U.S. Congress vetoed it, claiming it threatened "to impair the national security of the United States." For the American government, free trade does not apply to energy.

China had been on the hunt even before that. In 2004, CNOOC made its biggest acquisition when it paid a whopping $4.18 billion for a small Calgary company called PetroKazakhstan. The company, which had traded at thirty-four cents a share in 1999 before the Chinese bought it at $65.76, claims it has proven reserves in Kazakhstan of 550 million barrels of oil and 25 billion cubic feet of natural gas. (The chairman of the Calgary company, Bernard Isautier, whose $93-million annual executive compensation was once among the highest in Canada, used some of his enormous profits from the sale to buy a tiny ten-acre Polynesian island and resort near Bora-Bora.) China then built a 987-kilometre pipeline linking Kazakhstan's Caspian oil fields to Chinese refineries. The pipeline is supplying 15 per cent of China's needs and that figure will increase as the network is expanded. That same year China brokered a thirty-year oil supply deal with Iran. Partial payment for the oil is being made in Chinese weapons, including a wide variety of short- and long-range missiles. China has also bought oil companies in Nigeria. In 2005, the Chinese company Sinopec partnered with Calgary-based Synenco Energy Inc. in the proposed Northern Lights oil sands mining project in Alberta. In 2006, India and China signed an energy co-operation agreement. Altogether, since 2000, China has spent about $15 billion buying more than a hundred companies and oil leases around the world in an effort to secure its energy future. China and the United States are, as the German magazine *Der Spiegel* put it, two supertankers on a collision course.

A third supertanker is also in the water. Like China, Russia is not simply ready to surrender control over the flow of oil and gas worldwide to the Americans. A new cold war has begun. This time it is all about energy.

In the Caucasus Mountains, Russia has been wielding its gas resources like a whip to lash its neighbours, particularly those who become too friendly with the United States or western Europe. In mid-winter 2006 it shut off the gas to Ukraine after that country rejected a Russian proposal for a common market while negotiating closer ties with the European Union. Ukraine is a major transit centre for Russian oil and gas to Europe, so Russia's message was sent not only to Ukraine but also to the European nations: Russia controls their energy future.

Consequently, Europe—and also the U.S.A.—has been scrambling to establish alternate oil and gas sources and transportation routes out of central Asia. U.S. Vice President Cheney, who in 1994 was on Kazakhstan's Oil Advisory Board, underscored this need when he visited Kazakhstan in May 2006 to convince its government to support supply routes that avoid Russia. American policy, as stated in a Senate report, is "the support of multiple pipelines for the transit of energy resources in order to diversify political and economic risks and enhance energy security." In 2005 and 2006, two new pipelines opened that avoided both Russia and the Middle East. Azerbaijan's corrupt leader Ilham Aliyev controls the main $3.6-billion pipeline linking the Baku and Caspian to Turkey's Mediterranean port of Ceyhan. This pipeline, built with European and American money, was opened on May 25, 2005, in the presence of U.S. energy secretary Samuel Bodman, who was pleased to be reducing the power of Russia and Iran by creating a new export corridor outside their control. A second gas pipeline was completed in December 2006 from Azerbaijan's new gas fields in the southern Caspian Sea to Georgia and Turkey. The planned $6.4-billion Nabucco Pipeline will then ship the gas through Bulgaria, Romania, Hungary and into southern Europe. The Americans need Azerbaijan's gas to supply Liquid Natural Gas (LNG) plants along the U.S. east coast.

Europe and America are also hoping to build a gas pipeline under the Caspian Sea that will bring gas from Turkmenistan and Kazakhstan to Azerbaijan and on to Turkey and then directly into Europe, again avoiding Russia. But that project may have been trumped. In May 2007, President Vladimir Putin struck a deal with Turkmenistan and Kazakhstan to build a new pipeline around the Caspian Sea that will bring another 10 billion cubic metres of gas per year into Russia. The deal, which was to be signed formally in September, goes a long way towards solidifying Russia's control of central Asia's oil and gas shipments to Europe, making Russia the dominant player in the "new great game" for control of central Asian resources. At the time of the signing, Russia was earning a 100 percent markup on the gas it bought from Kazakhstan and resold to Europe.

Stretching almost five thousand kilometres along Russia's southern border, Kazakhstan, which is geographically bigger than western Europe, has the largest oil reserves in central Asia. They are estimated at anywhere from nine to forty billion barrels. Reserves of nine billion puts Kazakhstan among the top sixteen oil producers in the world. With a population of only 15 million, it is and will continue to be an exporting country. Its oil fields are still underdeveloped and its infrastructure is relatively primitive. Lacking sufficient pipeline networks, some oil companies still truck their crude to market. Aside from the new Kazakh-China pipeline, all of its pipelines travel through Russia. A small oligarchy of businessmen and corrupt politicians run the country. At the top is President Nursultan Nazarbayev, a former Communist Party leader who since the demise of the Soviet Union has never failed to win less than 90 per cent of the vote. The economy is controlled primarily by the Nazarbayev family and a handful of businessmen that includes what Kazakhs call "the Trio": Alexander Mashkevich, a former professor of philology who also holds Israeli citizenship, and Muslims Patokh Chodiev and Alijan Ibragimov. These men serve as a pipeline to the president. Their string of European-based companies including Eurasian Natural Resources Corporation (ENRC) is said to control at least a quarter of Kazakhstan's resource-based economy. Western companies soon learned that the road to Kazakhstan goes through the Trio as well as Nazarbayev's half-brother Bulat whose various companies own large stakes in Kazakh oil and gas fields. Belgian prosecutors charged the Trio in 2001 with money laundering, fraud and being part of a criminal organization. The case involves a Belgian company called Tractebel which paid US$55 million in commissions to the Trio for the purchase of a Kazakh power station. At least three journalists critical of the Nazarbayev regime have been killed in hit-and-run accidents. Political opponents as well as businessmen who are not part of the elite have been murdered. In a business environment defined by violence, "fees" and "commissions," it's not always easy for Americans to function, particularly when the U.S. Foreign Corrupt Practices Act forbids bribery of foreign officials. But America's need to be a player in Kazakhstan—and in all of central Asia—means ignoring or bypassing that law.

Oil executive James Giffen learned this lesson in 2003 when the U.S. government charged him under the act claiming he funneled US$84 million to Kazakhstan officials including President Nazarbayev. Prosecutors claim Giffen, a former ExxonMobil executive who ran a private New York bank called Mercator, was acting for Mobile Oil and other American companies in the mid 1990s when he made the bribes. Giffen, who was a confidant of the Trio, has claimed the bribes were authorized by the CIA and the U.S. government which had instructed him "to stay close" to top Kazakh officials and to "continue to report" on their activities. By 2007, his case had still not gone to trial. Swiss officials seized the bribe money, which had been deposited in Swiss bank accounts. Swiss and U.S. officials have said the money will be deposited into an education fund for poor children in Kazakhstan.

In another case involving the U.S. Foreign Corrupt Practices Act, a unit of U.S. oil services giant Baker Hughes Inc., pleaded guilty in May 2007 to payments of US$4 million made in 2001–2003 to officials of Kazakhoil, now called KazMunaiGaz, which is Kazakhstan's state energy company. The company president was Timur Kulibayev, the son-in-law of President Nazarbayev. A U.S. federal court in Houston fined Baker Hughes US$44 million.

Navigating central Asia's unruly version of capitalism is a shadow game. Small to mid-sized western energy companies often partner with local Kazakh firms to get financing only to find that the money doesn't show up. Houston-based Transmeridian Exploration in 2004 sold a 50 percent stake in its valuable South Alibek oil field lease to Kazstroiproekt Ltd. for a mere US$15 million. Kazstroiproekt then morphed into a new company called Bramex Management, which was set up in the corporate fog of the Caribbean's British Virgin Islands, where a company's ownership can be hidden. Bramex was owned by 37-year-old Yerzhan Tatishev who controlled Kazakhstan's second-largest bank, Bank TuranAlem (BTA). BTA is Transmeridian's banker in Kazakhstan, and Transmeridian's president Lorrie Olivier was hoping to get favourable financing to develop the deal.

These hopes were dashed, however, in December 2004 while Tatishev was apparently on a hunting trip. The young banker was behind the wheel of his SUV when one of his bodyguards, who was sitting in the back seat, shot him in the back of the head. Police called his killing a "hunting accident," claiming the gun accidentally fired when Tatishev hit a bump.

Then in October 2005 Transmeridian purchased all the shares in Bramex from Tatishev's family for US$168 million. According to a former Transmeridian executive, the company just wanted to rid itself of a burdensome partner. Bramex ended up with a huge profit and Transmeridian regained 100 percent control of the oil lease.

Three years earlier Olivier had created another British Virgin Island company called Green Grove Holdings Inc., of which he made his Moscow mistress the sole director, according to documents in a Florida court case. He then parked US$10 million in Transmeridian bearer bonds inside Green Grove. When he took the company back from the mistress in 2005, the mistress sued him in a Miami court claiming he had gifted her the company and then tricked her out of the US$10 million plus ownership of a Miami condo.

Investors put Transmeridian up for sale in March 2007. It reported losses of $53 million and was unable to raise the money to develop the South Alibeck oil field despite its close relationship with Bank TuranAlem.

This was not the first time Tatishev has used his bank to gain personal control of oil leases. In 2003, he secured 85 percent control of the Kazakh oil leases of another Houston-based company called American International Petroleum Corporation (AIPC) in return for exploration funds. In the end it paid only a small fraction of these funds. A year later, AIPC declared Chapter 11 bankruptcy and was liquidated without the company ever suing Bridge for the unpaid exploration funds. From 1991 to 2000, Olivier was vice-president of AIPC's Kazakhstan operations.

Rivalling Kazakhstan's corruption is its southern neighbor Turkmenistan. Until his sudden death from a heart attack on December 21, 2006, President Saparmurat Niyazov had been the country's "supreme ruler" since the collapse of the USSR. The commissar of the local Communist Party when the country was a Soviet republic, he grabbed control in 1991, declaring himself president for life and "Great Father of all Turkmen." Turkmenistan has the fifth-largest natural gas reserves in the world, producing an estimated $6.3 billion a year for a country of just five million people. Yet there are no public accounts and the country is one of the poorest in central Asia. More than half of its people are unemployed, and most regions have no health care. The London-based human rights and natural resource watchdog Global Witness said in a 2006 report that Niyazov stashed much of the country's billions in gas revenues in foreign bank accounts, including account number 949 924 500 at the Deutsche Bank AG, Frankfurt, Germany, where much of the country's gas is sold. The gas is transported to Ukraine in pipelines controlled by Gazprom, which is owned 51 percent by the Russian government. It is then resold through intermediary companies to western Europe. Why these intermediary companies, whose ownership remains hidden behind a network of front companies and nominees, are necessary has never been properly explained. It is likely that they are merely tools to siphon off millions of dollars in gas revenues. So not only does the dictator of Turkmenistan park the country's oil and gas revenues offshore with the help of Western banks, but unnecessary and totally unaccountable intermediary companies hive off millions of dollars to stuff their owners' pockets. This is another reason Russia opposes the Caspian Sea pipeline.

While bribes and bank secrecy smooth the flow of energy in Turkmenistan and Azerbaijan, the U.S.A. has an equally complicated problem in its own backyard. It comes in the defiant form of Venezuela's leftist president Hugo Chávez, a staunch anti-American. The man who launched a failed military coup in 1992 only to be elected president in 1998 calls Bush "the biggest terrorist on earth." In a now-famous speech at the United Nations on September 20, 2006, he attributed satanic qualities to Bush. The day after the U.S. president had delivered a speech to the UN, Chávez told members: "Yesterday the devil came here and this place still smells of sulphur." This would be little more than a sideshow if it weren't for the fact that Chávez controls 80 billion barrels of oil, making Venezuela's nationalized petroleum industry the world's fifth-largest producer and one of the United States' major suppliers. Since he was first elected in 1998, Chávez has threatened to cut off oil shipments to the United States, and he is actively attempting, in concert with Brazil, to reduce U.S. influence in South America. This includes opposing the Washington Consensus, which is an initiative by the World Bank and International Monetary Fund, both of which are largely controlled by the United States, to impose free market forces on Latin America.

Chávez's stated policy is to increase Venezuela's sovereignty over its oil and gas resources. Like his hero Simón Bolívar, who in 1811 drove the Spanish out of Colombia, Chávez wants to rid the continent of America's colonial interests and unite South America under one trading bloc. Houston-based Citgo, which is a subsidiary of Venezuela's state-owned Petróleos de Venezuela S.A., has 14,000 retail outlets in the United States. The U.S. convenience store chain 7-Eleven refused to renew its contract with Citgo after Chávez's UN speech. As a result, Citgo lost 2,100 gas outlets. But that's of little concern to Venezuela. Unless it greatly reduces consumption, America's reliance on Venezuelan oil will only increase in the future.

If that weren't enough of a headache for the States, in 2006 Chávez visited Russia, China, North Korea, Iran and Syria to make what he called "strategic partnerships" that would reduce Venezuela's dependence on U.S. energy markets. He also purchased weapons, including Russian attack helicopters. In August 2006, his visit to China bore fruit: the Chinese promised to invest $5 billion in the Venezuelan oil business by 2012 in order to boost sales to China to 500,000 barrels a day from a mere 150,000. This will inevitably cut into American supplies.

Meanwhile, the situation in Africa only worsens. Nigeria has 36 billion barrels of sweet, light crude oil, which is the easiest and cheapest to refine. Yet, like Angola, which has reserves of 5 billion barrels, Nigeria is racked by corruption and by rebel insurgents who frequently attack offshore oil platforms, shutting down production. Both nations are hostile to American interests.

Finally, the Middle East—which has the largest amount of oil in the world at 798 billion barrels, or about 65 percent of the world's proven reserves, plus 80 trillion cubic metres of natural gas—has become America's new Vietnam. The cost of the Iraq invasion has gone beyond almost anybody's estimates. The Pentagon said that it was spending at least $200 million a day, and as of 2006 had spent a total of $216 billion on the war. Americans are asking themselves, to what end? The answer lies in the Iraqi oil fields.

The country has 115 billion barrels of proven reserves. It has seventy-three major wells, but only fifteen have been developed. More important, it is the least explored country in the Middle East as far as oil is concerned. Figures for Iraq's potential oil reserves differ wildly. Various U.S. petroleum associations, the International Energy Agency in Paris and the United States Geological Survey have predicted that Iraq has anywhere from 45 billion to 300 billion barrels in undiscovered oil. What's more, it's the cheapest oil to recover and to refine. With world-proven reserves and undiscovered wells at about 2.1 trillion, this could mean that Iraq has about one-fifth of the world's reserves if the wildest projections are true.

Yet hardly a week goes by without terrorists blowing up Iraqi pipelines and threatening major oil fields in the region. Much of the violence is sponsored by the Islamic government of Iran, which remains a declared enemy of the United States, as it spends an estimated $100 million a year financing terrorists such as Hezbollah and pushes its nuclear agenda. Here again, the approximately $60 billion a year Iran earns in oil export profits is totally unaccounted for. While unemployment sits at more than 12 percent and 40 percent of the population lives in poverty, Iran's Islamic regime clings to power through an aggressive anti-Western foreign policy.

So, as America measures its long-term energy security, the future is not promising. About 90 percent of the oil and gas is in countries that are unstable, corrupt and hostile to American interests. At least 80 percent is controlled by Muslim countries, none of which cherish friendship with America. What's more, the expanding economies of countries like China and India are creating greater competition for oil supplies that will soon begin to dwindle. With such growing turmoil in the world's largest oil patches, it is no wonder that America's recent foreign policy has been all about oil—and more specifically, oil sands.

◆

When Bush finally signed his energy policy into law on August 8, 2005, he called it America's "energy strategy for the twenty-first century." The United States Energy Policy Act calls for Americans to reduce their consumption by one million barrels per day. But that reduction will only begin in 2015. In other words, the U.S.A. has no intention of reducing its present consumption by a single barrel. The year the act came into force, U.S. consumption rose 4.3 percent—the biggest increase since 1984. According to the British oil company BP, it was the largest volume increase ever.

Europeans consume about half the oil Americans do while enjoying a similar lifestyle thanks to better energy conservation. (The amount of energy used by American industrialized farming in petroleum-based nitrogen fertilizers and transportation is greater than France's total energy consumption. In fact, if all countries adopted U.S. farming practices, the world would be out of oil by about 2014.) Despite global warming, international terrorism and diminishing oil reserves, Americans just can't seem to stop consuming. And their government won't take steps to slow them down. With a national debt of $8.2 trillion, real energy conservation would trigger an economic slowdown. "It will be essentially impossible to service that debt if our economy does not continue to grow," Senator Roscoe Bartlett told the U.S. Congress in 2005. To keep the engine running, America has turned its hungry eyes towards Alberta. The Energy Policy Act makes that clear. It calls for a continental plan that will make North America energy self-sufficient by 2025. The cornerstone of that plan is the oil sands.

The act established a United States Commission on North American Energy Freedom, with a budget of $10 million. "The chairman shall select staff from among qualified citizens of Canada, Mexico, and the United States of America," the act states. The commission will submit a report to Congress within twelve months of the date of the act on "recommendations regarding North American energy freedom."

In a section entitled "Use of Fuel to Meet Department of Defense Needs," the act states that the

> Secretary of Defense shall develop a strategy to use
> fuel produced, in whole or in part, from coal, oil
> shale, and tar sands that are extracted by either
> mining or in-situ methods and refined or otherwise
> processed in the United States in order to assist in
> meeting the fuel requirements of the Department
> of Defense when the Secretary determines that it is
> in the national interest.

In other words, it has become law in the United States to process as much Canadian crude oil from the oil sands as possible in American refineries to meet the needs of the American military.

Another section of the Energy Policy Act establishes a task force to organize a special relationship with Alberta. Not Canada. Alberta.

> PARTNERSHIPS—The Task Force shall make recommendations with respect to initiating a partnership with the Province of Alberta, Canada, for purposes of sharing information relating to the development and production of oil from tar sands.

Following the signing of the energy policy, Bush told Congress that Americans were "addicted to oil." U.S. energy secretary Samuel Bodman was quick to point out that this was mere rhetoric, and that Americans shouldn't worry that the government would impose any inconvenient conservation measures. Bush's concern was to reduce reliance on foreign oil. By 2025 at the latest, he wants Americans to reduce their reliance on imported oil from unstable regions such as the Middle East by 75 percent. According to Bodman, Canada is to fill the void.

Immediately after the election of Stephen Harper's Conservatives in January 2006, Canadian government officials with Natural Resources Canada travelled to Houston to meet with U.S. oil executives and officials from Bodman's department to discuss ramping up oil sands production. This meeting was followed by another one in January 2007 to assess progress. (Neither Bodman's department nor Natural Resources Canada responded to repeated requests for interviews about these meetings.)

Following the 2006 meeting, Bodman went on a speaking tour to romance Canadians. In a speech in March 2006 at the Canadian embassy in Washington, he said that since Americans consume about eight billion barrels of oil a year, or about one-quarter of the world's production, Canada's oil sands represent "a big fraction of it, so it will be very important. We certainly are very anxious that the oil sands development be as swift as possible."

Bodman then headed north to Fort McMurray and the oil sands. On July 13, 2006, as oil prices closed in on almost eighty dollars a barrel, five helicopters took Bodman and his entourage for a flyover of the open-pit mining. Bodman also got to ride one of the big yellow 400-ton trucks that cart the sands to the upgraders. News photographers took his picture with his eager host, Alberta premier Ralph Klein, clinging to his side. Noting that the tar sands' output will quadruple over the next fifteen years to four billion barrels a year (or enough to furnish America with half its oil at present consumption rates), Bodman said: "The United States is the natural market for much of this production and the Canadians are willing to work with us to make that happen. Additional pipeline and refinery capacity is needed on both sides of the border to make the best use of the output from the sands." He reminded a luncheon meeting of oil executives that the U.S.A. is committed to reducing its reliance on oil imports from "unstable regions by five million barrels a day by 2025." He added: "No single thing can do more to help us reach that goal than realizing the potential of the oil sands in Alberta."

This more than pleased Klein, who quickly assured Bodman that "development will continue," implying that it will not be interrupted by any concerns over the environment or community resources. In fact, the Alberta government has basically imposed a moratorium on serious environmental regulations until the sands have been fully exploited. "The United States is increasingly looking to our province to help meet its energy needs, and that spells good news for the U.S. and for Alberta," Klein told reporters. "While our two jurisdictions already enjoy a vibrant integrated energy market, I believe there's room for that relationship to grow."

Even the aging Alan Greenspan, the retired chairman of the U.S. Federal Reserve, hobbled north to pay homage to the sands. His was a message of trust. "When you sign a contract, it doesn't have a Russian signature on it," Greenspan told his audience.

◆

A year before the Bodmans and Greenspans came to town, former Alberta premier Peter Lougheed received a visit from a U.S.

cabinet secretary, whom he refuses to name. The official had been sent up to probe the Canadians on the sands and to explore what Lougheed described as a "real hot issue."

Lougheed and the secretary were sharing a drink and talking about the North American Free Trade Agreement, which Lougheed had helped negotiate. In Lougheed's words: "He was saying, 'You *have* to send us oil. You can't send any of your oil to China 'cause we have a free trade agreement with you and you are obligated with anything in excess of your own needs to send it to the U.S.' I said: 'Mr. Secretary, you're wrong. I was there. It doesn't say that at all. There's nothing expressed that requires us to in fact function that way. We can sell it to a third country such as China, and we have the opportunity to do so. Obviously for trade relationships we would be working our first market to the United States. But I believe as a seller I want two buyers. And I want a buyer like China to make sure we're getting the maximum price.'"

The secretary became visibly upset, so much so that he almost dropped his glass. "In fact I'm not sure he didn't," Lougheed recalls. The visit ended abruptly. And the secretary reported back to Washington that the U.S.A. could very well find itself in competition with China, India and South Korea for crude oil from the Canadian sands.

That brief discussion went to the heart of Canada's obligations to the United States under NAFTA and how far the Americans are prepared to go to ensure that we don't sell elsewhere.

◆

Critics of NAFTA say that it requires Canada to sell as much oil as it can to the United States. That's not entirely true. But NAFTA does hamstring any move we might make to conserve our supplies. Former prime minister Brian Mulroney made sure of that when he deregulated the oil and gas industry and then agreed to the American demand for a proportional sharing clause in the 1989 Free Trade Agreement (FTA), which in 1994 became the North American Free Trade Agreement (NAFTA) with the addition of Mexico. In NAFTA, one clause was added—Article 605. Mexico did not agree to it; the Mexican negotiators realized that the clause could severely limit the country's sovereignty over its own vital energy resources. Canada, on the other hand, surrendered to U.S. insistence.

Under both the General Agreement on Tariffs and Trade (GATT) and NAFTA, Canada is obliged to allow the free flow of goods across its border. GATT allows a country to prohibit or restrict exports "to prevent or relieve critical shortages." The definition of "critical shortages" is left largely to the home country. NAFTA recognizes that restrictive right but with one important rider. This rider is Article 605, which is referred to as the proportionality clause. Article 605 says that Canada, in the event it decides to reduce its production for reasons of, for example, environmental protection, conservation or national security, must maintain the exact percentage of exports to the United States that prevailed over the previous three years. So if over the last three years Canada has exported 60 percent of its gas and oil production to the United States—as is the present situation—it must continue to export that percentage even if this means that Canadians will not have enough for their own domestic needs. Under Article 605, Canada can't even tax its oil and gas exports if it means Americans would have to pay more for their Canadian fuel—and petrochemicals—than Canadians.

Peter Lougheed helped negotiate this clause. This is the same man who in 1973 faced down the oil companies, raising royalties to 30 percent from a measly 16.33. This is also the man who faced down Prime Minister Pierre Trudeau over the National Energy Program, describing the federal government's policy to tax oil and gas exports and to impose volume restraints on shipments as a "declaration of war on Alberta." I asked him how such a tough guy could have agreed to Article 605. He was unrepentant: "That was a difficult part of the negotiations. I think that when it comes down to it—and this was a judgment call we made—if for some unusual reason we have a problem with Canadian supply, I think that what would happen is the Canadian parliament, including support by the government of Alberta, would say, 'We've got to serve the Canadians first.'"

"So that would mean an end to NAFTA?"

"It would create an issue under the North American Free Trade Agreement. But I think that that would be an issue that politically and publicly, if I were involved, I would take on at the time. But that's a very remote set of circumstances. I mean, my concern is the other way. My concern is that Americans say you have to sell everything that you have produced to us and you can't sell it to another buyer."

"Why is this 'remote'? We're already running out of gas."

"At best we can stay even," he conceded. "And then we are losing on the conventional oil side." But he added that, on the supply side, we're saved by the oil sands.

It's the approaching high stakes game of oil politics that concerns him—what America will do if we start selling to China, as a proposed pipeline over the Rockies to the west coast would allow us to do. Lougheed says Americans react to this prospect in two ways. "One of them is what I call the foreign service reaction—which I just had at lunch about four days ago—and that is, 'Well, I don't think that will ever be a problem,' you know, minimizing it. But I will not forget the dropped glass by the United States secretary when I told him what I just finished telling you. No, there would be a hell of a reaction. And the instability factor in the Middle East, Venezuela and Russia and Africa and you name it is why when the time comes . . . the Americans are going to act very vigorously if we start shipping significant quantities of oil to China. No doubt about it."

In May 2006, Lougheed was in Beijing talking to Chinese officials about oil and gas exports. The Chinese asked him to get involved in Chinese purchases of Canadian oil sands companies and leases. "I said, 'I'm not going to be involved because I don't think you should try to get a controlling interest in an oil sands plant. Because if you do, you are going to really create a problem for us by having a foreign government having a controlling interest in one of our resource operations.' And they didn't like it."

At that very moment the Chinese were signing a deal with a small Calgary start-up company called Synenco Energy Inc. to purchase a 40 percent interest in Synenco's Northern Lights oil sands project. The project is designed to produce 100,000 barrels of oil a day. Synenco was incorporated out of nowhere in 1999. Its only revenue is from interest on capital raised through the Toronto Stock Exchange. Its only assets are its 60 percent share of the oil sands lease for the Northern Lights Project plus land near Edmonton for a bitumen upgrader refinery. Synenco's 2005 cost estimate for the project was $5.3 billion. That cost has probably doubled by now. The only partner in this project that has deep pockets is the Chinese government through CNOOC.

"Keep your eye on whether the Chinese take a controlling interest," Lougheed says. "You have the interesting issue of whether or not Alberta, i.e. Canada, shouldn't constrain the ownership control. I'm not talking about having a minority interest, that's fine. If you get into the position that the Chinese are the actual owner, they can manipulate the supply much easier and all of the production from that oil sands operation would be going to Prince Rupert and then overseas. I would restrict ownership. Do not allow them as a foreign government—India or China, and even South Korea—to do that. And I wouldn't get buffaloed by the view where they are saying, 'Well, this is the China National Offshore Oil Corporation,' which we all know is controlled by the government."

Calgary-based Enbridge Inc. has proposed building a $4-billion two-way pipeline across the Rockies to Kitimat. It would ship a light oil diluent, which is needed to dilute the heavy bitumen so it can flow through a pipeline, to the oil sands projects and then bring back the crude oil for shipment to Asia. Enbridge has been negotiating a deal with PetroChina to ship the crude to China. The Chinese want at least half the pipeline's capacity.

Ownership is the crucial issue. As Lougheed emphasizes, the Alberta government owns the resource, but the Americans have locked up a large percentage of control. With NAFTA and American lease contracts with the Alberta government, it would be difficult to impose curbs on oil sands production, not to mention natural gas. Alberta under Ralph Klein, Lougheed says, essentially surrendered its control over its own resources to the free market, and the Americans have walked in and taken control—partially because of the free market deal that Lougheed himself helped negotiate. Yet one vital fact is still undeniable: Albertans own the resource. "Why is it a free market if I own the resource? I'm not a regulator here, I'm an owner. And Klein didn't get it in his mind, the difference between regulator and owner." The market is Alberta's to control. It's just a question of will.

With Canada's vast petroleum shipments to the U.S., we are quickly running out of conventional oil and gas. This leaves Alberta with only the sands and methane gas trapped inside coal and shale beds. Extracting both resources is environmentally disastrous for the province and a huge contributor to global warming. Alberta's new premier, Ed Stelmach, shows no sign of veering from Klein's free market vision.

"When you think that Canadians send more than half their natural gas to the United States, you might think that, well, they are not that bright," U.S. energy conservationist Randy Udall says. "You hope that sooner or later they will figure out that they live in a cold climate."

Trouble is, the money's too good.

CHAPTER 7

GETTING THE JUMP ON THE ENERGY GAME

IN WHICH WE TAKE THE PULSE OF AN OILMAN AND FIND OUT HOW TO GET RICH

By 1987, Jeff Tonken had had enough. For the past eight years he had been watching hundreds of oil and gas deals go down and not one of them included him.

He wasn't exactly an outsider. But he wasn't inside either. In fact, he felt he was in limbo. Not a good thing when you're thirty years old. As a law partner in one of Calgary's biggest firms, he had helped hammer out his share of million-dollar deals. But working fourteen hours a day, week in and week out, with nothing to show for it but an hourly rate of a few hundred bucks wasn't something he wanted to do for the rest of his life. After all, this was Alberta, where you were only in the game if you were drilling the earth. As it stood, he was grinding out deals and somebody else was having the fun. That's no way to live, he told his wife. Tonken wanted a seat at the energy poker game. "Just don't lose the house," his wife told him.

Tonken didn't know anything about oil and gas exploration. His father, who grew up in Toronto, had been a veterinarian in the tiny Alberta town of Vulcan before moving sixty kilometres north to Calgary, where Tonken and his two brothers grew up. This was a city driven by one thing and one thing only: energy.

But none of it had touched Tonken until 1982, when he joined the firm of Howard Mackie. "Lawyers were doing acquisitions, divestitures, securities law, banking, employment, all to do with the oil and gas business," he says. "There was and is nothing else." Which is why he finally caught the bug. He didn't realize that the world of oil and gas is a lot different from the varnished offices of an established law firm. He never dreamed that his entry into the game would eventually shake the entire industry to its core.

When Tonken jumped into the patch, the timing was good. Oil prices had dropped to as low as US$11. Politicians worried that conventional oil and gas reserves in Alberta were peaking. More wells were being drilled for less payback. The big discoveries had been made and now it sometimes seemed as if all anybody was doing was licking the bowl. But this only encouraged Alberta towards an open door policy. The province had a few rules, but even less oversight. "You could do pretty well whatever you wanted," one geologist says. It was a wild west that set the stage for what was to come. And the way it was set up, it took neither brains nor brawn. Just determination—and there was plenty of that around. A large number of Canadians and Americans were eager to chance the pitfalls of trying to get rich off Alberta's resources. Over the next twenty years their companies would drill more than 117,000 oil and gas wells in Alberta, adding to the already vast number of wells and the extensive grid of over 300,000 kilometres of pipeline. Tonken became a big part of that.

Tonken's entry into the industry came via a football team. In 1986, the Calgary Stampeders went bankrupt. When the community started a campaign to save the team, Tonken volunteered to join a new Stampeders board of directors that would fashion a rescue plan. On the board were several wealthy Albertan businessmen, including Scotty Cameron, president of Pan-Alberta Gas Ltd.; Larry Shaw, owner of Shaw GMC Trucks; Jim Silye, president of Western Seismic Exchange and a veteran Stampeders football player; and Vern Siemens, vice-president of Agra Industries.

At that time, Alberta had a unique and highly successful investment tool. It was called the Junior Capital Pool (JCP), and it allowed a business person to raise a ton of money on the stock exchange without having any assets. "You could raise $150,000 to $200,000 and now you would have a public company, on the basis of nothing," Tonken recalls. "It's a great concept." Without the Junior Capital Pool many Canadian energy companies would never have got off the ground, and Tonken saw it as a means of building a major oil and gas business.

Tonken seized the opportunity presented by his fellow Stampeders board members, all of whom had credibility in the Calgary business community. "I said to those gentlemen, 'You know, we should start a junior capital pool because someday I want to run it.' They said, 'Fine.'" So they created a company called Stampeder Exploration. Each of the five investors put in $6,000. Tonken had to borrow his stake. Then they sold stock on the JCP at one cent a share rising to ten cents. They raised about $200,000. Now they had a shell company with a bank account. Tonken operated it out of his law office. "We just had the $200,000. We had nothing else." So he went looking for leases.

To an oil and gas company, Alberta is nothing more than a checkerboard comprising tiny square sections each measuring 640 acres, or one square mile. This is the playground of the oil business. Geologists, geophysicists and engineers pore over section maps and, backed by seismic survey charts, try to locate the little square piece of land that will make them rich. To date there have been more than 300,000 oil and gas wells drilled in Alberta. Many are concentrated in core drilling areas in the central and southern part of the province, such as the Turner Valley, Edmonton and Lloydminster, and more recently in the northwest, around Grande Prairie. After a century of drilling, these maps have become crowded with tiny black dots and stars denoting old and existing wells. Finding that energy-rich acre of land that has not yet been staked can be needle-in-a-haystack work.

When a company wants to stake a section or part of a section, they "post" it by notifying Alberta Energy, a department of the Alberta government that oversees oil and gas leases. Because the Alberta government owns 81 percent of the subsurface mineral rights in the province (the rest is held by the federal government through Indian land or parks or by private landowners who hold pre-federation freehold rights), companies have to lease from the government as the owner of the resource. They can either post an entire section or just a quarter section. They can choose to buy the rights "to the basement," which means they have drilling rights all the way down to the bedrock, or they can lease only to a certain depth. Tonken says it's a bit like leasing space in an office building; you might want to lease only the eighteenth floor. In other words, you can purchase the rights to drill only, say, 1,400 metres below the surface. Other companies might have the rights just above or below you. So it can get pretty crowded in one section. Dozens of companies might be drilling the same section at different levels, in which case they usually pool their resources by sharing, for example, the drilling costs.

Once a company has posted its intention to lease a section, the government publishes an offficial notice of the posting and welcomes counter bids. Unless you work in the industry, chances of you finding out that a section of land has been posted are slim. You have to have an Electronic Transfer System account that gives you access to the posting and bidding system. The province makes no effort to notify the landowner, who is more often than not caught off guard when an energy company calls to say it intends to drill his or her land.

Every second Wednesday, Alberta Energy holds a blind bid for oil and gas leases. Companies send in their concealed bids and the highest bidder gets the lease. It's that simple. And this means that every second Wednesday millions of dollars pour into the Alberta Treasury. "Your dog could be the premier of this province," Tonken jokes, referring to the ease with which Alberta earns resource revenues. Buoyed by increased drilling and a scramble for oil sands leases, the take from these Wednesday Internet poker games has been steadily climbing over the last five years as drilling rates soar. The province's take tripled to $3.43 billion in 2006 from $1.1 billion in 2004. The lease gives the company five years to drill its wells and prove that the lease is productive. After that, unless it renews its stake (meaning more money for Alberta), the lease reverts to the Crown. So you have to get moving and start drilling, otherwise you'll lose the investment.

Alberta's policy is that no landowner should be allowed to hold up exploitation of an energy resource even if that exploitation ruins his land. Once the company has secured its leases, it then has to make a deal with the local landowner to access the property. This is where the "landsman"—or "land agent"—comes in. The landsman negotiates with the landowner the right of access. The price is usually a few thousand dollars plus a fee for every well drilled. The landowner can fight and try to hold up the process, but in the end landowners can't win. The land agents, of whom there are about 1,600 in Alberta, are paid by the oil companies. That's where they get their business and that's where their loyalties lie. Which is why they are the most hated and distrusted people in rural Alberta. Farmers fondly repeat an old joke: "How can you tell when a landsman isn't lying? When his mouth stops moving." If the two sides can't agree, the case goes to a government arbitrator, who with few exceptions inevitably rewards the energy company. It's against the Land Agents Licensing Act in Alberta—on pain of a $5,000 fine or six months in jail—for a landowner to hire an unlicensed land agent to advise the landowner in negotiations with the energy company. ExxonMobil and EnCana Corporation complained to the Alberta government in 2006 that an unlicensed land agent named Raymond Strom had given advice to a farmer in negotiations with three oil companies. The government charged Strom, who argued in Alberta Provincial Court that the law is unconstitutional, violating his right to free speech and a farmer's right to hire whomever he wants as a representative. The judge agreed that the law "creates an unbalanced playing field favouring the oil and gas industry," but still found Strom guilty and fined him $517.

"There's not much a landowner can do to stop it," Tonken says. "Up in the middle of nowhere, there's nothing up there, and the landowner is begging you to come on. Other guys who have a magnificent view of the mountains say, 'I don't want some drilling rig on it.' And farmers don't want it ruining their fields, because once you have a drilling rig there's a gazillion trucks going up and down the roads throwing dust and creating noise, and then if you hit a gas well you have to pipeline it to the infrastructure that's close by and it can become very complicated, and then you have to drill larger wells on his land, so it's not the one well, it's the twenty you drill behind it." Throughout Alberta, farmers and energy companies are increasingly at loggerheads over the intrusive nature of oil and gas drilling—which sometimes results in violent confrontations, such as the case of Wiebo Ludwig, who bombed gas company equipment.

◆

Tonken soon became enmeshed in the machinery of oil exploration. Roads have to be built. Rigs have to be brought in. Test wells have to be drilled. With the clock ticking on leases, nobody can stop the drilling. The machinery of energy exploration and extraction acquires a mind of its own. Once it's up and running, it's almost impossible to shut off. Every step demands more money, and with that comes a heightened urgency to recoup mounting investments. Stress levels rise. You're not digging for oil or gas, you're digging for money. Shareholders are eager for a payback. Everyone wants to get rich. But for Tonken and his fellow investors, the first wells came up dry, and so did their bank account. "We were almost goners," he recalls.

Tonken decided Stampeder was going about it the wrong way. Rather than starting from scratch, he should have bought an existing company with a steady flow of oil or gas revenues that he could use to finance explorative drilling. He started looking for a cheap company that would produce a fixed amount of oil or gas revenues over the long term and also offer the opportunity for infill drilling (drilling in a section with existing wells in hopes of finding sister pools). In 1992, Tonken found what he was looking for just across the border in Saskatchewan. It was a company called Allheart Resources. He had no idea what he was getting into.

Owned by local businessman Murray Paulin, Allheart was pumping about eight hundred barrels of oil a day out of the Kerrobert field. This was the cash flow Tonken believed he needed to build Stampeder. Paulin wanted $15 million for his company, but oil and gas prices were in the basement, so Tonken offered $9 million. They settled on $12 million. "I'll never forget the day," Tonken says. "I was standing in my kitchen on the telephone with Paulin, who turned out to be one of the great gentlemen of the oil and gas business. And so we struck the deal and I phoned Larry Shaw and we had sixty days to raise the money. I always thought we could leverage on their financial expertise. So we raised $2.5 million [on the JCP] and borrowed $10 million from the Bank of Montreal. And we had our eight hundred barrels a day of production."

Finally Tonken had a real company. He quit his job at the law firm, leased new offices in downtown Calgary and embarked on his quest to build a major oil company. He immediately began looking for his next acquisition. But he was about to get a tough lesson in the energy business's equivalent of a dogfight.

"Murray drove us out to the property and said okay, if you like these assets and want drilling opportunities, next door is a larger company and you should think about trying to buy them," Tonken recalls. The neighbouring company was originally called Big Heart. Paulin and Ed McNally, the owner of Alberta's home-grown Big Rock Breweries, had started Big Heart and then sold it to BC Resources, who in turn sold it to Vancouver billionaire deal-maker Jimmy Pattison. Pattison held it through his Westar Group and renamed it Westar Petroleum. It wasn't, however, one of Pattison's smartest deals. He bought it in the early eighties at the top of the market. Now Westar Petroleum was heavily lever-aged to the Bank of Montreal, which also had tied down Westar Group. With the price of oil and gas still dropping like a stone, Pattison was looking for a way out.

Oilmen like to concentrate resources in core areas, so they will buy up leases within a patch of land maybe 145 kilometres square or smaller. Concentration creates economies of scale by cutting travel, management and exploration costs as the company saturates the section by doubling or quadrupling drilling. Westar Petroleum had several high-producing wells yielding about 1,800 barrels per day. It also had good infill possibilities for further exploratory drilling. And it was right next door to Stampeder's new Allheart acquisition. But it had something even more enticing: about $100 million in tax losses. If Stampeder could get its hands on those, it could pump oil and gas for years to come without paying a cent in taxes. In the energy business, playing with tax losses is a business in itself. So it was no wonder that Westar caught the eye of two other Calgary high flyers.

Murray Edwards and Jim Grenon were two lawyers with big profiles in Calgary's oil patch. Edwards, who is part owner of the Calgary Flames, and Grenon ran a merchant banking firm called Colborne Capital Corporation. The company operated out of Calgary's biggest oil and gas investment firm, Peters and Company. Their business plan was simple: using investor money from Peters and Company, they purchased companies full of tax losses. These companies then bought oil and gas assets, using the tax losses to offset profits. Westar Petroleum seemed a perfect fit.

Each side thought they had their own ace in the hole. Stampeder was close to the Bank of Montreal, which appeared to prefer Tonken's team. Edwards and Grenon, however, were close to Westar Petroleum president Tom Pointer. They had been working with Pointer to restructure the company. At the same time they had been trying to persuade Westar to give them the right of first refusal on any sale. But Pattison and his board refused; they wanted the sale open to all comers. It was soon apparent that the key player was the Bank of Montreal, which preferred Tonken and his management team.

To a guy like Edwards, Tonken was just an upstart. "Edwards told me I was just a lawyer and knew nothing about business," Tonken recalls. "Hell, he's a lawyer also.

"So people are circling around, looking for the opportunity to buy the shares of Westar Petroleum from Westar Group. We own the assets right next door. We are trying to buy those assets because I see all the upside drilling. I see a ton of drilling. There's no question that the tax losses are an opportunity not to pay taxes in the future. In fact, we had bought other assets that were short on tax pools because we thought we could buy Westar. But our number one goal was to buy Westar Petroleum because it had all those infilling opportunities, full stop."

By 1995, it was clear that Tonken was ahead. Westar owed the bank about $38 million and Tonken offered to buy out their position for $32 million, which the bank accepted. Westar then sold Stampeder its shares for $2 million.

"So I got a phone call from Murray Edwards and he said why don't I sell him the tax losses and I said, 'Why do I want to do that,'" Tonken remembers. Two days later, Tonken closed the deal. Tom Pointer was present at the closing but didn't say anything. Tonken thought he was angry because he was about to lose his job.

Westar Petroleum now belonged to Stampeder, but the transition wasn't going to be so easy. Edwards and Grenon hadn't given up. Without Tonken's knowledge, Pointer had signed a right of first refusal favouring Edwards and Grenon. Not even Westar's board knew about it. In fact, as it later came out in court, Pointer had no power to sign such a document. And oddly, he didn't mention it at the closing. But that didn't matter—Edwards and Grenon just wanted to use it as leverage.

On the Friday of the signing, just after the deal was publicly announced and just before Tonken was to take Stampeder on a road show to persuade investors to buy 5.5 million shares at $5.50 each to finance the Westar purchase, Edwards and Grenon struck. "Friday at about two in the afternoon a press release comes out issued by Murray Edwards's company saying he's got a right of first refusal on the shares of Westar Petroleum," Tonken says. What's more, Edwards and Grenon were threatening a lawsuit.

This was news to Stampeder's owners; nobody had ever mentioned a right of first refusal. This unexpected announcement by two respected oil patch players could destroy Tonken's deal. "And then we go to our law firm and get a phone call from a lawyer, who's representing Colborne Capital, and he said, 'Now, you can either sell us the tax losses or we'll go ahead with this lawsuit.'" Tonken says that the lawyer then added: "Do you want a little old man with grey hair to decide this in a few years, or do you just want to sell us the losses and go away?" Tonken, who was on the local boxing commission, wasn't about to lie down. "We said 'Fuck you' and they sued us."

Edwards and Grenon hoped the threat of a lawsuit would coerce Stampeder into cutting them into the Westar deal. The two men calculated that they could force a $15-million settlement with Stampeder. They didn't know Tonken.

Tonken was mystified at the Edwards team. The right of first refusal was clearly worthless. Why would he pursue the case? Tonken wanted a meeting. So the two met at a Calgary drive-in, ordered hamburgers and talked. "I said to him why don't you just go away because . . . you are going to destroy a number of people's careers," Tonken recalls. Edwards replied: "My lawyers tell me I have a fifty-fifty chance of winning." Tonken said: "You're crazy. You guys fabricated the documentation and now you are going to let these guys get hurt—for what?"

Edwards wouldn't back down.

Colborne Capital sued Stampeder for $27 million and Stampeder countersued for $35 million. In 1994, the case went to court. A year later, Tonken's refusal to cave in paid off. Stampeder won hands-down.

Judge Charles Virtue awarded Stampeder $3.63 million in damages plus $1 million in punitive damages. The judge lashed Grenon and Edwards in a 140-page judgment for fraudulently using the legal system for their own greed. He described their actions as a deliberate "plan of deception" and "a benighted and devious effort" filled with "concoctions falsely created," "deceitful," "dishonest and fraudulent" and "unlawful." The judge wrote:

"Colborne sought to employ a devious and tortuous scheme, and to abuse the process of the court, to gain a profit which Grenon predicted, at one point, to be in the vicinity of $15 million."

Colborne Capital had to cut a cheque immediately. A triumphant Tonken photographed it, framed the photo and stuck it on his office wall. It was his trophy. "A lot of our shareholders wanted us to settle on the basis that it was taking up too much of our time," he says. "My position was it was a real matter of principle. I had never seen someone fabricate a bunch of documents, sue you and then say, 'Hey, you do this and I'll do that.' Forget it."

It was a big win for Stampeder against two of Alberta's most aggressive players. Two years later, Júdge Virtue's judgment was substantially upheld on appeal. Damages, however, were reduced to $1.8 million. The appeals court denied the $1-million punitive damages but imposed additional legal costs on Colborne. "We are satisfied that the trial judge did not err in his conclusion that the conduct of Pointer, Grenon and Colborne was dishonest and deceitful," the appeals court ruled. An appeal to the Supreme Court of Canada fell by the wayside. By 2004 the case was closed. Any company venturing to use the court system to extort payment from rivals would now think twice. Judge Virtue finally had slammed the door on the practice. Stampeder's victory was complete.

Any setback for Murray Edwards was only temporary. He helped build Canadian Natural Resources Ltd. from a tiny start-up to a $22-billion company with a major stake in the oil sands. *Forbes* magazine in 2006 ranked Edwards number 562 on the list of the world's richest people, with assets of $1.4 billion.

Tonken and his partners in Stampeder quickly became heroes in the oil patch. The Calgary company was clearly on a roll and becoming a big name in energy circles. By the end of 1995 it had almost doubled its oil production to 9,478 barrels a day from 4,800 a year earlier, most of it "through the drill bit," as Tonken put it, meaning the company found it and drilled it. From a penny stock, they now were a mid-sized energy company with net cash flow closing in on $290 million. "We look to be a significant player in the oil and gas industry," he told a local paper at the time. "We'd like to be in excess of 100,000 barrels a day in five years."

By the end of 1997, Stampeder was well on its way to fulfilling Tonken's predictions. More acquisitions pushed its daily production to 38,000 barrels and catapulted it into the category of "senior producer." His company was now among the top twenty Canadian producers and was trading on the New York Stock Exchange. Then it caught the interest of the Americans and became an acquisition target.

Like any business, the oil patch has its fads. In 1997, the buzz was around heavy oil. It was thought that heavy oil reservoirs, although more expensive to extract, had greater reserves. J.P. Bryant, CEO of Gulf Canada Resources Ltd., was eager to do a significant deal in heavy oil. Stampeder fit the bill. When its stock suddenly slumped, Bryant made his move. In July 1997, Gulf Canada Resources offered a staggering $1.3 billion (including debt) for Stampeder. The five-cent company was now a billion-dollar player.

Tonken and his investors jumped at the deal. They believed the oil patch was entering a slump and they wanted out; it was time to ring the cash register. Ten years after he started Stampeder, his original investment of $6,000 had grown to $7 million. "It was an excellent run," he says with a smile. Of course, Tonken made a lot more than that; he had been buying stock all the way down the line. And now his dream was complete. He had played his hand in Alberta's biggest game and won. He had bested two of Alberta's major oilmen and now was a champion of the patch. In a few years he had become one of Alberta's newest multi-millionaires, quoted in newspapers and welcomed at the Petroleum Club. A beacon of hope to all those who longed to share the dream of the Alberta advantage.

Then it all came crashing down.

CHAPTER 8

THE MAULING OF BIG BEAR

IN WHICH 16 MILLION CUBIC FEET OF GAS PER DAY GOES MISSING AND TONKEN GETS DECKED

CASH RICH AND FOREVER EAGER TO PLAY THE GAME, JEFF Tonken was not about to retire.

A mere three months after selling Stampeder Exploration for $1.3 billion, he and his four principal investors were back in the game, ready to rebuild an empire around another miniature company—Colony Energy Inc. of Calgary. The company produced about 1,400 barrels of oil a day from Alberta properties—small potatoes for Tonken, but a good start. Once again he had big plans for a tiny oil company.

As part of the Colony deal, Tonken also acquired a tiny oil company with a bold name: Big Bear. He liked the name so much that he ditched the quieter Colony for the predator Big Bear Explorations Ltd. Tonken soon proved it had claws.

Tonken launched Big Bear on the same business plan used to build Stampeder Exploration—acquisitions and infill drilling. Tonken was betting that commodity prices had hit rock bottom and were set for a run. He knew there were a lot of small and medium-sized oil companies burdened with debt and bleeding red ink. His first target was a Calgary natural gas producer with solid core wells in Alberta and across the border in British Columbia.

The company was called Blue Range Resource Corporation and it was managed by two veteran oil patch executives, Gordon Ironside and Robert Ruff. Its estimated value was about $300 million. Big Bear's market value was a mere $30 million. The bear was about to swallow a whale.

Tonken saw Blue Range as a cash cow that could strengthen Big Bear, which was losing money at the rate of $2 million a quarter. Jockeying for hot properties in the oil patch was becoming intense and Tonken was eager to make his mark again and prove that Stampeder wasn't a fluke. (Under Gulf Canada's management, Stampeder suffered a major meltdown. Heavy oil prices had slumped to $7.76 from a high of $15.54, and Gulf had to take a writedown of $465 million, most of which was Stampeder. So Tonken got out just in time. It's a question of playing the commodity price cycles. Or so Tonken thought.)

Essentially, Tonken and his management team, which was the same one that built Stampeder, would replace management at Blue Range. This meant Ironside and Ruff would be looking at a pair of pink slips should Tonken buy their company. For this reason alone, Tonken figured they probably wouldn't be amenable to a takeover. So he approached Blue Range's institutional investors. To his surprise, they were dissatisfied with Ironside and Ruff's management and supported the takeover. "I signed a letter with four institutions to back the takeover bid, so I had about 35 percent of the shareholders," he recalls. He also bet that he could avoid a bidding war because most oil and gas companies were already carrying too much debt. He bid $299 million for Blue Range and gave the company twenty-one days to take it or leave it. Big Bear's stock was trading at only fifty cents. His bid was eleven Big Bear shares for one Blue Range. In effect he was just printing paper, issuing stock against the target company's presumed profits, betting that Blue Range's numbers were accurate.

Ironside and Ruff tried to fight the deal, but they were up against not only Tonken and his vaunted Stampeder attack squad of buyout specialists but also the four big institutional investors who controlled one-third of Blue Range. The institutions thought Blue Range was underperforming and Tonken could give it a testosterone boost. After all, the Stampeder success story spoke volumes about Tonken's prowess.

Ironside countered Big Bear's unfriendly bid by launching a publicity campaign designed to ridicule Tonken's management of Big Bear, which Ironside claimed had lost $19.4 million that year alone. Ironside convinced the Blue Range board to recommend that shareholders not accept Big Bear's offer. He initiated a shareholder rights plan that would at least delay the sale for forty-five days, buying him time to shake out supporters and rival bidders. He opened the company's books to about twenty potential suitors; strangely, none of them bit.

Tonken didn't see the warning signs. He didn't know, for instance, that Ironside had once been caught in an insider trading scandal. In 1987, Ironside bought and sold 666,666 shares of Olympia Energy Inc., a company controlled by another brash oil patch maverick, Gregory Noval, without filing insider trading reports. (Noval and four other principals of the company were also nabbed.) Tonken was blinded by his own eagerness to grab the bigger company. He was about to create another Stampeder and nothing was going to stand in his way. He believed he was getting in on the ground floor of what would become a steady rise in gas prices over the next ten years. "Had it worked out, we would have made out like bandits," he says. Greed was taking flight. "We're going to create a substantial producer," Tonken boasted to the media at the time. "We're going to build something that's bigger than Stampeder."

"If you've got to grow quarter by quarter by quarter, the only way to do it is to buy, drill and exploit," he says. "Blue Range can give us the production base we need."

With Tonken back in action, investors were licking their chops. For instance, Belco Oil & Gas Corp., a small New York producer whose market capitalization hovered around $800 million, invested $200 million of that money in the Bear.

On December 12, 1998, Tonken, after padding his bid to

$307 million, got what he wanted. Blue Range buckled and Big Bear took over. Once again, Tonken had won.

The takeover earned rave reviews from all the right analysts, who applauded the institutions that had initiated the buyout. "This is shareholder activism at its best," John Ing, president of Maison Placements Canada Inc. of Toronto, told the Canadian Press. "Management can no longer hide behind the veil of the board of directors . . . shareholders are saying enough is enough." Victor Flores, an analyst at HSBC Securities of Toronto, said: "Sometimes you need someone to stir the pot and get things going."

It was some pot and some stirring.

When Tonken took over on December 13, 1998, his strategy was all set. All he had to do was maximize the leases and gas production and then leverage that towards more buyouts. It seemed simple. Money would flow. But within twenty minutes of arriving at Big Bear's newly acquired asset, his plans went up in smoke.

Tonken's first inkling that something was wrong came when he saw the piles of shredded documents in Blue Range's corporate headquarters. A technician was hooking up a new shredding machine and told Tonken: "This is the third machine they have gone through in three weeks." That scared him. He knew that his hostile takeover meant he hadn't been able to conduct a complete due diligence on the company; he had to rely on its public statements. Given proper accounting procedures and securities laws, he had no reason to believe the figures would be wildly inaccurate. He was wrong on all counts.

"They were misrepresenting their production," Tonken says. "The production is not 13,000 barrels per day, it's 10,000 . . . 35 percent is missing." He says the second thing that floored him was the company's bank debt, which was $156 million and not $123 million as reported. The newly acquired company's total debt was a surprising $234 million and growing. Finally, Blue Range had hedged a lot of its gas sales at below market value. The company's production was actually falling and most of its gas sales were locked down either by long-term fixed price contracts or by transportation cost obligations. This meant the company couldn't take advantage of the increased gas prices, which Tonken had relied on when he made his bid. The lion's share of Blue Range's production had been sold to Enron Corporation, the giant Texas energy dealer.

Tonken summarizes the company's position this way: "They were topped up on their lines. They were short on gas. They had hedged all their gas. Their debts were way out of whack. Their production is short, and now we find out they had mortgaged all their infrastructure, which they didn't show on their balance sheet. So there was another $30 million in debt that didn't show."

It was the perfect recipe for bankruptcy. Within two days of taking over, Tonken was issuing revised numbers to his shareholders and investors. He then spent the next four weeks desperately trying to rescue the company. But it was pointless. Blue Range's credit was maxed out and its cash flow was dwindling. Because its production was dropping, it was forced to buy gas at a loss to meet its production contracts. The institutions that had originally backed Tonken dumped their stock at the first sign of trouble. Tonken and his fellow investors watched helplessly as Big Bear shares fell to 12 cents from $5.50. In February 1999, Blue Range was petitioned into bankruptcy and Tonken was completely undone.

The bankruptcy court cancelled Enron's fixed price contracts, which were valued at $49 million. This gave Blue Range breathing space, but it angered Enron. Enron's Canadian subsidiary sued and then launched a bid to take over the Blue Range assets for $200 million. But it was all to no avail. Enron itself was teetering. Loss of contracts such as these would soon help tip the Texas trader over the edge and into one of America's most spectacular business collapses.

Things got so weird that Tonken sued himself. Big Bear launched a $151-million lawsuit against its own subsidiary, Blue Range. Tonken hoped to grab Blue Range's gas wells, which without the encumbrance of fixed price contracts would be highly lucrative. But it didn't work out.

Tonken had clearly overstepped himself. As a hostile bidder, he hadn't had access to the company's books and had to rely on analysts' reports and annual statements. He made the mistake of trusting Blue Range's public statements and ended up buying a lemon. "You can't look under the hood at all when you launch a hostile takeover on another company," David Stenason of Scotia Capital Markets said at the time. "The Big Bear guys, they took that chance and they've had their heads handed to them."

"Every guy in Canada who watches you build up your company from zero to forty thousand barrels per day loved it that you were getting creamed," Tonken says with a certain amount of bitterness. "It's just the psyche of Canadians. They just can't stand to see people do well and they love to see people get beat up."

♦

The Big Bear/Blue Range case became a lightning rod for critics who claimed oil and gas reserve reports and energy company accounting methods were unreliable. Assessed reserves in the oil and gas business are a subjective gauge of an energy company's assets. They include current reserves and anticipated growth, which are assessed by independent petroleum engineers using past experience and probability calculations. Companies can then use their own methodology to report the engineering figures, which are speculative to start with. The game can be, as Tonken discovered, a total crapshoot not only for investors but also for a nation trying to assess its energy future.

Alberta's regulations basically left the description of a company's reserves to the company's discretion. No independent audit was required. So when a company claimed it had a million barrels of oil in the ground, an investor basically had to take it on faith even though the reserve numbers could mean almost anything from proven to simply estimated. Blue Range, for example, had concocted a method of reporting gas production and reserves using "heat adjustments" that increased their reserves by almost

10 percent and their production by as much as 14 percent. Executives Ironside and Ruff didn't bother to inform the public about these "heat adjustments." It seemed too many investors were getting burned by Alberta energy companies. Blue Range was the last straw. The credibility of the entire market was brought into question. In response, the Alberta government established a task force to look into this problem and the Alberta Securities Commission opened an investigation into Blue Range.

One result of the task force was the establishment of a system for categorizing reserves: *proven reserves* means there is at least a 90 percent probability the oil or gas is in the ground and recoverable; *proved and probable* means at least 50 percent probability; *proved, probable and possible* means at least a 10 percent probability. Each company would henceforth have a special committee of independent directors to assess the reserves annually and approve public statements. Admittedly, the system was still one part science and one part guesswork; it simply reflected the one-eyed optimism that says a company will be able to extract the oil or gas it claims is in the ground. It was thought that imposing an industry-wide quasi-mathematical calculation reflecting this confidence was the best anybody could do.

Tonken's one consolation was that the investigation into Blue Range led to a tightening of the rules. Blue Range had proved the system was seriously flawed. "It shook the whole place up. There was no standard way of doing these engineering reports. The oil and gas guys knew it. The industry thought that if an engineering report said the value was this, the value was that. But it's not. It was what the company was saying it wanted its engineering report to say."

◆

As for Blue Range, four companies bid for its assets, including Big Bear and Ironside Energy Ltd., a new company owned by Gordon Ironside. The court finally sold the company to Canadian Natural Resources Ltd. for $235 million cash. Ironically, Canadian

Natural Resources was owned by Murray Edwards. Freed from the vise-grip of Enron's fixed price contracts, Blue Range's gas wells were suddenly worth a lot of money and helped vault Edwards into the big time. Within two years Canadian Natural Resources became a billion-dollar earner and launched a $10.8-billion oil sands project north of Fort McMurray called Horizon, slated to open in 2008. Started in 1989 with nine employees and $1 million in the bank, Edwards's company now has 2,500 employees and a value of $22 billion. Tonken's dream had been fulfilled—but by his once-vanquished adversary.

Tonken, however, picked himself up and got back into the game. Big Bear survived, but barely. It was left with about $1 million in the kitty. No longer interested in the Bear, Tonken later sold it to Avid Oil and Gas Ltd. for $6 million.

Over the next five years, Tonken bought and sold three small oil and gas companies, earning investors tidy profits all along the way and restoring his reputation.

Meanwhile, the Alberta Securities Commission (ASC) continued to investigate the Blue Range scandal. Finally, in December 2006—eight years after the buyout by Big Bear—the ASC issued its report. It found that Ironside and Ruff had issued misleading financial reports, hid documents from its auditors, misrepresented the company's debt and overstated its reserve and production figures. As Ironside casually told the ASC hearing when explaining his company's reporting practices, it was a case of "buyer beware." The ASC imposed no sanctions against the two men, leaving these decisions for later hearings.

One of the unstated reasons for the delay in the ASC report was that the conduct of the ASC itself had come under investigation. Employees and various aggrieved businessmen, including Gordon Ironside, claimed that the ASC played favourites in its investigations, that it was incompetent, and that one of its senior staff had invested in a company that was a target of an investigation. At one point there were three separate investigations into the ASC: one by a Calgary lawyer who conducted an independent investigation, another by the RCMP and a third by the Alberta auditor general. The commission, which is the second largest in Canada next to the Ontario Securities Commission, almost crumbled under the weight of the serious charge that its investigations were sloppy, its record keeping inadequate, and that it was controlled by the oil and gas industry and the Conservative Party of Alberta. If true, the credibility of Alberta's market regulator would be shattered—a good reason for investors to shy away from the oil patch.

Alberta's auditor general, Fred Dunn, investigated eighty-two case files and concluded in 2005 that there were indeed serious problems at the ASC. There was a "lack of information in the files to support key decisions," he claimed. He added that he "found the most sensitive or potentially high-profile cases to be the most poorly documented." Dunn also found that the ASC's head of enforcement, John Petch, was in a conflict of interest when he bought shares in a company the commission was investigating. The auditor claimed Petch had bought the shares the same day he ordered the investigation. Dunn said Petch sold the shares three months later and made "significant profits." Petch claimed the transgression was inadvertent because he was not aware of his own agency's conflict guidelines. It also emerged that ASC chairman Bill Rice stayed on as chairman of Tesco Corp. in Calgary for three months after he had taken charge of the ASC. He also filed a late insider trading report for which he was fined one thousand dollars. While several other employees had recently been fired for violations of ASC regulations, neither Rice nor Petch were forced to resign. After Petch's stock play was revealed, he gave his profits to a food bank and apologized to his employees. But the scandals left a bitter taste and continued to raise questions about the ASC's credibility as a regulator.

After buying and selling several small energy plays, in November 2004 Tonken established Birchcliff Energy with his old team of investors: Larry Shaw, Scotty Cameron and Vern Siemens. They put in $15 million of their own money—"skin in the game" as oilmen like to say. Tonken raised $60 million in a junior pool and in 2005 paid $255 million for oil and gas assets in the Peace River

Arch near Grande Prairie in northwestern Alberta. Birchcliff has put him back on the twenty-ninth floor of a glass high-rise at the corner of Fifth Avenue and Fifth Street in the heart of Canada's energy sector. By the end of 2006, Birchcliff's revenues were $93.8 million. But the memory of Blue Range still rankles.

Even though Tonken had nothing to do with the demise of Blue Range, Ironside claimed in the media that Tonken had driven a healthy company into the ground. It stretched the imagination to believe that anybody could destroy a $250-million company in a few days—but plenty of investors believed it. "It killed my reputation," Tonken says. "It took me a long time to build my reputation back with common shareholders because they wondered, 'How stupid is this guy that he walks in, does a hostile takeover bid and he's in bankruptcy? Didn't he see it?'"

The answer is no. He was blinded by ambition hedged on prospects that were enormous. In the oil patch, the upside can be huge. There are plenty of happy Alberta investors who have cashed out of the game after watching their penny stock take flight, as Tonken experienced with Stampeder. Their instant wealth buys a scenic ranch in the foothills and winters in Arizona. But there are plenty more who get caught up in the great game, watch their investment disappear down a hole, and are left wondering why a company that had so much promise died so swiftly.

PART III

ALIEN
INVASION

◆

CHAPTER 9

LIFE ON MARS

IN WHICH WE EXPLORE ALBERTA IN 2100,
EXPERIENCE DEATH BY A BILLION BEETLES
AND CONTEMPLATE THE END OF SNOW

DAVID SCHINDLER LIVES IN A TWO-STOREY POST-AND-BEAM house on a hill overlooking a small river called the Lobstick. It meanders around the rolling hills west of Edmonton before flowing into the Pembina River, which in turn flows into the Athabasca. It's part of one of Alberta's most important watersheds. In fact, ultimately it's part of one of Canada's most important river systems, the Mackenzie. The only problem these days is that the Lobstick no longer flows after the spring runoff. For most of the summer it's dry.

Schindler began to notice progressive problems with the river in about 2000. The Lobstick drains Lake Chip near the small town of Wildwood as well as all the rivers that drain into the lake. Even in the hot summer the Lobstick didn't usually run dry. But the lake level had decreased enough that it was no longer draining into the river. At about the same time, another change also caught Schindler's eye.

He and his wife raise sled dogs as a hobby on their 160 acres of land. He needs that much land because the dogs are bred to run. He used to race them in "the ten good sled races" held every winter in the region. But in recent years there has been so little snow that the races had to be cancelled. Snow no longer falls as often as in previous years, and when it does it doesn't stay. Racing is now a past pleasure.

As a scientist who has studied the ways of rivers and lakes most of his life, the issue of water has acquired a fresh urgency for Schindler. In his view, it is the key issue around climate change: will we have enough water?

Schindler holds the Killam Memorial Chair in the Department of Biological Sciences at the University of Alberta, to which he was named in 1989 because of his knowledge of aquatic ecology and because he had proven that phosphates in laundry detergent and fertilizer were killing Canadian lakes and rivers by sapping them of oxygen. Ontario's Lake Erie in particular had been turning into pea soup because of all the phosphate-based detergents dumped into its water from cities and industries. Working at the time for the federal Department of Fisheries and Oceans, Schindler found himself up against a phalanx of not just soap manufacturers but also other commercial interests that used phosphate detergents in their industrial processes. These corporations blamed the greening of Canadian lakes on naturally formed nitrates and carbon—although they were hard pressed to explain this sudden natural phenomenon. Schindler proved them wrong.

His experiment was lengthy but simple. He placed an enormous plastic curtain across the narrows of an hourglass-shaped lake, which he dubbed Lake 226, near Kenora, Ontario. Over an eight-year period he added carbon and nitrogen to both sides of the lake, but on one side he also added phosphorus. The side receiving phosphorus immediately developed blue-green algae while the other side did not. The aerial photos dramatically showing the difference had a global impact. After years of resistance from industry, governments around the world finally had the proof they needed to restrict or ban the use of phosphates. In 1991 the Swedish government awarded Schindler the Stockholm Water Prize for this research. But while he was showered with praise abroad, back home Ralph Klein, who was Alberta's environment minister, was trying to discredit him.

The fight was over the construction of a bleached kraft pulp mill on the Athabasca River in 1990 by Alberta-Pacific Forest Industries Inc. (Al-Pac). Al-Pac is owned by the Japanese giant Mitsubishi Corporation, whose gross profit in 2006 was $10.4 billion. Despite the fact that Mitsubishi is one of the world's most profitable companies, the Alberta government awarded it a cornucopia of goodies. The province lent the company $275 million in income debentures to finance construction of the plant, threw in a $75-million grant to cover the cost of roads, railway lines and utilities, gifted the company the land on which the plant was built, and then added a huge forest management agreement that gave the company 73,426 square kilometres of boreal forest with the lowest stumpage fees in the country. But when Alberta quietly permitted the plant's construction without any environmental impact studies, ignoring the province's own environmental laws, Schindler stepped in.

Schindler publicly protested that the plant would pollute the Athabasca River with dioxins and furans, which are chemical by-products of bleaching paper pulp. Both are stable chemical compounds that accumulate in the body and in large enough doses can cause cancer and other health problems, such as liver disease and serious skin rashes. The public responded to his concerns by demanding hearings into the mill's construction, which forced the Alberta government to create a citizens' panel that included Schindler. It also included three friends of Premier Don Getty plus local business people who would benefit from the plant. For the government, it seemed like a well-stacked committee. But the government hadn't figured on the persistence of Schindler. "What I did was make sure they heard from government scientists who knew about dioxins and furan production," Schindler recalls. The panellists became so concerned about the health of the river and the local communities that they recommended against construction of the plant.

The government was furious. "In 1990, they actually tried to get the university to fire me," Schindler says.

I had heard from other Alberta academics, who had opposed

the government in one way or another, that the Conservatives had tried to kill their funding or had threatened their jobs. So I called Rod Love, who had been Klein's chief of staff, and asked him about Schindler.

"We didn't like him much," he said. "No question about that. And maybe somebody said, 'I wish that prick was gone.' But no, nobody tried to get him fired."

Love added that the Conservatives regarded most of the professors that opposed the government as "flakes."

"They weren't scientists, they were politicians . . . We would say 'This is not science. This is a political agenda not an environmental agenda and they didn't like it. Fuck'em."

"What did you say?"

"I said they didn't like them."

"I thought you said 'fuck'em'?" No response from Love. "You rejected [their science] because it was against the government?"

"We believed that it was a political agenda. Schindler was just a professor over there, a professor who sets political agendas.

"All professors?"

"Many."

Whatever words were exchanged between Klein's office and the university, Schindler didn't care; he was determined to face down the government on an environmental issue where the government had done its best to avoid scientific inquiry by dismissing critics as simply politically motivated.

Pressure was also put on panel members to change their conclusions, and many were ready to buckle. "All the other members of the panel pretty well ducked," Schindler says. "I said, 'I'm not ducking.' Klein and I had some pretty nasty exchanges in the papers." In the end, Al-Pac came up with new plans for a much cleaner plant. It was eventually built in 1993 and is still considered one of the cleanest pulp mills in the world.

For Schindler, the Al-Pac affair again put his name out there as a serious adversary and scientist. Which was a good thing when you consider what was around the corner.

◆

In addition to his own experience of watching his backyard river run dry, Schindler began to receive information about other disturbing occurrences involving water systems in Alberta. "In the last several years I've had repeated calls from people about bad alga blooms, increased intensity of blooms, people whose wells are going dry, fish kills on some of the southern Alberta rivers. It's been really clear that a trend was happening." This time, however, he thought the problem was more complex than the phosphate-induced algae he had earlier studied. Water flow has a major influence on nutrification of lakes and rivers. "It's very basic. If there is less water to dilute the nutrients, there's higher concentration of nutrients and therefore more intense alga blooms." The question, of course, was why. This time he couldn't simply blame it on phosphates.

But even these concerns weren't enough to really get him going. "I think the final thing that got me thinking about looking at the long term was evidence from the University of Regina, Dave Sauchyn, who works on tree rings, and Peter Leavitt, who works on the paleolimnology of the lakes." Limnology is the study of lakes and their ecosystems, which is Schindler's specialty. Paleolimnology, as Leavitt describes it, is an "aquatic archaeology of things that live in lakes." Essentially, he digs up the sediment and examines it for fossilized creatures.

Sauchyn and Leavitt compared historical data on precipitation over the last century to tree ring patterns and to sediment development in lakes during the same period. There was a definite correlation. Tree ring development, for example, was much thicker during periods of high precipitation. During periods of reduced precipitation, lake and river sediments showed heavier growth of diatoms. These are microscopic communities of algae that expand with increased salinity in water, which occurs during periods of drought. In other words, tree rings and/or sediments could be used to project back in time to reveal periods of high precipitation and periods of drought in centuries past.

Sauchyn examined logs that were as much as four hundred years old. Leavitt studied sediments dating back six thousand years or more. (Scientists can carbon-date lake and river muds, thereby revealing the age of the sediment. The fossilized algae content in the sediment is then an indicator of climate conditions during that period.) They further verified their findings by examining written documents from the Hudson's Bay and North West trading companies as well as the diaries of early explorers such as Captain John Palliser. Palliser in 1857 led the British North America Exploring Expedition from Winnipeg to the Rockies. He is best known for his comments on the drought conditions of southern Alberta and his observation that most of southern Alberta "will forever be comparatively useless" for farming because of drought. This dry area became known as the Palliser Triangle. A prolonged drought also occurred there between 1878 and 1896. Despite drought conditions, Canada was determined to lure settlers to this area. This sparked the *Medicine Hat Times* to write an editorial on February 5, 1891, stating that "it would be almost criminal to bring settlers here to try to make a living out of straight farming."

Sauchyn's and Leavitt's studies indicated that droughts in the eighteenth and nineteenth centuries were much more severe than those in the twentieth. Some lasted as long as forty years, which makes the devastating drought of the Great Depression from 1928 to 1936—when a quarter of a million people abandoned the Prairies—look puny in comparison. In earlier centuries, data indicate that droughts lasted seventy years or more, with the odd spike in precipitation. In other words, over the last century Albertans have been lucky. Going back even further in time, to about nine thousand years ago, warmer temperatures and prolonged droughts had dried up most of Lake Manitoba and Lake Winnipeg. "[Nine thousand years ago] you can find grass right across most of Lake Manitoba and a good fraction of Lake Winnipeg, and these are massive lakes tens of thousands of square kilometres," Leavitt says. "They just weren't there. So it was either a lot drier for a lot longer or quite a bit warmer or both. When we are reconstructing climate, we seem to be looking mainly at water availability, and I would actually argue that it is the main thing that we have to worry about."

Sauchyn and Leavitt concluded that the twentieth century was an unusually wet century, the likes of which we haven't seen before. Leavitt's research shows the twentieth century to have been the wettest in twenty centuries. "I think the bottom line is we have probably been fooled into thinking the twentieth century was normal weather here," Schindler says. "It seems very unlikely we'll get a second wet century in a row. When I considered the terrific increases we've had in Alberta in population and industry here, and this of course translates directly into demand for water, I thought we could be in big trouble."

The prairies are, of course, naturally dry. The Rockies block Pacific moisture. Minor changes in trade winds can have a big effect. "If you look back at history, First Nations people, prairie populations, were nomadic," Leavitt notes. "We believe that this was partly in response to the fact that you could go a decade without significant precipitation. I think there is a message there for modern society, that as we build these fixed-emplacement cities and towns and that sort of thing, that this isn't the way to adapt to droughts and we are becoming more vulnerable rather than less vulnerable as a result. So with the economic boom driven largely by natural resources in Alberta, we are certainly seeing a situation where we are developing infrastructure based on the idea that the twentieth century's water supply is the norm, and when we look back in time we don't see any evidence that that is the case."

What Sauchyn and Leavitt had done was use the past to predict future droughts. Schindler wanted to take their work one step further and see what was happening now with river systems in the western prairies. He was particularly interested in water sources and river flows, the crucial indicators of the long-term health of any watershed.

Alberta has seven river basins and major sub-basins. All of them are sourced through a spidery grouping of capillary-like rivers and streams that drain the snowpacks and glaciers of the Rocky Mountains. In most cases, the foothills and prairies do not produce enough runoff water to sustain these rivers. Precipitation during any given season is too light and evaporation rates are too high to make a significant impact. This is particularly true in the south, where the golden brown grasslands and dusty soil serve as a constant reminder that Calgarians live precariously on the edge of drought. In other words, the snows and glaciers of the Rockies supply the lifeblood that courses through the river and lake systems of Alberta, creating a habitat that can sustain only moderate human populations.

Schindler and fellow scientist William Donahue first had to examine what was actually happening with Alberta's climate. The federal environment department maintains a climate database that tracks temperatures throughout the country. Until Schindler came along in 2001, nobody had really bothered to analyze this data. The two scientists chose seven locations right across the province where data dated back before 1925. They chose areas that would not be affected by urban hot spots such as airports or other massive heat-reflecting concrete structures. It was immediately apparent that not only were these areas warming, but they also were getting reduced amounts of precipitation and increased rates of evaporation. These were not signs of a healthy future.

Alberta keeps records of river flows, but here again nobody had bothered to track them. Schindler discovered reductions that ranged from 20 to 84 percent. In the north, the Peace River was down in the crucial summer months by about 40 percent. The Athabasca, which is the only river in Alberta that has no dams, had decreased 30 percent since 1970 alone.

"Worst affected is the South Saskatchewan River, where summer flow has been reduced by 84 percent since the early twentieth century," Schindler later wrote. The South Saskatchewan basin is heavily taxed for irrigation. About 70 percent of Canada's irrigated farmland—about one million acres—is located south of Calgary. Each year approximately 2.5 cubic kilometres of water is taken from the river for irrigation. The province has been handing out water allocations since 1910 and stopped only in September 2006 because areas of the Bow sub-basin had almost slowed to a trickle.

"The confusion is we look at Canada and we think, 'Oh, there's lots of water there,'" Schindler says. "But only a couple of percent is renewed per year. The reason it's all lying around is, number one, we have lots of basins left by the glaciers to catch it and, number two, there's not much evaporation 'cause it's cold. But the warmer weather is increasing evaporation."

Schindler next examined the rivers' sources. He discovered that snowpack melt on the mountains had accelerated and winter snowfall was increasingly replaced by rain. This means the late spring thaw that swells the rivers is coming earlier and is less intense. Also, because of rising temperatures, the rate of evaporation is higher and the period over which evaporation occurs lasts longer due to shorter winters. Therefore, there are reduced amounts of water for summer irrigation. What's more, glaciers feeding all the major river systems have receded dramatically since 1970. "The Saskatchewan glacier has declined about 1.5 kilometres," Schindler says. "It's attributable to global warming—probably 95 percent certain that it's greenhouse gases." The same is true for the Athabasca glacier. Schindler says he can't predict when these glaciers will actually dry up; it all depends on the rate at which Alberta warms and also how much it warms. What he does know, however, is that glaciers have now receded so much that glacial melt is declining.

A major problem is a lack of data. Donahue discovered that, because of budget cuts, since 1993 the Alberta and federal environment departments have greatly reduced their monitoring of river flows and snowpack cover. Alberta has gutted its environment department. Since 1993 it has eliminated about a third of its positions and closed its chemistry laboratory. So the department now has neither the manpower nor the tools to monitor climate change, or even to enforce environmental laws. "It can't even patrol the once-thriving cold water fisheries because it doesn't have a budget for gas," Schindler says.

Consequently, as Donahue discovered, almost all the record keeping has been done in easily accessible southern urban areas. In some cases Donahue discovered that government scientists had monitored snowpack not in the winter, as one would expect, but in the summer, in which case he just saw a lot of zeros on their charts. "So there is less and less data available at a critical time for critical locations, and it's almost all coincided with budget cuts," Donahue says. "I would argue that [gathering data] is probably the most important thing, period. It's more important than terrorism, more important than Afghanistan, more important than the oil boom. We have not got any understanding of the major ecological processes and the limits under which we are going to start getting ecological collapse. And I don't mean birds are going to disappear or trees or whatever. I mean what most people don't seem to understand is that everything relies on environmental services, processes, water supply, rivers as pipelines that carry away all our waste. Clean air, clean water, you name it, the services the environment provides allow us to do what we do. The degrees of change that are evident and the projection for future change are pretty extreme. Likely what's going to happen is we are going to hit some break points. We're going to get collapses in systems that people rely on and we will suddenly realize that we have been fiddling while Rome is burning."

To make things even worse, Alberta has permitted and con- tinues to permit the mass destruction of its wetlands in rural and urban areas. Almost half of Edmonton is paved-over lakes or wet- lands. Fifty major wetland areas in the water-hungry region south and east of Calgary have been destroyed to make way for farm- ing. Oil and gas drilling throughout the province has also laid waste to countless wetlands. The biggest destruction so far is in the region of the oil sands. Here, oil companies have destroyed thousands of acres of boreal forest wetlands, including rare fens. The boreal forest represents three to four thousand years' accu- mulation of peat, with pine trees surrounded by wetlands, natural canals and shallow lakes. Many of the wetlands have been plowed up and drained in order to get at the oil sands beneath.

According to a 2006 report by the federal Department of Fisheries and Oceans, nobody yet knows what impact this ongoing destruction has had on the Athabasca River, its downstream flows to the Peace-Athabasca delta, and its fisheries. "A key concern is the ongoing removal of tributary streams that contribute food and nutrients and are used for spawning and rearing habitat within the mineable Oilsands area," the federal report states. In other words, the federal and Alberta governments have been handing out water licences for the extraction of almost 400,000 cubic metres per day without knowing the effect on the river and its marine life. Furthermore, no one has figured out how to restore the fens and wetlands devastated by the oils sands companies. Without wetlands to soak up the water, floods are becoming more frequent. "We just have a habit of stripping the defences of our ecosystem," Schindler says. "We're setting ourselves up in several ways both for floods and for droughts."

Southern Alberta experienced a long drought beginning in 2000. By 2005, Albertans had pronounced it over because the rains returned and in some cases caused spring flooding. Schindler says drought is a long-term process that is often punctuated with relatively brief wet spells. "This year [2006] we're dry again. This year actually is the driest I've ever seen." During the drought many ranchers survived only because of the fees they received from energy companies for the right to drill on their properties.

For Schindler, Leavitt and Sauchyn, their studies into tree rings, mud sediments, glaciers and precipitation all point to one thing and one thing only: Alberta is running out of water.

"What we're going to see is we've got a trend of increasing population and industry, a trend of increasing temperature doing all the things I talked about with glaciers, snowpacks and evaporation," Schindler says. "The wild card we really can't predict is if and when we get a prolonged drought. I think when all of those things collide, that is when we will see a water shortage. And as I mentioned, we could be in it now."

The effect, he says, will devastate Alberta. Agriculture is near collapse because of drought and debt, and forestry is in crisis because of the mountain pine beetle infestation. "Plus we've had more forest fires this year [2006] than in any year in Alberta's history. Luckily they have done a good job in containing them. It's been also a low-wind year. Pine beetles are just starting to move into the province from Bristish Columbia. Give it five years and every pine tree in Alberta will be dead pretty well, and once they are dead that is a classic set-up for fire. So forestry will be toast."

The mountain pine beetle is usually killed off each year by prolonged cold of minus twenty-eight degrees Celsius and by forest fires. But the last sixteen years has seen only two winters that have been cold enough. Rising temperatures due to global warming combined with fire suppression techniques have created since 2000 the largest North American pest infestation in recorded history. By the end of 2005, the tiny black beetles had killed 450 million cubic metres of pine—equivalent to six years of harvest in Canada, according to the Canadian Forest Service. The climate has warmed up so much that in 2006 the beetles spread to the western pine forests of Alberta—including Banff National Park—and eventually will move into Saskatchewan. (Meanwhile, warmer temperatures in the Yukon have caused an infestation of spruce beetles that by 2006 was in its fifteenth year, according to the Yukon Department of Energy, Mines and Resources.)

A prime target of the pint-sized pine beetle are the lodgepoles. The tall, thin pine is Alberta's official tree. The Canadian Forest Service predicts the little black beetle will munch its way through 80 percent of British Columbia's and Alberta's mature pine trees by 2013, killing off Alberta's official tree, before spreading through the northern boreal forest of Jack pines and into Ontario and Quebec, devastating Canada's forests. (Quebec, however, has pre-empted most of the work of the pine beetle by logging 80 percent of its boreal forest.) To make matters worse, scientists have recently discovered that the pine beetle is also beginning to feast on spruce trees. Schindler points out that the effect on ecosystems and watersheds of a treeless environment will be enormous because the deforested lands will be unable to retain water.

Alberta's cities already are feeling the strain of overpopulation and reduced water supplies and are taking steps to conserve water. Schindler is not optimistic: "I don't think it will be enough because the growth rate is too fast." Alberta has a plan to divert water from the Peace River to the south, as California has done with its northerly rivers. The cost would be in the billions and the environmental destruction to the Mackenzie River system would be enormous. But the province sees no alternative.

Reduced water flow will also affect the expanding oil sands projects, which require two to six barrels of water to produce one barrel of oil. It is predicted that water extraction from the Athabasca River will triple over the next ten years as more oil sands projects come on stream. By 2020 oil sands operations could be using the equivalent of half of the Athabasca River's low winter flow.

"The oil sands are very close to oversubscribing [taking too much water out of] the flow of the Athabasca," Schindler says. "The difference there is that we have a different critical point in the river. In the southern parts, where there is no ice on the rivers in the winter, there's a big stress on the cold water fisheries in the summer. We get lethal temperatures for some of the species exceeded every year. In the north, the critical period is in mid-winter, and it's [related to levels of] oxygen. With all of that organic matter in the form of petrochemicals coming in, the Athabasca and many of its tributaries have a pretty good oxygen sag [reduced oxygen content] during winter under ice . . . If you have less water in the river, of course, there is less oxygen as well, because there is less volume. The concern there is winter low flow conditions. Overall, it is the same sort of effect. The people downstream in the Peace-Athabasca delta have already, due to climate warming and the Bennett Dam [on the Peace River], seen a lot of their resources simply dry up, and if they get

Oil Sands effluent

less water coming from the Athabasca as well, it will just accelerate what is happening. It's mostly Aboriginal people in this area."

Forest fires and the destruction of peatlands enhance climate change by sending carbon and methane into the atmosphere. The most conservative climate model forecasts for Alberta indicate that mean temperatures will rise a further two or three degrees by mid-century. This is only if we lower our greenhouse gas emissions. If we continue at the present rate, temperatures will rise six to eight degrees Celsius. "If that happens, I don't think there is a scientist who will tell you that we can adapt."

Schindler is a stocky, muscular man with powerful arms and hands, a broad mouth and facial features that remind you of Raymond Massey. He speaks his doomsday words in a disarmingly clinical manner that leaves you wondering if he really said what you thought he just said or was he just describing the art of dissecting a frog. So you ask the key question. Is Alberta doomed?

"We're doomed in terms of the sort of lifestyle and fauna and flora around us that we see. Most people don't connect things like mountain pine beetle outbreaks to global warming. They think all those foresters running around cutting down trees are going to stop it. Well, they've had four years now and they haven't stopped it. It's spreading faster than ever. It's time for a second look. They know the river behind their house is low, but either they think it must be a local coincidence or they think they really have to divert the Peace River to southern Alberta and it will all be okay, not realizing the cost of doing that, not to mention the environmental damage. I don't think people look very far ahead."

Schindler was born in Minnesota, where he did his under-graduate work. He won a Rhodes Scholarship and obtained his doctorate in environmental sciences at Oxford University. He also has eight honorary degrees and a long list of academic awards. He says he immigrated to Canada because it offered a chance to be close to his laboratory—our endless expanse of lakes and rivers. Despite his clinical tone, there's a touch of panic in his voice.

I describe a doomsday scenario, thinking he will say I'm going too far: "By the end of this century the southern half of the province will be a desert. The northern half will be dug up for oil sands. The entire province will simply be a network of coal bed methane and in situ mining operations, most of which will have been abandoned; the forests will be destroyed by the pine beetle, forest fires and clear cutting; and there won't be any water for anybody. So at the end of the day you will have a pot of gold with no place to live, except maybe the odd oasis."

Without flinching, Schindler nods his agreement. "Yeah, and all this would be like Palestine, with a huge population of people with a small land base. It's going to be like Newfoundland after the cod was gone."

"It sounds pretty stupid to me."

"It is pretty stupid."

"Why are Albertans so stupid?"

"A dollar in hand is worth two in the future. Remember the Garden of Eden. Most people here are bible smackers and faithfully believe all that. Go to Newfoundland. Newfoundland had a huge population increase. They cut down all the trees and got rid of all the fish. Now their livelihood is gone and so is the means by which to keep warm. So what do you have but a bunch of people sitting on a rock. And most of them are moving to Alberta, and their successors will suffer the same fate unless we put on the brakes."

"Can we stop it?"

Schindler sighs. "We can survive and at least do a fairly good job of adapting to 2050 conditions with projected increases in temperature, with no population increases and some restrictions on digging. We're still going to have huge forestry damage, things like that. I think we can adapt to that. It's going to be a costly adaptation, though. But 2100, I don't think we have a hope in hell."

"What do you mean?"

"By 2100, with business as usual, we would be so far out in extreme temperature ranges. We're out there by eight degrees centigrade by 2100, that's just a huge increase in temperature. We'll probably still have a few humans scurrying around on the Prairies, but it won't be anything like as affluent. They'll be moving to other areas if they can find them."

CHAPTER 10

HELLO! IS ANYBODY OUT THERE?

IN WHICH THE FEDS IGNORE WARNINGS
FROM A SENIOR GEOLOGIST,
TERRORISTS BLOW UP A HOSPITAL, ALBERTA TRIES TO BRIBE
QUEBEC, AND A RELUCTANT ENVIRONMENT MINISTER SHUTS
DOWN HIS BRAIN

For over a century, the Geological Survey of Canada, an arm of the federal natural resources department, has mapped and remapped Canada's surface and subsurface rock formations to such a minute degree that there is barely a square metre—or cubic metre for that matter—of this country that hasn't in some form or another been surveyed by this body of geoscientists. The GSC also researches new technologies for probing deeper into Canada's subsurface rock formations both on land and under the sea. As fossil fuels get harder and more expensive to find, demand grows for more precise tools to locate what treasures might be found down there and for knowledge on how to extract them with minimal environmental damage.

More recently, however, the GSC's research has taken a new direction. Canadians have been so good at locating mineral and fossil fuel deposits, so thorough at plumbing the depths of Canada's rock formations—as well as the rock formations of almost every continent—that geologists are trying to get a more precise reading on just how much is left down there and what a downward slide in reserves would mean for Canada's future. It's an area of inquiry usually reserved for economists. But some geologists realized that their broad expertise not only in locating ore bodies but also in the complex techniques required to get them out of the ground, together with the accompanying environmental issues, give them a more complete picture of the mining and drilling business than that held by economists who crunch reserve numbers and hypothesize about future economic trends. The geoscientists thought they had substantial expertise to add to this more politically sensitive aspect of managing Canada's resources.

In compiling the data, geoscientists were finding that, when it came to conventional fossil fuels, our reserves were showing definite signs of stress. By the beginning of this century they began to realize that Canada's conventional oil and gas reserves were peaking and Canadians were riding the downside of the energy curve even as they increased consumption and exports to the United States. The implications were huge. A pending shortage of Canadian and/or world reserves could undermine our entire free trade economy. So it was not entirely surprising that politicians didn't want to hear about it. Which is why, in 2001, David Hughes suddenly found himself ignored.

Hughes was one of what you might call the new geologists—men and women who use their geoscience expertise not just to find energy but also to assess long-term reserves. For more than thirty years he has worked out of the GSC's Calgary offices, studying Alberta's geological formations. Consequently, few people know this underground world of seismic lines as well as he does.

More recently, his expertise has concentrated on the exploitation of coal bed methane. The southern half of Alberta from Grande Prairie in the west to Lloydminster on the Saskatchewan border and then south to Montana is one enormous coal zone. The Alberta Utilities and Energy Board estimates there are about 500 trillion cubic metres of methane gas—or almost ten times our current natural gas reserves—bonded to the coal seams found within this area. Since 2001, gas companies have drilled more than 7,700 wells, concentrated primarily in a section of the Horseshoe Canyon formation east of Calgary, in the rolling ranchlands and farmlands around Drumheller. The industry projects it will drill about 60,000 wells in total by 2020. Extracting the methane is an expensive process which requires that the companies fracture the coal seams and use chemicals to help free the gas. Environmental issues include contamination of water wells with methane gas and petroleum pollutants, the release of a highly potent greenhouse gas, and the digging up of huge areas of the Alberta plains. Such a dense array of wells has to be drilled per section that the area around Drumheller, as Hughes puts it, looks as if it has been "carpet-bombed." The mere fact that energy companies are going to such lengths to extract natural gas is just another sign that Canada is running out of conventional natural gas. It shows a certain desperation, considering that conventional gas wells are much easier to exploit.

As he watched gas companies drill more and more wells with less and less payback, Hughes began to speculate about when Canada will run out of oil and gas and what will happen when it does. In other words, he found himself probing the realm of King Hubbert and his mathematical calculations for peak oil and how they applied to Canada. He didn't like what he saw. "When you look at it, it's a tad shocking," he says in his typically understated style.

♦

Hughes discovered that Canada's natural gas reserves could run out by 2014, if not earlier. His research showed that Canada's conventional gas reserves peaked in 2001, which was one reason gas prices began to skyrocket. We have to drill an increasing number of gas wells just to keep up with demand. In 1996 we drilled 4,000 productive wells to get 15.7 billion cubic feet per day of gas. By 2001 we were drilling 10,757 wells to get 17.4 billion cubic feet per day. These drilling figures have continued to rise. In 2005 we drilled 15,000 wells to get 17 billion cubic feet per day. Decline in the average productivity of wells is 21 percent in Canada and 28 percent in the United States, where reserves peaked in 2000. "We have to drill more and more and more to get the same amount of natural gas," Hughes says. Canada's gas reserves declined to 56.4 trillion cubic feet (TCF) in 2005, from 62 TCF in 1998.

Coal bed methane, which is another form of natural gas, was supposed to be the saviour. In 2002 the government claimed there were 500 TCF—ten times more than our current reserves of natural gas. These reserves, Ottawa claims, will last at current production rates until 2080. Hughes's studies, however, showed that most of the 500 TCF of methane gas the government claimed was in the coal is not recoverable. In 2006, he came out with figures that showed recoverable gas was between 11 TCF and 45 TCF—enough to replenish our reserves for maybe another eight years at most.

◆

By 2007, Alberta energy companies were cutting back their conventional natural gas exploration programs because they were too costly and the payback was too small. Despite this decline in exploration, our gas consumption is rising and we are exporting more each year to the United States. In 2005, Canada produced 6.2 TCF of natural gas. Of this amount, we shipped 3.7 TCF south of the border.

Oil sands companies are also consuming increasing amounts of natural gas. Demand for gas to heat the water that extracts oil from the sands continues to climb. In the last six months of 2006 demand rose about 300 million cubic feet a day. The Alberta government predicts that by 2015 gas consumption in the oil sands will triple. This will be equivalent to about one-third of Canada's current annual domestic consumption. The present daily burn rate of natural gas at the oil sands is enough to heat more than three million homes. Natural gas not only heats nearly half of all homes in Canada—more than six million—it also supplies thousands of industries with energy to produce value-added goods and is the basic feedstock for the petrochemicals industry, which manufactures plastics and other synthetics plus fossil fuel–based fertilizers that allow us to maintain our food production. Without natural gas, these companies will leave Canada. Yet Canada now sells 60 percent of its natural gas to the U.S.A., and these exports are growing as American gas reserves continue to decline. This is a vital resource, and Canada is running out.

The news is no better for conventional oil. By the end of 1998 we had reserves of 4.8 billion barrels, according to the Canadian Association of Petroleum Producers. By 2002 this was down to 4.5 billion, and by the end of 2004 it was 4.3 billion. Alberta has basically been drilled out and we cannot expect any new important finds that will stop the downward curve, Hughes says. Which leaves the oil sands. And Hughes's research shows that the oil sands reserve estimates are overblown.

The Alberta Energy and Utilities Board (EUB) claims the sands hold 174 billion barrels of marketable oil. This, says Hughes, is speculative at best. He claims the figure could be as low as 11 billion. "Oil sands don't represent a resource problem, they represent a deliverability problem," he says. Although we know the oil is in the ground, there are still too many unsolved variables that could prohibit extraction in the longer term. The question of deliverability involves a complex assortment of factors that includes geology, engineering, the wholesale destruction of Alberta's environment, global warming and the availability of water and raw materials such as natural gas. Says Hughes: "My conclusion—bottom line—is when conventional oil goes into decline, we will get a little bit of incidental boost from unconventional oil [oil sands] but it is just not possible to offset a significant decline in conventional oil. If you look at Alberta's oil sands, it's a mess right now." Hughes's essential point is that there are still too many unanswered questions to put much stake in the long-term viability of the oil sands.

To begin with, the gas needed to heat the bitumen and extract it from the sands is a huge question mark. We need about one barrel equivalent of natural gas to obtain two barrels of oil. To achieve production of four million barrels per day, Hughes says the industry will need all the daily production of the Mackenzie Valley, which is Canada's last remaining untapped major gas field.

The same is true of water. We need two to five barrels of water for every barrel of oil. The Athabasca River is already strained from the amount of water extracted by just three oil sands operations—Syncrude, Suncor and Shell. And at least twenty more projects are either under construction or awaiting approval from the EUB, with projected capital expenditures—so far—of about $110 billion.

We also need enormous amounts of light synthetic oil to dilute the heavy bitumen so it can flow through pipelines to the refineries in Edmonton and the United States. Much of this will have to be brought in by pipeline as the sands are exploited. It's a crazy economic equation: we are piping oil to the oil sands to dilute bitumen so we can pipe it to refineries. "It's like bringing coal to Newcastle," Hughes says. "We'll need to import 40 percent of the global production [of synthetic oil dilutants]."

The Alberta government forecasts oil sands production will rise from the present one million barrels per day to three million by 2015 and four million by 2020. Hughes says the economics cannot justify such predictions; the cost per barrel makes no sense. In 2002, Shell Canada estimated capital costs at $4 billion to increase oil sand production at its Athabasca mine by 100,000 barrels per day. By July 2006, cost overruns had almost doubled to $7.3 billion. Just a few months later, Shell announced they had increased again to $12.8 billion. So Shell will have to spend $128,000 in capital costs for each barrel of extra production capacity. By comparison, the cost of taking a barrel out of the Saudi desert is about two dollars. Despite these costs, however, Shell announced in November 2006 that it was proceeding with the project designed to raise its production to 255,000 barrels a day. The following month the company received government approval.

Other companies are taking drastic actions to keep costs down. Synenco and its Chinese partner SinoCanada Petroleum had by December 2006 decided to ship jobs to China. Synenco claimed its estimates for the Northern Lights mine north of

Fort McMurray had almost tripled to $4.4 billion from $1.7 billion. To keep costs from rising even higher, the company has an ambitious plan that includes constructing most of its equipment in China. The company will build thirty modules of up to two thousand tons and ship them around the top of Alaska and then down the Mackenzie, Slave and Athabasca Rivers to their mine site. One problem still to be overcome is the Slave River's four main rapids—all of which are like walls of rock and one of which is called the Rapids of the Drowned. Canada classifies them as "very violent and dangerous rapids, not navigable." That will be quite a portage.

Petro-Canada, on the other hand, decided in 2006 to delay start-up of its Fort Hills oil sands project until at least 2008 because it predicted costs at between $13 billion and $19 billion, or as much as $190,000 per barrel per day on infrastructure. That's a huge discrepancy and indicates the companies are flummoxed by inflated costs as their project designs become more detailed and reality sets in. Petro-Canada's stock immediately fell 5 percent. French oil company Total SA also announced a postponement.

Hughes says that, despite the hype, Canada is not the energy superpower politicians like to pretend it is. Rapidly running out of conventional oil and gas, it is now in a blind race to sell off the oil sands. And if we put our faith in renewable or alternative energy sources, we're dreaming, Hughes says. Eighty-seven percent of the world's energy comes from hydrocarbons. Most of the balance is nuclear and hydro. Windmills, solar energy and the like account for less than one percent. Furthermore, alternative sources of energy don't have the same calorie kick as hydrocarbons, nuclear or hydro. "You can't smelt aluminum with a windmill," Hughes notes. Nor will ethanol meet our needs; it takes too much energy to produce it. Hughes thinks Canadians have to begin preparing themselves for the inevitable transition from a fossil fuel society to a more sustainable energy society. "The longer we wait, the more chaotic the transition will be," he says.

His message, put simply, is about the need for conservation. The problem is, nobody in government wants to listen. Hughes says that his bosses told him in 2001 that the federal government was not interested in oil and gas conservation. Long-term energy policies were not on the government agenda, they did not figure in the Throne Speeches of 2001, and so he should just forget about his research into international energy reserves. "The official prognosis of some people in the government is don't worry about a thing, the markets will take care of it. The party line is business as usual—let's get on with liquidating our resource."

In 2002, Hughes published an official CGS report on his analysis and sent it to the then deputy minister of Natural Resources Canada, George Anderson. Anderson immediately made copies and sent them down to the department's economists. And that was the end of the road for the report. Anderson never heard back. Preparing for a future with limited oil and gas was just not on the government's agenda.

Looking back five years later, Anderson himself is surprised at the lack of concern about Canada's energy future. "Remarkably, it wasn't an issue during the period," he says. He notes that while the United States and many other countries keep strategic supplies in stock in case of a national emergency such as a sudden interruption in supply, Canada has never done this because it has always felt it had enough. Nor does Canada keep reserves to last at least thirty years, as it once strived to do. "The Americans maintain these very large strategic stocks," Anderson says. "It's become a bit more of an issue in the last two or three years as people become more and more concerned with the continuing growth of American energy imports. And not just the U.S.A., but virtually all the OECD [Organization for Economic Co-operation and Development] countries . . . are all facing declining oil production, but Canada is not. But that doesn't mean there are no issues around energy security. But they really haven't had much public attention."

While the Canadian government ignored Hughes, others did not. When Ontario announced in 2003 that it would close down its coal-fired electricity plants by 2007 and replace them primarily with natural gas, the chemical industry, worried about yet another competitor for increasingly limited natural gas supplies, brought in Hughes, the acknowledged expert in the field, to talk to Ontario officials. His message was that by 2011 there might not be enough gas in Canada to supply these plants. Ontario has since delayed its conversion plans, and it is now in a terrible quandary. Its coal-fired plants are among the largest contributors to global warming in Canada, but because of this country's huge gas exports to the United States as well as the fact that the oil sands companies continue to plunder our gas resources, Ontario cannot convert to natural gas for fear supplies will run out.

The rest of eastern Canada is in no better shape. The Sable Island gas fields off Nova Scotia are already showing signs of decline. A bid to build liquid natural gas (LNG) plants near Quebec City that would help replace our dwindling stocks has so far fallen through. This is not because of security issues; worries that an LNG tanker could explode are generally overblown. The problem is that gas companies are finding it difficult to sign long-term supply contracts with countries such as Russia and Iran. The main issue is reliability of supply.

The GSC has become redundant. Since Canada surrendered sovereignty over its energy resources to the North American Free Trade Agreement, which obliges Canada to sell oil and gas to the United States, the GSC's mandate is to act as little more than a cheerleader for energy companies. Canada doesn't have a sovereign national energy policy. NAFTA is its energy policy. If Canada wants to change it, it will have to change NAFTA. And that is not in the cards.

◆

Twelve years before Hughes's analysis was buried, the government of Alberta had interred a groundbreaking report on global warming.

Long before Kyoto, long before United Nations reports on climate change and long before Al Gore, the Energy Efficiency

Branch of the Alberta government's Department of Energy began studying the effects of climate change and how to reduce greenhouse gases. Its report was entitled "A Discussion Paper on the Potential for Reducing CO_2 Emissions in Alberta, 1988–2005." It begins by recognizing that global warming is a threat to life on earth and is caused by the increasing accumulation of "carbon dioxide, methane, oxides of nitrogen and chlorofluorocarbons." The report's stated objective was to "identify a CO_2 reduction potential in Alberta through more efficient energy utilization and fuel substitution."

In 1988, Alberta produced approximately 22 percent of the CO_2 emissions in Canada, the highest per capita emissions in the country. The paper correctly predicted that that percentage would continue to rise substantially. The report outlined a strategy for reducing by 2005 Alberta's greenhouse gas emissions by 20 percent of 1988 levels. It contains a detailed list of about three hundred energy conservation measures—from better driving habits to improved home insulation and stepped-up use of alternative energy sources—most of which would also reduce costs for industry and Alberta residents. Essentially, the report charted a strategy of greenhouse gas reduction that would have set emissions reductions below levels later demanded by Kyoto while saving Albertans money and going a long way to improving the environment.

The report went nowhere. It was filed away in government archives in 1990 while Ralph Klein was environment minister. When he became premier, Klein gutted the Energy Efficiency Branch and cut back the budgets of the environment and energy departments. He campaigned throughout Canada against Kyoto, joking that global warming was caused by dinosaur farts. Members of his party, the oil industry and the former Reform and Alliance Parties then helped create an Alberta-based organization called Friends of Science, which campaigns against Kyoto. Its chief scientific adviser, Professor Timothy Ball, denies global warming is a man-made phenomenon.

One of the founders of Friends of Science was Barry Cooper, a political science professor at the University of Calgary and a confidant and fishing buddy of Prime Minister Stephen Harper. Cooper is part of a group of seven professors at the university whose right-wing political and economic theories have shaped the thinking of Harper and his Conservative Party. In 2004, Cooper set up a University of Calgary Science Education Fund to help funnel anonymous donations to the Friends of Science.

"Just think where we'd be today if we had paid attention to that report," Kevin Taft, Alberta's Liberal leader, says. "The branch that produced this report is gone and this report was buried deep. They were twenty years ahead. That's where Alberta was before these people [the Klein gang] came along."

◆

Taft himself has known the sting of Klein's government. In 1993 he produced what he thought was a harmless report commissioned by the government of Alberta on its services to senior citizens. The report made it clear that the services were inexpensive and the costs were under control. That didn't conform to the policies of Ralph Klein, the new Conservative Party leader, who ordered all two thousand copies of the report shredded. "They spent a million bucks, but clearly it didn't fit with the message they wanted to create of a government that was spiralling out of control," Taft recalls.

Klein then launched his government on a slash and burn policy, gutting the departments of the environment, health and education. He even went so far as to blow up Calgary General Hospital. The biggest hospital in Calgary was reduced to rubble. He claimed it was too expensive to run. "I would rate that as the dumbest political thing I've seen in Alberta in my lifetime," says one senior Conservative politician who wished to remain anonymous. "I mean, to blow up a hospital. And it was just at the time he was receiving reports of the population growth in the province."

To control the flow of information, Klein centralized the government's public affairs departments under the umbrella of the Public Affairs Bureau. He also reduced the power of community education and health boards and loaded them with hand-picked Progressive Conservatives. Anybody who challenged him was threatened with job loss or a cut in funding. For example, Taft wrote in 1996 a small polemic called *Shredding the Public Interest.* The book detailed government expenditures over the previous decade in an effort to prove that there was no debt crisis, as Klein had claimed. Taft showed that the only spending that was out of control were the mounting subsidies to the energy industry. Klein called Taft a "communist" and tried to pressure the University of Alberta Press not to publish the book. "He sent his henchman Rod Love over to try and intimidate the president of the university," Taft says. "It was very intolerant. You were either for us or against us, and it felt like speaking out against the government was almost treasonous. If you spoke up, you might get personally denounced. There was a whole abusive kind of power play coming out of the premier's office. So that politicized me. I knew that a lot of what they were telling the public was untrue and even openly deceitful." Until then, Taft had regarded himself as a consultant and civil servant. He had never been involved in partisan politics. In 2001 he won a seat for the provincial Liberals and became leader of the party.

Other university professors were also disciplined for speaking out against the Conservatives. Klein tried to cut funding to the Parkland Institute because of its constant criticism of his social, economic and environmental policies. Gordon Laxer, the institute's director and co-founder, had a running battle with Klein. A professor at the University of Alberta, Laxer says Klein tried for years to persuade the university to cut funding to the Parkland. At one point Klein addressed a letter to the university's president demanding they shut down the campus offices of the Parkland Institute. "I am dismayed to see yet again another one-sided and ideologically biased report from the factually challenged Parkland [I]nstitute," he wrote.

But Albertans loved his style. They re-elected Klein and his Tories three times.

♦

Bribery is another method Alberta has for dealing with the opposition. In 2005, Alberta tried to buy off Quebec.

Quebec's hydroelectric energy dams make the province the cleanest economy in the country. For this reason Quebec supports Kyoto and has publicly contested Alberta's opposition to the treaty. Quebec also has opposed the federal government's offer to pay Alberta billions of dollars in compensation for cleaning up its pollution while not offering Quebec similar compensation for the cost of dam construction. In November 2005, Alberta saw an opportunity at least to soften Quebec's point of view, and maybe even create an ally.

During the 2005 Kyoto conference in Montreal, Alberta's environment minister, Guy Boutilier, sought out Tom Mulcair, who at the time was his opposite number in Quebec. Few words were exchanged, but Boutilier took the opportunity to slip Mulcair a handwritten note. Mulcair read it quickly, smiled politely at Boutilier and then stuck it in his pocket.

The note offered to funnel billions of Alberta's energy dollars through Quebec brokers and the Montreal Stock Exchange in exchange for Quebec's support of Alberta's position. "Recent media reports has (sic) positioned Quebec vs Alberta on this file. Considering our Premiers are good friends . . . (sic) We may want to discuss a couple of positive initiatives relative to finance and the Montreal Exchange with the billions Alberta industry has," Boutilier wrote. He ended the note with a cheery: "Let's Talk!" and signed his name.

Mulcair, who was and still is a committed supporter of Kyoto, didn't have to ask about the quid pro quo; the fact that Boutilier gave the note to Quebec's environment minister spoke volumes. What particularly irritated Mulcair was the invocation of an alleged friendship between Klein and Quebec premier Jean Charest. It signalled Mulcair to "get out of my way, get out of here."

"I knew exactly what was going on," he said. "He was telling us to stop talking about greenhouse gas emissions and take the pill that he would give to us."

For Mulcair, it was a brief, furtive exchange during a busy week at the conference. He says he never followed it up. But he kept the note as a reminder of how Alberta does business.

I tried to set up an interview with Boutilier to discuss the many environmental issues facing the province as well as question him about the intent of his note to Mulcair. Initially, his staffers appeared eager. But when I emailed them a copy of Boutilier's note they immediately declined my request for an interview.

◆

In 2006, Boutilier made a rare appearance before the EUB at a hearing into a new Suncor project. As MLA for Fort McMurray, he claimed he wanted to express the region's concern over the unbridled growth of the oil sands mining and the failure of education, health care and other services to keep pace. Local politicians hoped he would support their call for slower growth of the oil sands and take a strong stand in favour of environmental conservation. But they were disappointed. He came armed with a government lawyer who told the commission he was there to protect his client by assuring that everybody played by the rules. As it turned out, he had little to worry about. Boutilier wasn't about to give anything away. His appearance was more show than substance, more obfuscation and egomania than clarity and precision. The people of Wood Buffalo had serious concerns but their MLA was not about to address them. He spent most of the time talking about his CV, his master's degree in public administration from Harvard, and his other accomplishments—"I was very pleased to be awarded the Alberta Urban Municipal Association Award of Excellence." When he finally got around to discussing the oil sands, he lectured the commission on the need to assure that energy companies make a "healthy return on their investments . . . That's simply Business 101." Little mention was made of the environment other than the following Norman Rockwell vision: "When I look into the future, I want to know I can be standing on the banks of the Athabasca basin fly-fishing with my grandson and granddaughter because we made the right decisions today."

Don Mallon, lawyer for the Mikisew Cree, picked up on that theme and questioned Boutilier how far he was prepared to go to protect the environment. Boutilier refused to answer his questions, claiming thirty-eight times that he was appearing before the board only as an MLA and not as the environment minister. Given that Boutilier rarely put himself in a position where he could be examined on his environmental record, it's revealing to see how Mallon's questioning unfolded:

> Q. I'm going to talk about the paragraph where you look forward to fishing with your grandson . . . but I gather . . . that you don't have a grandchild yet, or am I mistaken?
> A. Actually my wife and I don't have a son or daughter yet, but we're in the process of privately adopting, so as a follow-up to our adoption, we expect to have grandsons and granddaughters.
> Q. Good. That's excellent. . . . I caught my first jackfish about a mile north of the bridge on the Athabasca River . . . I'm assuming it's enjoying that thrill with your grandchildren that you're looking forward to doing, is it not?
> A. It's the fact about being out in this incredible blessed environment that we have, that we enjoy, that my wife and I chose to make it our home over thirty years ago. And it is a thrill and it remains a thrill to be able to do that in the Athabasca basin.
> Q. Sure. So for you and I, fishing is for a thrill, but you understand that for the Mikisew—
> A. It is a—
> Q.—it's sustenance?
> A. Yes.

Q. And it's part of their traditional way of life?

A. That's correct.

Q. Well, you'd agree with me that the Government of Alberta, and particularly Alberta Environment, has the responsibility to protect the environment?

A. Yes, I would agree . . . I'm here, I repeat, as the MLA.

Q. And you are the MLA but you are also the Minister of Environment. And so the responsibility that falls to that department falls to you?

A. Mr. Chairman, I would like to say—yes, is the answer to your question . . .

Q. Right. And you're the number one guy in that department, so I'd like to ask a few more questions of you . . . and your responsibility to the environment.

A. As the MLA, I'm quite prepared to answer any questions that impact my constituency as the MLA, as I obviously indicated at the beginning.

Q. Okay. So when you say that we have this absolute responsibility, I'm assuming that what you mean is that we must do everything that we can to absolutely ensure the viability of the ecosystem, the river ecosystem, that you want to go fishing in?

A. As citizens of Alberta, which I was making reference to, it is clear that the ecosystems and the habitat within the basin is something that all Albertans I know share with in that value that you speak of, yes.

Q. Right. And, as we've discussed, so does the Department for Environment and so do you as the head of that department?

A. Yes. And I remind you, Mr. Chair, through the Chair, that I am here today as the MLA, not as the Minister of Environment.

Q. All right. So I'm going to assume that your grandson is precocious . . . And has become a river ecologist, a river biologist. And your [grand]son advises you as the Minister of Environment that the Athabasca River system's ecosystem is in danger of imminent collapse and that you and he are not going to be able to fish in that river anymore. And the reason for it is that the flows are too low and that we're removing too much water. Now, the responsibility that you have, which is an absolute responsibility, then, is to protect the river, right?

A. . . . It's important to recognize that, Mr. Chair, that I'm here as MLA, I'm quite prepared to answer any question, but not as Minister of Environment . . .

Q. Well, I'm sorry, sir, you don't get to pick and choose who you are one minute and who you are not the next. You are the Minister of the Environment.

A. Right.

Q. . . . So let's assume that your grandson is even more precocious than that, and that tomorrow, or let's say five years from now, he tells you that the river ecosystem is in danger of collapse because there's been an extended drought, the flows are too low, and something has to be done or the fisheries will collapse . . . And I suggest to you that the way that you would react is to, one of the ways that you would react, is to look to reduce the withdrawals from the river. Wouldn't that be correct?

A. I think, again, you're posing the question as a hypothetical Minister of Environment five years or, well, actually five years from now with my hypothetical grandson. But I would say, Mr. Chair, I'm here as MLA. Your conclusion that you arrive at, it appears you're asking as a Minister of Environment, but you are asking, just to be clear, you're asking me as the MLA for this region that question. As the MLA, I'm not an expert . . .

Q. Do you know what an IFN is?

A. I'm sorry?

Q. Do you know what an IFN is? Instream Flow Needs?

A. Instream Flow Needs?

Q. Yes.

A. I know there's hundreds of acronyms out there, but I remain—I continue to be amazed in the number. But I know now that IFN does mean inflow needs . . .

Q. And you're aware that that Instream Flow Needs Management Framework does not have a provision for cutting off the water entirely? Are you aware of that?

A. I'm sorry, the technical knowledge that you're talking about, I cannot speak to, but I would certainly defer that, Mr. Chair, to the very capable people within the Ministry of Environment or whatever appropriate department is required.

Q. Well, don't you think as the Minister of that department who has absolute responsibility that you ought to know that?

A. Mr. Chairman, I am here today as the MLA representing the region and citizens . . . I want to be assured both as the MLA elected that I will be able to enjoy my grandson and granddaughter in the hypotheticals that you described about, to be able to enjoy that river well into the future and future generations . . .

Q. And we know that Alberta Environment is the protector of the environment in this province.

A. Yes, I'm here today, though, not as Alberta Environment but as the MLA.

Q. And we've heard that many times. And would it be appropriate, then, for Alberta Environment to set specific targets and timelines for objectives that they saw were important?

A. I think, Mr. Chairman, you asked would it be appropriate for Alberta Environment? I am here as the elected MLA for the citizens of Fort McMurray . . .

Q. You don't know if your department should be setting targets and bench lines over the things that they think are important?

A. I'm here as the MLA today . . .

Q. When you appear here as the MLA, do you just turn off an area of your brain where you were the Minister of Environment?

A. Yes, I do.

CHAPTER 11

HEAVEN ON THE MOON

IN WHICH TALK OF THE ENVIRONMENT IS FORBIDDEN,
MONSTER MACHINES DIG FOR MONEY AND ALBERTA TAKES A
BACK SEAT TO KAZAKHSTAN

THE HEAVY SMELL OF OIL AND DIESEL FUEL AND THE NOISE OF angry engines, grinding gears and hissing air brakes are overwhelming. Moving along the highway or parked on the roadside and in paved lots, apparently waiting for their marching orders, are flatbeds loaded with graders, bulldozers, diggers, cranes, compressors, drilling rigs and machinery I've never seen before—most of it of monstrous proportions. This whole region for about a hundred kilometres around is the biggest construction site on earth. And Fort McMurray is at its core—a once-quiet town turned into a massive work camp.

This is the staging area for the final assault on the many oil sands projects under construction around Fort McMurray. It's also the supply route for the constant refits of giant spare parts required to keep the mines of Syncrude, Suncor and Shell's Albian Sands producing about a million barrels of oil a day. This city belongs to machines. But Mayor Melissa Blake is trying to take it back.

Melissa Blake is thirty-six years old and is already serving her third term on council and first term as mayor. Like most people in Fort McMurray, Melissa is from someplace else. She was born in Danville, Quebec, where her father worked in the nearby asbestos mines as a heavy equipment mechanic. With the decline in asbestos mining, he moved his family in 1982 to Fort McMurray, where he got a job in the oil sands.

Hers is a common Canadian story made even more common in Fort McMurray. It's about miners following the unpredictable and often jarring cycles of commodity prices and mineral wealth. Fort McMurray is the Mount Everest of this boom-and-bust cycle, whose ending has yet to be told. About half of the population of Fort McMurray comes from dead or dying mining towns in the Atlantic provinces and Quebec. And more are coming every day, primarily Newfoundlanders.

The city is the biggest boom town Alberta has ever seen, and it's seen its fair share. Forty years ago it was populated by a few thousand trappers and salt miners. In the 1960s the oil companies began to take control, and by 1996 Fort Mac had 34,000 people. Now it has 64,031 and is on its way to 100,000 by 2010. Then there's the shadow population, which comprises the thousands of construction workers temporarily billeted in hotels, trailer parks and work camps all around the city. Some stay for only a few days, some for months and some for years. Nobody knows for sure how big the number is. It spikes and falls and plateaus and spikes again with each new project. But in the meantime it strains the town's resources to the breaking point, because these people don't pay taxes and have no stake in the city. They're hard-hat drifters.

Melissa's realm is much more than Fort McMurray. She is mayor of Wood Buffalo, of which Fort McMurray is the commercial centre. Geographically, Wood Buffalo is one of the largest amalgamated municipalities in the world. At 68,450 square kilometres, it is twice the size of Belgium, equal to Ireland and only slightly smaller than Austria. Its eastern border runs along the Saskatchewan line all the way up to the Northwest Territories. The southern and western lines zigzag about a hundred kilometres south and east from Fort McMurray and include Pony Creek and Manley Natland's atomic bomb test site.

Most of Alberta's richest oil sands lie beneath its soil. This means that Wood Buffalo's 79,810 people produce a Gross Domestic Product of about $72 million a day or $26.3 billion a year in crude oil alone. Per capita, that works out to $329,282 per resident. Government forecasts indicate production will triple by 2015. Who knows what world oil prices will be in eight years. But any way you look at it, it's a lot of money. Wood Buffalo ought to declare independence.

Running a boom town is no picnic for anybody, but this is particularly true for Melissa. For one thing, she's an environmentalist. In a city ruled by oil, heavy machinery and brand new pickup trucks with gleaming paint jobs and giant V8 engines driven by heavy-footed hard hats, Melissa is committed to conservation. She drives a hybrid, electric car—a little Toyota Prius. Half the trucks in the city could drive over her and think they hit a speed bump. But that's not all. She has outfitted her home with the latest energy-efficient light bulbs and slow-flow water faucets and tries to teach her three-year-old the importance of preserving the environment. She insists that community construction projects employ the latest in energy-saving devices. She formed a municipal housing corporation that requires that all future housing be heated with geothermal units. Yet her conservation and environmental policies are tempered by the fact that just up the road are the most environmentally rapacious industries in Canada, consuming vast amounts of fresh water, natural gas, boreal forest and entire ecosystems in one of the dirtiest oil production processes on earth. And it's her job to promote these industries and make sure they are happy campers as they plunder her community.

Blake used to work for Syncrude, Canada's largest oil sand producer. Her husband is a chemical engineer and manager at Suncor, the oldest oil sands operator. Since 1967, Suncor alone has extracted more than 1.1 billion barrels of oil from the sands, tearing up the land just north of Fort McMurray to supply civilization with combustible fuel that's destroying the world as we know it. In the face of this, Melissa is committed to taking any personal steps she can, however small, to mitigate this destructive force while at the same time promoting the continued growth of the oil industry. It's a Sisyphean task. Her satisfaction is in the striving. She's a hopeful pragmatist.

"The need [for oil] is not going to go away over the next number of decades that I'm around for. And so responsible stewardship over the life of that asset is something that I have expectations for." That's about all she'll say on the subject. In the end, she confidently puts her faith in technology. Science will mend the atmosphere and help restore the broken land. "Yes, I believe that. But in the meantime I am in the government and there's a reason for that: I want to have an assurance of orderly control over my municipal development."

As events have played out, however, she admits that none of this has happened. There is no orderly control. Wood Buffalo has no say in the projects that are being built on its territory. The sands have become an unstoppable juggernaut that is squashing her town like roadkill. And part of that is the town's own fault.

♦

Fear is what former city councillor John Rigney says makes the city reluctant to take on the oil companies. Fear that they might get up and leave. "Fat chance of that ever happening," he laughs. Or that new ones might not come. Fear that the boom will bust. He suggested in 2003 that council hit the oil sands companies with higher tax rates. "Well, somehow that got out and right away the oil company people, all their presidents, came and met with our council and basically convinced the council don't bite the hand that feeds you."

With such hugely profitable companies within their boundaries, most municipalities would be rolling in cash. But that's not the case in Wood Buffalo. It's a poor orphan begging for handouts from a provincial government that persists in bestowing largesse only on the rich. All other businesses and residents in Wood Buffalo are taxed on 100 percent of the market value of their business, but this is not the case with the oil sands companies. Alberta tax laws created in the 1980s to encourage oil sands development require that oil sands companies be taxed according to a formula that works out, at most, to only 40 percent of their market value, according to Henk van Waas, the city's chief tax assessor. Furthermore, the province forbids the city to levy taxes on any oil sands project that is still under construction. "So the city has to pay to provide services [to an oil sands project], yet we don't get to tax it," Henk says. Every other business project is taxed annually according to the percentage of the project that has been completed. In 2006, Wood Buffalo's ten oil sands companies paid a total of $71.2 million in property taxes. Henk says that if they had been taxed on the same basis as any other business, they would have paid at least triple.

There's yet another twist to taxing oil sands companies. Every other business in Wood Buffalo is evaluated for municipal taxes according to its revenue streams. But not the oil sands companies. Their unique tax formula is based on the depreciated value of their property. This means that as their plants age, the oil sands companies will pay less tax. "Property values are based on the ability to pay, and the oil sands companies who have the highest revenues have the best ability to pay, but pay the least taxes," Henk says. "So, you know, talk about fairness and equity."

But that's not the end of the property tax giveaways. Henk notes with undisguised contempt that energy companies in Alberta do not have to pay school taxes on their machinery and equipment assessments. In the energy sector, equipment and machinery make up at least 90 percent of their property assessments. This means that oil sands companies in particular and the energy sector in general pay relatively little, if any, school taxes. Of course, they occasionally donate a tiny portion of their vast profits to university research into the energy sector. In return, they get their name on a donor's plaque and access to advanced technology. The donation, of course, is tax deductible.

The city has asked the province to change the rules, but without success, Waas says. "What happens is the heads of the oil companies have so much power that they go to the minister in charge and they walk in and they get their way. We shouldn't delude ourselves into thinking that the government can do anything, because really and truly the oil companies run the country. They don't pay income taxes. They don't pay their fair share of property taxes. I'd love to have that deal."

◆

In her own quiet way, Blake has pleaded with the government to stop future oil sands projects until "there is a comprehensive plan for all future growth in the region." She was the first mayor to intervene in Alberta Energy and Utilities Board hearings where she is up against a fortress of eight mulish, white male suits who comprise the EUB board plus a male bastion of division heads. Their mandate is to regulate the industry in such a way as to "ensure that the discovery, development and delivery of Alberta's energy resources take place in a manner that is fair, responsible and in the public interest." But fairness, responsible conduct and "public interest" are woolly concepts floating in the nether realm of the undefined. Basically, the EUB's history indicates that the public interest lies exclusively in the unfettered development of the industry.

Blake's pleas to the EUB to delay projects and impose some order on the development of the oil sands to assure they are in the public interest have been in vain. The EUB keeps pumping out permits at an unheard-of rate. Multi-billion-dollar projects are rubber-stamped after little more than a few days or weeks of hearings. Its speed is Mach 2. Opposition is simply overwhelmed and outmanoeuvred. There's little time to react. Blake wanted the EUB to delay Suncor's $12.8-billion mine and refinery expansions. The proposal involved thousands of pages of technical reports detailing everything from construction plans and manpower to mining technology, as well as environmental impact studies. The province approved the project a mere four months after it was proposed. Blake wanted Imperial

Oil's massive Kearl Lake mine stopped. Here again the concerns of Fort McMurray were ignored. So far, she says, the province hasn't cared whether the town can bear the stresses caused by its ballooning population of people and machines, just as it hasn't given much thought to the environment.

Melissa's town is at the epicentre of this boom, and it's behind the eight-ball. Its water treatment and sewage plants are inadequate. Construction costs have gone through the roof. She says she needs about two billion dollars for health, education, transportation and recreational facilities, but costs keep going up at a rate of 50 percent a year. When I suggested to Patty King, the city's acting chief financial officer, that the city might go bust, she replied: "Basically, that's where we see ourselves heading if we don't get some grants." To date, nothing has been forthcoming from the Alberta government other than a $136-million loan for a new sewage treatment plant. At least Wood Buffalo doesn't have to start paying the interest until 2010. Kind of like a furniture warehouse deal.

The city competes with the oils sands for workers. Most migrate to the highest paycheque. That means they choose the oil sands projects, of which there are fifty billion dollars' worth under construction and another fifty or sixty billion dollars' worth promised. Which in turn means spiralling inflation for the city.

This is a world where a teenager can clear at least $100,000 a year driving an oil sands truck. But it's also a world where a small jerry-built bungalow will cost you on average $469,000; where a mobile home will set you back $300,000; or a tiny two-bedroom apartment will start at $3,000 a month plus utilities. Billions are pressure-pumped into this tiny river crossing. Everything just ratchets up. The government claims the poverty line is $60,000 for a couple, $93,000 for a family, which sounds ridiculous, but it's a reflection of supply and demand in an inflated economy. Here the free market rules with rapacious hunger. Its motto: "Where's mine?" This is wonderland.

Most people, as soon as they retire from the oil sands, cash in and leave. One survey put the figure at 95 percent. For young people it's hit and run. As local pilot Rob Elford says, "You do your two or three years here, pay your debts and get out."

Melissa's only hope is that things will naturally slow down. But it's a faint hope. In fact, she agrees it's not really in the cards at all. "This boom doesn't fit the typical characteristic where you have a peak and then a tapering or decline. We don't have that on our radar at the moment."

♦

It's a cold, crisp morning. The sky overhead is as broad and blue as the sea, and I'm standing in the middle of a 100-metre-deep open-pit mine surrounded by a horizon of black earth stretching about two and a half kilometres across all points of the compass. It's a perfect moonscape. Not a living thing in sight. Just Pete and me and the machines.

Repairing the underbelly of the beast

Peter Duggan is a tall, robust miner originally from Toronto. He came in 1978 and now works as a production adviser to Syncrude Canada Ltd., which is the largest oil sands operator in Canada, running the largest open-pit mining operation in the world. Despite the fact that he's fifty-six years old and has been in the mining business for decades, you can tell by his strong voice, facial expressions and use of exclamations such as "Ohhhh yah" or "You better believe it" that he still finds the size and scope of the oil sands operations awesome.

As we stand chatting in the middle of the pit, Pete reaches down and picks up a fistful of earth in his gloved right hand. He pokes a finger through it and the soil splits into wet clumps of black sand and clay. "This is what it's all about," he says with undisguised wonder. "Just put that up to your nose and you can smell the oil."

I don't have to. This whole place stinks of oil. I tell Pete that he's been working here so long he can't smell it anymore. He says that I should smell it in the summer heat. "It's like working on an asphalting crew."

At peak production, Syncrude puts out about 240,000 barrels a day of what it calls Syncrude sweet crude. That's a golden liquid that looks like canola oil. Syncrude claims that their oil is equivalent in quality to what the industry calls West Texas Intermediate or just plain WTI. This is the benchmark for North American oil pricing. Syncrude president Jim Carter boasts that his company's refining methods can sometimes produce an even higher grade than WTI, meaning it's about the best quality a refinery can hope for.

If you go to the home page of Syncrude's website, the company has a counter that shows split-second production tallies from the moment it shipped its first barrel on July 30, 1978. As I write this paragraph, the counter shows the company is producing oil at a rate of 2.8 barrels a second. That's phenomenal. The total as of this split second of writing is 1,696,239,543. In fact, by the time I finish writing this paragraph, Syncrude has added another 411 barrels to the world's supply.

And there's plenty more where that came from. So far all the oil sands projects have taken less than 4 percent of what Alberta claims is 174 billion barrels of recoverable oil in the sands. At present production rates, Syncrude says its leases contain enough oil to keep it in business until 2050. "My grandchildren if they want will still be working here," Pete says.

This is why the world is coming to this once-pristine forest. The technology challenge has been met. The politics is trustworthy, biddable and compliant. It's now just a question of paying the bills. Almost every major international oil company plus a host of smaller, mostly Canadian-based companies have bought leases and forged partnerships, spending billions in risk capital despite inflated costs. It's living proof of a world desperate for oil and of a certainty that prices will only rise. This is why they're digging up an area equivalent in size to the state of Florida.

♦

Probably few employees of Syncrude Canada Ltd. know this mine the way Pete knows it. He has watched as thousands of acres of boreal forest have been slowly peeled back to reveal the black gold within. And now he patrols the mine daily to ensure that production is maximized. He's big and muscular, and even though he spends most of his time either in his office or driving around the mine in a company SUV, he still looks to be in good shape.

Syncrude runs two mines. The North Mine is thirty-four kilometres southwest of where Pete and I are standing and it's quite a bit older and almost twice the size—three by five kilometres. But that is just the size of the pit. The dimensions don't give a full appreciation of the real size of the Syncrude operations, including its refinery, crushers, tailings ponds and older sections of mines that have been partially refilled or left for future reclamation.

If you just took the North Mine area and measured the full extent of its triangular shape, its overall perimeter would stretch roughly 22 by 21 by 21 kilometres. The Aurora Mine, which opened in 2000 and is more rectangular in shape, is 12 by 6 kilometres. These two mines represent only about a quarter of Syncrude's eight oil sands leases, which total approximately 250,000 acres—almost twice the size of Toronto. These leases are in what the company refers to as the "sweet spot" of the oil sands region. In other words, Syncrude claims its leases contain the greatest concentration of oil reserves—an estimated five billion barrels—in the oil sands. This means Syncrude has more oil than half of the world's top forty-eight oil-producing countries.

Preparation of these mines can take several years. As Pete explains: "The area is drilled with vertical drills in a 100-metre by 100-metre pattern so we can pick the location that has the least amount of oil sands to put the offices and maintenance buildings, and where to dump the soil, and where is the best place to start the pit. We also of course want to find the area with the biggest concentration of oil. The oil sands are everywhere, but they vary in geology."

No one knows for sure how the oil sands were formed, but it is thought that underground upward pressures pushed the oil into the sands. While the pressure may have been uniform, the amount of oil pushed up was not. So the concentration of oil in the sands, as well as the size of the oil sand seams, can change quickly. Companies don't want to put buildings overtop of rich deposits. And they want to make sure their pits, which could be in operation for decades to come, depending on the rate of extraction, are located in the richest areas.

Once they've charted the geology, they start tearing up the earth. They redirect rivers and streams, drain aquifers, lakes, ponds and fens. Fens are shallow strips of water found in peat bogs and unique to this area of the boreal forest. Logging companies clear-cut the forests. "All this is viewed as a resource that belongs to the province of Alberta," Pete says. "So whether it's the trees above the oil sands formation or there's bands of gravel and sand that have commercial value, the expectation is that we maximize the use of that resource before we extract the bitumen." The land becomes a smorgasbord. In preparing the mine, everybody gorges.

Open pit mining

After the surface table is stripped, the oil companies peel off the topsoil, peat and muskeg, piling it up at the edge of the mining area. Finally, they dig up what miners call the "overburden," which is the soil and rock above the ore body. This could be anywhere from a few metres to forty or fifty metres deep. This colossal amount of earth is pushed aside to reveal the raw oil sands, what they call the "feed." It extends over about 1,000 square kilometres and averages thirty-five to sixty metres in depth. Miners dig down through the seam to the base of the feed. The pit takes form and the wound expands as they extract more and more of the oil sands. Soon the place looks as if it had been hit by an atomic bomb. This is what miners call the "footprint."

Mankind has been scarring the earth in this way since the Bronze Age, often for the most frivolous of reasons. Rio Tinto, a British mining company, has just begun open-pit mining in the coastal rainforest of Madagascar, considered to have an ecosystem unique on the planet. The company is mining titanium dioxide, otherwise known as ilmenite. Ilmenite produces a pigment used to whiten textiles, paper and paint. To minimize the impact, Rio Tinto has paid Kew Gardens in London to preserve rare seeds from threatened plants. It's not as if the people of Madagascar, a poor country, are benefiting greatly from this intrusion. All of the nation's ilmenite is being shipped from a harbour paid for by the World Bank to Sorel, Quebec, where it will be smelted. Essentially, Rio Tinto is digging up a forest with an estimated 175,000 unique species so businessmen can wear gleaming white shirts.

Pete and I are surrounded by giants. Nothing at the oil sands is on a small scale. It's all supersized. About one hundred metres away, a huge bright orange shovel that stands about four storeys high to the top of its cabin is digging into a wall of oil sand with a 100-ton shovel. It has *Syncrude 84* stencilled in large white letters on the back and sides. A Canadian flag flies over the cabin, which also has the call number 4100BOSS painted above the windows. Pete points to a thick black cable that snakes over the base of the pit close to our feet. The shovel is run by an electric motor and that's the extension cord. "You've got 110 volts in your home. There's 15,000 volts going through this cord." He kicks it lightly with his foot. The cord is attached to a grid fed by a cogeneration plant that uses heat from the oil sands extraction process to produce electricity.

We climb the thirty-four narrow metal stairs that lead up the side of the shovel. At the controls is Collin Dakin, who comes from the small town of Terrace in northwestern British Columbia. Operating this $30-million machine, Pete says, is "the pinnacle of machine operations," which is why Collin is the highest-paid man in the pit.

Collin is forty-nine years old and has been working for Syncrude since 1979. He has two sons who are also machine operators for the company. Syncrude carries on the mining tradition of hiring the children of its employees, fathers passing on their skills to the next generation. And for the first time, this includes daughters. Twenty percent of the machine operators at Syncrude are women.

Collin sits in a captain's chair from which he controls the giant shovel using two simple swivel sticks, one on each arm, much like a Game Boy. In front of him is a large bay window stretching from floor to ceiling. It gives him a commanding view of the steel shovel as it chomps into the wall of sand, which rises at least sixty metres above him. Collin spends fully a third of his life now eating away at blackness. Barely visible at the top of the pit is a relatively tiny yellow bulldozer. "The shovel by law can't go above its height to extract the sands," Pete says. It's a safety precaution so the shovel doesn't somehow drop a hundred tons of oil sands on itself. "So dozers up on top of the 'bench' push the sand down the side of the pit to the feet of the shovel so it's safe for the shovel to mine it."

A dump truck backs into position beside the shovel. This is the poster child of the oil sands. It's the biggest dump truck in the world, weighing about four hundred tons, with a payload of another four hundred tons. It's called a Cat 797—like a jumbo jet. Other open-pit mines have similar trucks, but nothing as big as these. As Collin begins loading the truck, another one backs in on his left side. Orange plastic cones hanging from the shovel help guide the drivers into position. The cones are probably the only non-hi-tech devices in the entire oil sands operation, and worth about a dollar each. Every driver is equipped with a radio and satellite global positioning device, all hooked into a central computer. If the truck's position isn't exactly right, Collin can always adjust his shovel—but only a little. These machines are not easy to manoeuvre. If the truck hasn't taxied into the exact position, the driver will have to do it again. Collin keeps in contact through his radio, which he controls with foot pedals, leaving his hands free to operate the shovel. "I can keep workin' and talkin' at the same time," he says. "There's $10 million worth of truck and a $30-million shovel. That's $40 million worth of equipment waiting right in front of your face there." Which is why, he says, only the best machine operators are allowed to operate the shovel.

As the electric engine throttles up into a high-pitched whirr, Collin lightly manoeuvres the two swivel sticks with little more than wrist action. The shovel dips and scoops up a hundred tons of oil sand, swings over the truck and dumps the load in one fluid motion. A video screen to one side tells him the precise weight of the payload as he fills the truck. Four scoops usually fills a truck to capacity, which is about forty times what the normal street dump truck carries. The loading takes no more than a minute or so. Collin toots a horn and the truck to the right slowly moves off, tooting its horn in reply. Without missing a beat, Collin immediately starts filling the truck on his left. When that's done, he announces that he has to move the machine farther down the ore body. I want to see how this manoeuvre is accomplished, so I leave the cabin, return along a small catwalk that runs over the top of the massive electric motor and descend the metal stairway.

The shovel sits on two steel caterpillar tracks that move about half a kilometre an hour at top speed. When Pete and I are clear, Collin swings the entire shovel 180 degrees. It is amazing how easily and quickly the machine pivots. Just behind the shovel is a ball-shaped steel cage attached to the extension cord. Collin carefully manoeuvres the shovel so that it picks up the cage, raising the cord high off the ground like a woman picking up the train of her ball gown. He then slowly "walks" the behemoth along the ore face. Cameras located at the rear and sides of the machine help him keep track of what's going on around him. His GPS system, which is installed in every truck and shovel, shows on a screen in his cabin the location of every vehicle in the pit. So far, they haven't had any collisions.

I tell Pete that I'd like to check out one of the trucks, so he calls a driver on his radio and asks him to stop by. Pete instructs me to stay in his pickup until the dump truck arrives. "The drivers can't always see people on the ground," Pete says.

Collin is loading another truck. When it's full, the driver steers it towards us and stops a good thirty metres or so away. The driver leaves his cabin and climbs down a metal stairway that runs across the front of his radiator. I count twenty stairs in all. His name is Damien Alexander. He's wearing work boots, jeans, a dark hooded sweatshirt and an orange hard hat. He's tall and lean and only nineteen years old.

Before I can introduce myself, Alain Moore, a young, wiry public relations officer for Syncrude, strides over to talk to Damien. Alain has been my host, tour guide and minder all day long. He moved here from Newfoundland when his dad got downsized and took a job in the oil sands. Alain grew up here, married, started a family and has just moved into a bigger house with a bigger mortgage in a better part of town. He trained as a journalist and now he's a propagandist who has staked his life and that of his family on Syncrude. As we drive through this vast destroyed environment, I can sense his nervousness. He glances over at me and I can feel him wondering: "What are you thinking?" Just like the woman at the Husky station when I complained about the Kickass coffee. This is his domain.

Alain tried at one point to lay down some ground rules. "You'll find our operators are really good ambassadors. There's only one thing, because we don't want to put our operators in a tough position: Bill, I just ask you not to ask them any questions about the environment and stuff like that. Just ask them what job they do and whether they like it and things like that. The environment side, that's for the bigwigs."

"Why is that?"

"Why is what?"

"Why is it only for the bigwigs?"

Perhaps Alain didn't hear the question above the din of machine noise, because he starts telling me a story about an American reporter who asked a truck driver what he thought of the Chinese buying up oil sands leases. He laughs and rolls his eyes as if to say: "What would a driver know about that?" I ask him what the driver said. Alain replies, laughing: "He had an answer!" He pauses before adding, half to himself: "It was consistent with ours, which was good."

"What is yours?"

"Our opinion is it's a free market."

Now Alain wants to make sure that Damien knows the score. "You can only talk about your job, and whatever he asks, just be positive. Tell him about your job and why you like it. He'll ask about the community, and I guess you grew up here."

"Yup. Born and raised."

"Oh, okay. Just keep everything positive."

Damien nods in agreement. There are no unions at Syncrude.

Pete cautions me to make sure I put on my seat belt. "And when the truck does dump at the hopper, make sure you brace yourself a bit, okay?"

I follow Damien up the staircase into his cab. It's not nearly as spacious as the shovel's. Nor does it offer the same panoramic view. In fact it seems a bit hidden and cramped, almost as if I've ascended into a dark cave. The steel front of the Dumpster, which extends over the cab like a giant visor, blocks out the sun. I may be two storeys up, but my vision is narrow and unidirectional— basically straight ahead. Laid out before me is an endless expanse of dark sand heavily indented with the thick tread marks of giant machines. In the distance, maybe ten kilometres away—distance is impossible to judge for lack of markers—the pit walls disappear into a hazy horizon capped here and there by the long white plumes of the refineries.

Damien climbs in behind the wheel and I settle into the passenger seat, which seems superfluous in a machine such as this, but Damien says it's designed for an instructor. A slim console separates the two of us. Damien's radio is crackling with the voices of other drivers, shovel operators and dispatchers. We snap our heavy-duty seat belts into place. They are wider than normal and really clamp you in. Damien politely asks if I'm ready and comfortable. When I reply in the affirmative, he puts the truck in gear, releases his emergency brake and the monster begins to move. Or I should say, float.

As Damien speeds up to fifteen kilometres per hour, I have the sensation that I'm not in a truck but a boat. A large cabin cruiser. This truck has none of the jarring, bumping, heaving feel of a normal street dump truck. Instead, it rides as if it were sailing over lightly rolling seas. This is partially because of the massive hydraulic suspension and partially because the tires are so bulbous. Every once in a while the truck seems to roll over a particularly high wave and I recall Pete's caution about fastening the seat belt. The truck could easily toss me against the steel roof.

I ask Damien about the visibility. "Thirty feet from out in front of me I can't see a thing. It's my blind spot. Like when I pulled up to you guys at the truck, I couldn't see you guys. That's why I stopped so far away. Something like this can block out a whole pickup truck on the road. You could drive a pickup truck right around me right now and I wouldn't see you. I might see your buggy whip in front of me. These are big machines, so you are cautious and safe about 'ifs.'"

Damien says his dad also works at the mine. "Hearing him talk about these kind of trucks . . . I always wanted to drive one. So here I am. I love it. I can come out here all day and do this for twelve hours, no problem."

Which is exactly what he does. He works a twelve-hour night shift for three days followed by a twelve-hour day shift for another three days, with one day in between for adjustment. After that he gets six days off before starting the cycle all over again. Syncrude has made access to his truck as easy and fluid as possible. The company has its own fleet of about one hundred buses. Night and day they travel through the neighbourhoods of Fort McMurray, picking up workers to take to the mines. The buses make 2.5 million passenger trips every year. Next to Edmonton and Calgary, Syncrude's is the biggest transit system in the province. These buses, however, are like intercity coaches—large and comfortable. All Damien has to do is roll out of bed and walk down the street, where the bus picks him up and takes him to the mine offices. There, a smaller bus transports him to the truck he'll be driving for that shift. He simply changes places with the existing driver who's heading home. When Damien's ready for his break, the bus comes out to his truck, delivering another driver to take over while Damien goes to the canteen. The idea is to keep the trucks hauling oil sands and feeding the oil extractor 24–7.

Damien trained for only six days before he took his first solo run. "This was easier to learn how to drive than my pickup," he says. The truck is simplicity itself. There's no clutch to slip or gearshift to grind. It's fully automatic. He puts the lever into drive, presses on the gas and the truck moves through its seven gears with barely a hiccup. Damien can turn the power steering with his finger. And the power disc brakes stop the beast on a dime.

We drive off towards the hopper where Damien will dump his load, which his computer tells him is exactly 395 tons. Damien says the truck can take up to 450 tons, but because each scoop is about 100 tons, they stop at four. It's not worth it for the shovel operator to try to gauge half a scoop.

Top speed is forty kilometres per hour, but Damien rarely goes that fast. With a full load he crawls along at fifteen. Ironically for such a mammoth machine, the one thing Damien has to be really careful about is stones. Road graders—the biggest in the world, of course—constantly level the broad dirt roads leading out of the pit. These graders have a tendency to unearth sharp rocks that are often concealed in a grader's wake and can easily puncture any one of a truck's six tires. It's like an elephant being felled by a mouse. With each tire costing fifty thousand dollars, it's an expensive blowout. It's also dangerous. "The littlest rock can make a tire blow. We had a driver blow a tire this morning and it made the window shatter. It doesn't take very much. I have to know where my tires are at all times. You get a feel for it."

We are proceeding up one of these graded dirt roads to the crusher. The truck's progress is constantly monitored by the central dispatch office. Through the GPS system, dispatchers know exactly where each truck is, how fast it's going and the load it's carrying. The computer also picks up the more than twenty electronic sensors in each truck that allow men like Pete to keep track of how the truck is performing. If something goes wrong or is about to go wrong, Damien is usually the last person to know. The first hint he gets is a call on his radio or a visit from a mechanic. If the problem is serious enough and can't be fixed on-site, the truck is driven to the maintenance hangar, about a kilometre away. The building's bays could shelter a jumbo jet. Syncrude keeps a fleet of thirty-four trucks. It rotates them through the service bays every seventeen days for checkups and oil changes (170 litres of oil per change) and other regular maintenance. The goal is to keep at least thirty trucks on the job at all times. Six maintenance crews work twenty-four hours a day to make that happen. Which is the point of the whole exercise. These trucks are at once the most important and the weakest link in the chain leading from oil sands to sweet crude. Blow a tire and production rates immediately decline and hundreds of thousands of dollars are lost. In the end, this massive undertaking can be slowed by a small rock.

At the moment, Damien is carrying about two hundred barrels of oil, worth approximately $14,000. He needs slightly less than that to pay for the 4,164 litres of diesel fuel required to keep his truck on the job for twenty-four hours. So he needs slightly less than one load to keep his truck moving. He makes on average about thirty-five trips per shift. That's about $500,000 worth of oil, depending of course on international oil prices. Ten days of hauling will pay for his $5-million truck. Seven trips to the hopper will pay his annual salary, which with overtime will be at least $100,000. In fact, ten days of work will likely pay his salary for the next forty-five years if he makes it to retirement. Every day, Syncrude takes about six thousand tons of oil sands out of the Aurora Mine. In 2005 this translated into about $4.4 billion worth of oil, against expenses of $2 billion. Like any business, this is about numbers. All of which show how Syncrude can afford these elaborately expensive machines and processes.

It's hard to give precise figures on Syncrude's revenues and expenses because technically the company doesn't have any. What it has are seven partners involved in a joint venture called Syncrude. The largest owner is Canadian Oil Sands Trust of Calgary with 36.74 percent. Imperial Oil Resources, which is owned by the ExxonMobil Corporation of Irving, Texas, has the next-largest share at 25 percent. Petro-Canada has 12 percent; ConocoPhillips of Houston 9.03 percent; Nexen Inc. of Calgary 7.23 per cent; and Mocal Energy Ltd. of Japan and Murphy Oil Corporation Ltd. of Arkansas each have 5 percent.

Syncrude distributes its production and costs according to the percentage owned by each partner. Each partner then sells its oil through its own marketing department. The amount of profit each partner earns depends on Syncrude's ability to keep its expenses down and the partner's ability to play the oil market. Whatever their individual market skills, profits flowing to the partners have been huge. Canadian Oil Sands alone earned $831 million in net income in 2005. Its profits since 2000 have risen so high that its unit prices have soared almost 500 percent. Canadian Oil Sands is a trust and therefore distributions paid to unitholders have been tax-free. Setting themselves up as trusts is one of several ways companies avoid paying the government for the oil they take.

The oil extracted from the sands belongs to the people of Alberta, but despite the huge profits they earned in 2005, the government of Alberta required Syncrude's partners to pay only a minimum one percent royalty to Albertans. In 2005, this amounted to a mere $19.6 million for Canadian Oil Sands Trust, despite the fact that it earned $2 billion in revenues and $831 million in profit according to its annual report.

In 1996, Ralph Klein's government passed a law that absolved oil sands companies from paying the full 25 percent royalty until they had covered the capital costs of their projects. This was supposed to encourage growth in the sands sector, but it wasn't necessary; increasingly high oil prices and the resulting profits have driven the industry's expansion. For years Syncrude's partners have paid the minimum one percent royalty on a large portion of its oil sands revenues despite the fact that throughout this time they earned substantial profits. From 2000 to 2005, Canadian Oil Sands' net income totalled $2.3 billion, an overall rate of return of 36 percent. Its contribution to the Alberta Treasury in royalties, however, was a mere $235 million according to the company's financial reports. If it had paid the full 25 percent, it would have turned over more than twice that amount in royalties to Albertans—$575 million—and still earned a handsome profit of $1.7 billion. And that's only one oil sands owner among many. Suncor, for example, during that same five-year period paid $575 million in Crown royalties against $6.29 billion in net oil sands profits before income taxes. This amounted to an average Crown royalty payment of $1.68 a barrel. Revenues for the industry as a whole were about $65 billion, while royalties to Alberta totalled just $2 billion, or a mere 3 percent. Lost royalties add up to billions of dollars. Under Alberta's giveaway royalty scheme, the $14,000 worth of oil—every grain of which is owned by Albertans—that Damien and I are carrying in his monster truck will produce a royalty to the government of less than $100. And even that paltry royalty is an illusion.

Government subsidies, environmental tax credits and other tax breaks have largely offset what little the oil sands companies pay in the way of royalties. From 1979 to 1985 the federal Energy Administration Act and the Oil Administration Act dished out $1.8 billion in subsidies to Suncor alone, which amounted to 72 percent of its profits for those years. Federal studies show that Ottawa's generous tax breaks on capital costs incurred by oil sands companies have saved the industry about $1.8 billion since 1996. Taken together with other subsidies and tax incentives, the taxpayer has been subsidizing Damien's load—while Syncrude's partners and their shareholders get rich.

This is one reason why Alberta's much-ballyhooed Heritage Fund, which was created in 1976, contained only $15.4 billion as of 2006. Compare this to Alaska, which also started a resource fund in 1976 to ensure that future generations get a cut of the earnings from non-renewable resources. The Alaska Permanent Fund contains $37 billion. The top prize, however, goes to Norway's fund, which began receiving oil revenue only in 1996. By the end of 2006, it contained close to $306 billion. Norway not only charges much higher royalties than Alberta, it also ensures that a state-owned company controls more than 50 percent of North Sea oil production. So instead of flowing into foreign hands, billions in non-renewable resource money stays at home. Furthermore, Norway invests all of its oil and gas revenues in foreign companies and assets so as not to create an inflationary spiral in Norway that would quickly eat up its oil revenues and drag down the section of its economy that is non-resource-based. It has basically created a massive pension fund for future generations. Even corrupt Kazakhstan has a bigger government oil and gas fund than Alberta has. The National Oil Fund of Kazakhstan contained $24 billion as of August 2006.

Alberta forgot about the second part of the Norway equation. It won the lottery and is fast becoming the guy who wakes up three years later in the gutter. It sold off its energy company—the former Alberta Energy Company Ltd.—in 1993 and poured its royalties into capital projects and into general revenues to meet daily government expenses. This has allowed the Progressive Conservatives to reduce income taxes, cancel the sales tax and boast that Alberta has the lowest taxes in the country, which in turn keeps the Tories in power. The Tories have basically treated oil and gas revenues as their own private slush fund. When they need votes, they buy them. The $1.3 billion in "Ralph Bucks" dished out in 2005 to Albertans in $400 cheques is only the latest example. This puts Alberta on the level of countries such as Turkmenistan, Azerbaijan and Kazakhstan, all of which have state oil funds totally controlled by the ruling party or local despot. The result is that most of the money vanishes.

The government's failure to curb oil sands expansion has caused double-digit inflation, which is in turn eating up the province's oil and gas revenues. "It should be a profound concern for every citizen of Alberta that more than $200 billion in today's equivalent in non-renewable resource revenue has flowed through the Alberta Treasury," Kevin Taft, Alberta's Liberal Party opposition leader, says. "None of that has gone to Ottawa or anywhere else. All of it has flowed through the Alberta Treasury since 1971, and it is virtually all gone." Fact: Alberta now makes more money from gambling than it does from oil sands royalties. Albertans recall a 1980s bumper sticker that read: "Dear God, let there be another oil boom and I promise not to piss it away this time." Well, it's already happening. This is the legacy of Ralph Klein marinated in free market economics.

Both the Alberta government and the oil industry have claimed that the actual cost of extracting oil from the sands is so astronomical that the oil sands companies can't do business without extensive royalty holidays, subsidies and tax incentives. But how much does it cost? It's impossible to get a straight answer. Pete told me "it's now $12 to $15 a barrel." Jim Carter says it varies from $15 to $25, depending largely on the cost of natural gas. Suncor claims it's $14.50 to $19.50. In any case, it's a lot less than the $35 to $40 often claimed by the Alberta government to justify its royalty breaks. The point, according to Pete, is simply this: oil sands are "extremely profitable." Except in 1988, when it lost $8 million, Suncor has over the last thirty years consistently earned healthy profits.

In 2006, Syncrude's partners began paying the full 25 percent royalty because it had covered its capital costs. This may sound pretty good, but it's not all that much. The 25 percent is based on net revenues, which means the partners get to deduct all their costs, including ongoing capital costs, before they calculate the amount they owe the government. The royalty is simply the price the company pays to the government for the resource. It's like buying a TV set or any other piece of merchandise, only the TV vendor doesn't allow you to deduct your transportation costs to and from the store or the cost of electricity to run the TV or the cable or satellite fees. In its 2005 annual report, Canadian Oil Sands Trust notes: "Even at the higher royalty rate, based on today's crude prices, we expect to be generating healthy operating margins [profit before taxes]."

The federal government finally announced in November 2006 its intention to tax all trusts, provoking an outcry from the oil patch, which had been earning billions in untaxed profits. Since such a large proportion of ownership in the oil patch is foreign, the federal government's decision stopped a massive leakage of billions of dollars in untaxed resource dollars out of the country. Unfortunately, the new tax rules won't come into play until 2011.

◆

Damien approaches the hopper and brakes. The truck bounces a bit on its balloon tires as he brings it to a halt behind a lineup of two other trucks. Truck number 506 is backing up to the hopper. The driver is a woman and she has a payload of 391 tons. You can tell what each truck is hauling because they all have a screen attached to the side that displays the weight. Damien points out a rip in one of her tires, probably from a stone. "That could blow at any time," he says as he watches her leave. He says it takes four to six hours to change a tire. Through the rear-view mirror I can see that another truck has come up behind us.

The ease with which Damien's truck manoeuvres has the effect of reducing its colossal size and scope to that of a pickup truck. When his turn comes, Damien smoothly swings his truck around to the left in a finely cut arc, stops, toots his horn twice and then backs up. He brakes as the back of his Dumpster edges over the hopper, striking another orange cone. He pushes a lever and the Dumpster quickly rises. I brace myself, recalling Pete's note of caution. But I feel nothing more than a slight swaying sensation. Other than the noise of the soil tumbling into the hopper, there's no suggestion that the truck is dumping 395 tons of earth. Once the load has disappeared down the hopper, the Dumpster automatically falls back into place, settling over the truck with a gentle thud. Damien toots his horn and we're off back to the pit for a reload.

It's a monotonous repetition of an assembly line process on a grand scale, for which Collin's and Damien's shovel-and-truck combo constitute the front end and most visible part. The rest of the process is hidden inside thousands of kilometres of pipes, crushers, tumblers, extractors and upgraders that lead from the mine to refineries in Edmonton and Chicago, and ultimately into our gas tanks. About half of Syncrude's oil is consumed in Canada; the rest is shipped to Illinois and other Midwest states.

The simplicity of the extraction process obscures the decades of work needed to develop and perfect it.

From the hopper, the sand drops into a crusher. This breaks up any pieces over fifteen centimetres in diameter to prepare them for the "hydro transport" system. Hot water and caustic soda are added to create "slurry" that's pumped through a pipeline to the bitumen extractor, located three kilometres away. The huge cone-shaped extractors aerate the liquefied sands, turning the slurry into froth. Heat then separates the oil from the sand. The froth floats to the surface, with the oil clinging to the bubbles, while the sand and clay sink to the bottom. The thick bitumen oil is scooped out, mixed with a diluting oil and piped to the upgrader refinery, thirty-five kilometres southwest, at Syncrude's base mine. The process is repeated several times as the leftover sand is recycled through the extractor to remove the maximum amount of oil. The tailings are piped to tailing ponds. The entire system is largely a hi-tech version of what Sidney Ells and Karl Clark invented almost a century ago. Modern technology has greatly enhanced the process and reduced the price, but essentially it's not much different from the original cone-shaped washing machine used by Clark. Which is why it's still called the Clark Hot Water Extraction Method.

To heat the water so that the oil molecules separate from the sand, Syncrude uses about 150 million cubic feet of natural gas a day, which is 2.2 percent of Canada's total daily consumption of 6.8 billion cubic feet. To put it another way, to create one barrel of oil they use enough natural gas to heat an average home for four days in mid-winter. By the end of 2005, the entire oil sands industry's daily consumption of natural gas could heat 3.2 million Canadian homes for a day, according to Alberta's Pembina Institute. With as many as ten new projects coming on stream by 2015, this consumption rate is forecast to triple. Any way you look at it, that's a lot of conventional natural gas. And we're fast running out of it.

There are many alternatives to natural gas. Suncor admits in its filings with the Alberta Energy and Utilities Board that it could easily make hydrogen or natural gas from gasified coke, of which it has "years of supplies." The company boasts that when natural gas supplies are gone, "the company will be in an excellent position to take advantage of its coke, butane and naphtha to make hydrogen."

So why do they burn valuable natural gas? The answer is simple: it's cheap and available. "We could get off the natural gas pipeline. By just gasifying more of the heavy end of the barrel we'd likely take out the asphaltines," Syncrude president Jim Carter says. "We can gasify those. But it's a big capital investment and it doesn't make sense as long as gas prices are in the range that we are seeing them in today."

The refining process also produces mountains of sulphur as a by-product. Syncrude used to blow a lot of its sulphur up the stack. Pollution Watch claims that in 2003 alone Syncrude released 821 tons of sulphuric acid plus one million kilograms of ammonia into the air. Alberta permits the entire industry to emit 245 tons of sulphur dioxide per day, but these astronomical levels are not always reached. Prevailing winds push much of the acid pollution to Saskatchewan, angering that province's government, which has complained to Alberta that acid rain is killing its lakes. The smell has occasionally been overpowering. More recently, Syncrude has installed scrubbers in the refinery flue stack. They emit a shower of water, which when mixed with ammonia absorbs the sulphur. Syncrude ships the sulphur to its fertilizer plant, where it's dried into tiny pebbles. The problem is what to do with it. At the moment, it's stockpiled. The company can't sell it because, Carter says, the market is flooded. But there might be another use— something so drastic it's both frightening and darkly comical.

Paul Crutzen, a Dutch climatologist and Nobel Prize laureate, proposed in 2006 in the journal *Climate Change* the idea of pumping sulphates into the atmosphere to create a cloud of pollution that would shade the earth from the sun. Crutzen wasn't serious. He admitted that he published the idea only to emphasize the serious situation the world faces with global warming. But he says this is the sort of extreme solution that will be necessary if the world doesn't take immediate steps to curb its carbon dioxide emissions. He suggested a delivery system consisting of balloons carrying cannons that would shoot the sulphates into the stratosphere. No matter how crazy Crutzen's idea sounds, some scientists are taking it seriously, believing that we might be reduced to such drastic measures. U.S. climatologist Dr. Tom Wigley put it through a computerized climate model and concluded that Crutzen's idea will work. He claims that injecting five million tons of sulphur into the atmosphere would indeed cool the earth. In other words, the industry that helps create climate change could supply the feedstock to reverse it. How great is that!

♦

Wood Buffalo coroner Dr. John O'Connor remembers the incident well. On April 28, 2006, Syncrude leaked a toxic cloud. Winds blew it upriver to Fort MacKay, a small Cree community located on the banks of the Athabasca River between Syncrude's North and Aurora mines. The gas entered the school's ventilation system. "There were twenty-nine kids treated, five in the hospital and the rest out in Fort MacKay," O'Connor recalls. The children suffered from nausea, headaches and eye irritation. They were given an inhalant to help them breathe and sent home. "There were various descriptions of the smell and it didn't entirely fit ammonia. We don't know in the end because they haven't really come clean with exactly what it was." Alain Moore said at the time that the leak came from the company's new desulphurization unit in the refinery flue. He claimed the problem was fixed and characterized the leak as a "low concentration of ammonia."

A few weeks later, another noxious cloud hit. This time the wind blew it south to Fort McMurray.

Dr. O'Connor and his wife, Charlene, were out jogging. "There was this horrible smell in the air," he says. "It was like burnt cake. It was just very, very strong. Charlene got a headache from it, her eyes watering. Both of us were a little wheezy."

Air quality in the oil sands region is monitored by the Wood Buffalo Environmental Association (WBEA), which calls itself "Your Independent Air Quality Reporter." This is one of three local environmental organizations created by the Alberta government and the oil sands industry to monitor and analyze the effect of the oil sands projects on the environment. The other organizations are the Cumulative Environmental Management Association (CEMA) and the Regional Aquatics Monitoring Program (RAMP). Essentially, the Wood Buffalo Environmental

Association monitors air and water quality while CEMA, in its own words, "develops recommendations on how to best manage cumulative impacts of oil sands development and protect the environment." RAMP's mandate is to "assess the health of rivers and lakes in the oil sands region." All three agencies, whose budgets totalled $10.8 million in 2005—a paltry figure when you consider their mandates—are funded entirely by the oil sands industry. Industry members make up either the majority or the largest single-interest bloc on their membership boards, which also include employees of Alberta's health and environment departments. Reports compiled by these organizations are included in applications for expanded or new oil sands projects before the Alberta Energy and Utilities Commission.

Mayor Blake expressed surprise when I suggested this is like putting the fox in charge of the world's biggest henhouse. "I think the companies that are responsible for the pollution should pay to clean it up," she says.

The effect has been to absolve the Alberta environment department and therefore the government of practically any responsibility for the environment in Wood Buffalo. It also has created a strange incestuous cycle. The companies hire the same private environmental consulting companies to write reports on the impacts of their projects. These reports are filed with the EUB, whose experts study them and inevitably approve the project. Then organizations financed by the companies—CEMA, RAMP and the WBEA—monitor compliance. Their monitoring data is used in turn to support environmental impact studies for new projects, which are again monitored by CEMA, RAMP and WBEA. And so it goes round and round.

The Mikisew Cree band at Fort Chipewyan on Lake Athabasca quit CEMA in 2006. The Cree are opposed to further expansion of the oil sands projects because of the environmental destruction and the threat to the Athabasca River. They feel they don't want to be the companies' dupes. "The Alberta government has given away its regulatory responsibilities to a group of people controlled by industry," Archie Waquan, a Fort Chipewyan elder and former chief, says. "Guess who puts the money in it? Industry. So who controls the whole group? It's like saying to the Alberta government, 'We control you.' It's controlled by one group that wants development to occur and yet they are given the responsibility to look after the environment. It's crazy."

Strangely, on the day the toxic cloud hit Fort McMurray, none of the thirteen air monitors put in place by the Wood Buffalo Environmental Association registered a problem. The WBEA claimed they had a software problem in the monitoring system. It was the people of Fort McMurray who sounded the alarm.

Following hundreds of complaints, the Alberta government sent in mobile units that picked up high concentrations of ammonia. Four days after the original incident, the government ordered the plant shut down. Luckily, the cloud dispersed quickly and there was no serious harm done. Syncrude blamed the incident on start-up problems with a new coker. Dr. O'Connor, who is the general practitioner for the outlying Native communities, says it didn't go unnoticed that when the Native children in Fort MacKay

The endless horizon of the oil sands

were hit several weeks earlier, the province took no action against the company. "When the white people of [Fort McMurray] complained, the local MLA, Guy Boutilier, said shut it down."

♦

Whatever weather the day brings, you can always see the distant gas flares of Syncrude and Suncor as well as the plumes of heavy white smoke and steam gushing out of the refinery cokers, pumping CO_2 into the atmosphere. These are visual reminders of what drives this area. The other reminder is the constant scent of oil. Residents say that you get used to it and after a while you don't smell it anymore. These emissions put Syncrude and Suncor among the top ten producers of greenhouse gases in the nation, according to Pollution Watch. In 2004, between them, they emitted almost 19 million tons. Together, they are number three in the nation behind Alberta's and Ontario's coal-fired electricity plants. The new mines slated to come on stream within the next five years will double the greenhouse gas emissions. None of these future projects incorporate any strategy for reducing emissions.

"The solution is in technology," Syncrude's Jim Carter says. Technological breakthroughs, however, are unlikely to come from Alberta's energy companies. None of them rank high on the list of Canada's top research and development spenders, according to Research Infosource Inc. of Toronto. In 2005 only ten Alberta companies made it onto the list of the top one hundred. The highest ranked was Suncor at nineteenth; it spent $108 million on R & D. That figure represents a mere 1 percent of its total revenues of $11 billion. The average is about 4 percent. Syncrude was ranked fiftieth with a mere $44 million in R & D spending.

Carter doesn't dispute global warming, although he claims the jury is still out on its severity. "There's more emotion than science on the table," he says. Still, he's resigned to doing something about it because it's "what society expects of you." Yet he opposes taking any action that will depress earnings or harm the economy. "There's no magic way of wishing [global warming] away or taking steps to change our economy to stop it. That would be so dislocating in terms of incomes for people. I don't think we need to do that. I think we can rely on technology to make us better. And as long as we have robust companies that can reinvest capital, we're going to see investment in that technology that is going to be energy efficient."

Carter can afford to be casual about global warming and the Kyoto Protocol. While Alberta has been fighting against Kyoto, claiming it will destroy the province's energy industry, the oil sands companies themselves don't consider Kyoto a threat to their bottom line. Suncor, for example, in its 2005 annual report calculated that, by 2010, adhering to Kyoto Accord standards will cost it a mere twenty to twenty-seven cents a barrel. "We do not currently anticipate that the cost implications of federal and provincial climate change plans will have a material impact on our business or future growth plans," Suncor states.

♦

There are disturbing industrial processes going on in the oil sands region that nobody sees or smells. Mainly, they have to do with water.

The oil extraction process uses enough water in a day to supply the needs of the cities of Calgary (population one million), Lethbridge (79,000) and Red Deer (82,900). As of December 2006, oil sands mining operations were withdrawing 215.2 million cubic metres of water each year. This figure will more than double as the new projects come on stream by 2010. In other words, the industry could soon be withdrawing more water from the Athabasca River than is used by the entire urban population of Alberta.

Most of the water has to be disposed of as waste material, referred to as "tailings." The ultimate safe containment and disposal of these toxic tailings remains an unsolved problem. Every minute of the day, thousands of litres of grey-textured tailings gush out of 36-inch pipes into ever-expanding settling ponds.

The mixture contains highly toxic hydrocarbons such as naph-thenic acids, which are deadly to marine life, plus a host of other chemicals, including arsenic. Over the last four decades these tail-ings have developed into huge toxic lakes that are now the largest bodies of water in the region. Propane cannons scare away birds and other wildlife. To stop the deadly water from draining into the Athabasca River, the oil sands companies have used oil sand itself to construct a system of dams around the lakes, mixing the sand with gypsum to stabilize the structures. By the end of 2006, Syncrude's dams alone contained about 600 million cubic metres of mine tail-ings, making this the second-largest dam system in the world after China's Three Gorges, which is still under construction.

Those same sands are being used to restore the land. Nobody at Syncrude claims that they can restore it to what it used to be. They can't replace the ecosystems, the vast networks of peat bogs, fens, rivers and wetlands. Those are gone, proba-bly forever, along with the unique flora and fauna that once inhabited this region. Only nature will decide to what extent the land is ever restored.

The government of Alberta requires that the companies have restoration plans. Nobody knows, however, what this entails. Syncrude claims it has restored over eleven thousand acres, but by 2007 the government had still not approved this restoration as meeting its standards. Syncrude is "on the sharp end of the arrow, and you're trying to work with people through a process that they haven't been through before," Carter says. In other words, this is virgin territory. After four decades of destruc-tion, nobody has any real idea how to fix it. "We're still working on it. It's like anything else—it takes time when you're the first one through the chute kind of thing."

At the moment, Syncrude and the other companies simply plow back the sand, cover it with overburden and topsoil, and create a series of toxic lakes and ponds where they hope the hydrocarbons and other toxins will sink to the bottom and biodegrade. Then they pump fresh water overtop. The reclaimed land, which is bulldozed into gently rolling hills looking a bit like an artificial golf course with water hazards, is sown with a crop of barley. When the barley dies, it restores a certain amount of fertility to the soil. Syncrude then plants spruce, pine and aspens. They hope nature will eventually take over. It's a lot more than most other mining companies have done in this country. The scars from the oil sands are so huge that some effort has to be made to hide the damage and blot out the memory of a once-thriving boreal ecosystem.

Alain takes me over to see the bison. If the dump trucks are the poster machines for the oil sands, the wood buffalo are the poster animals for reclamation. Huge wood carvings of wood buffalo decorate the entrance to Syncrude. The wood buffalo has become the emblem and mascot of the very industry that is destroying its habitat. The company has installed a herd of about three hundred bison on land leading to the entrance to their refinery and base mine. There is a small viewing area where visitors can park their vehicles and watch the animals. The bison are penned in corrals and pastures and fed with hay trucked in from southern farms. If they had to live off the reclaimed land around Syncrude, they would starve to death. So the company contracts a First Nations company from Fort MacKay to manage the herd. The buffalo play a key part in Syncrude's attempt to convince Canadians that the destruction of vast parts of the North is relatively harmless and can be reversed. Just check out the happy bison.

Shell also has its herd of promo bison. The company runs a national television advertisement to convince the Canadian public that Shell is acting responsibly in restoring the land to its former state. The ad shows a few grazing bison and a Shell employee in a field of barley talking to a group of local Aboriginal elders. The voice-over claims that Shell is getting advice from the Natives on how to restore the land. This begs the obvious question: what do Natives know about restoring the land? They'll teach you how to gut a moose, but they don't know how to restore the land for the simple reason that they've never destroyed it.

Jim Carter claims that Syncrude is actually rendering the land "more productive than it was when we got here." He can't explain how he calculates that other than in terms of barley, bison and planted trees. But the statement has legal meaning. The Alberta government requires that Syncrude return the land to "equivalent capability." The government has never clarified what that means; it's hoping the companies will come up with an answer. Carter's pretension that Syncrude's restoration program makes the land "more productive" implies that it now has more than "equivalent capability." Pete says that the company is actually "doing nature a favour" by "cleaning out this dirty oil out of the oil sands." Damien says, "Truthfully, I don't think about it at all. I mostly just come around here and do my job and a lot of times you have a lot of time to think and you can think about a lot of things. But I don't think about that."

The mines are already so big that you can see the craters from the moon. Yet ten years down the road, this area will be unrecognizable. That's because it will have grown tenfold, dwarfing the present projects. There will be further expansion by the existing players plus the addition of at least six major new projects, including ExxonMobil and Chevron, France's Total, Imperial Oil, Husky and Canadian Natural Resources. They are projected to spend $110 billion. With that kind of money on the table, the beast will be unstoppable. "Obviously you can stop anything, but it's not very elegant to stop one of these things," Jim says of Syncrude's oil sands operations.

◆

Pete and I drive back to the main parking lot, over the extensive dam system. Until nature hopefully takes its course, Syncrude's dams will have to hold back the toxic soup. It's a precarious situation. Suncor admitted in 1997 that its Tar Island Pond just south of here leaks approximately 1,600 cubic metres of toxic fluid into the Athabasca River every day. Not surprisingly, the company's studies show, according to the EUB, "there is no measurable impact to the river from this seepage." While the engineering of tailing ponds has improved since construction of Tar Island began in 1966, Syncrude followed the same construction design when it built the dams that we are now travelling over. A thin finger of sand separates the tailing ponds from the river. Were any of the dams to rupture, say because of torrential rains, the consequences for the river could be disastrous.

For the Cree and Dene living downstream on the Athabasca delta, the consequences have already arrived.

CHAPTER 12

DOWN NORTH

**IN WHICH MYSTERIOUS DEATHS RATTLE FORT CHIP
AND DR. O. SWINGS INTO ACTION**

FROM FORT MCMURRAY, THE ATHABASCA RIVER FLOWS
225 kilometres north into the Peace–Athabasca delta before emp-
tying into Lake Athabasca. Situated just across from the delta on
the northwestern shore of the lake is Fort Chipewyan. Whatever
comes down the river ends up at its doorstep.

On its way from Fort McMurray to Fort Chip, the river
meanders through the boreal forest, past hundreds of tiny sandbars
and silted islands capped with pines, before finally disappearing
into the delta's confused swirl of channels, lakes, ponds and
marshes. Stretching one hundred kilometres east-west and seventy
kilometres north-south, it is the world's largest freshwater delta.

As Joe Marcel and I drive through the maze of delta channels in his open aluminum powerboat, ducks of every variety
madly flap their wings to get out of our way. I make a mental note
to Google the ducks, find out what kind they are. Then I remember I have an expert right here with me. A Cree hunter, trapper,
fisherman and guide, Joe knows these waters probably better
than anybody.

"They're mallards, northern pintails, American widgeons,"
Joe says.

He points out three trumpeter swans sailing overhead. These are the aristocrats of the delta. Once hunted almost to extinction, their numbers have grown from a low of 77 to about 550 in western Canada. They find refuge in the delta. Millions of migratory birds use the delta as a nesting or staging area in the spring and fall. The roar of the outboard only partially drowns out the birds' honking and quacking. A thin blanket of fresh November snow covers the riverbanks, where tiny black muskrats huddle down and scurry back and forth over the mud and reeds. Joe says the forest and grasslands are full of lynx, moose and wood buffalo, but we don't see any. All we see is a wall of forest on each bank occasionally broken by clearings of tall brown grasses and marsh reeds waving their soft, furry heads.

It's cold out on the water. Joe's hunched over the wheel staring down the channel from behind a pair of wraparound glasses, keeping an eye out for sandbars. The river has been getting lower each year, Joe says, partly due to increased water withdrawals for the oil sands—they take up to 20 percent of the river flow—and partly because of rising temperatures and higher rates of evaporation. You never know when you are going to hit bottom, so you have to be extra vigilant even when you know the delta as well as Joe knows it.

Joe Marcel

He's a big burly Cree packed inside a down-filled hunting jacket, coveralls and a peaked cap with earflaps. I've got my toque pulled down around my ears and my parka zipped and buttoned up to my chin. We've been riding now for about three hours and it's another hour at least before we get to Fort Chipewyan. Joe steers the boat over to a clearing and says we'll build a campfire and warm up a bit before making the final leg of our journey.

I'm almost too cold to move. But when the boat slows to a halt, we both immediately feel more comfortable with no more icy wind on our faces. I jump out of the boat and into ankle-deep water, secure the tether to a fallen tree and climb up the muddy embankment. Throughout the delta the riverbanks are unusually high, rising three metres or more out of the water, revealing their heavy silt content. "This year is the worst I've ever seen it," Joe says, referring to the river's low water level. "You see reeds like you've never seen before. And the delta is getting bigger every year. It must gain two or three hundred yards with all the sediment coming down and the water running low."

In the 1980s, the delta lakes and ponds began to dry up because the water levels in the river weren't high enough to replenish them. The delta gets water mainly from the Athabasca River. A secondary source is the Peace River, which doesn't actually touch the delta, shying by to the northwest. Water from Lake Athabasca flows through two channels into the Peace as it turns north to become the Slave River. Before the 1960s, during the spring runoff the Peace was so full and the ice jams were so heavy that the river flooded and backwashed over the delta, refilling and fertilizing shallow lakes and ponds, which then became havens for migratory birds. When British Columbia built the Bennett Dam in the eastern shadow of the Rockies in the early 1960s, its two-kilometre-long wall of concrete reduced the river flow and pretty well killed the spring flooding cycle. Since then, Parks Canada says, the once-lush marshes have declined 50 percent. Oil sands water removals that started thirty years ago added to this problem. More than fifteen years ago the Chipewyan Cree dug trenches by hand between the main channels and the interior lakes. The Cree hoped the trenches—some almost half a kilometre long—would redirect water from the channels and replenish the lakes. It worked for a while, but the water levels have continued to fall. From our temporary camp we can see one of these trenches. The water in the delta is so low that it is about three metres below the entrance to the trench. Joe says the lakes are pretty well empty.

◆

Despite three decades of increasing water withdrawals by an ever-expanding oil sands industry, neither the federal nor the provincial government has ever studied the effects of reduced flow rates on the thirty-one species of fish that populate the Athabasca River. With more than half the fish species found in Alberta, this marine habitat is among the most important in the province, yet no studies at all have been done on the delta. Nor have the governments studied the effects of the oil sands projects on tributary streams that feed nutrients into the Athabasca. Many of these streams have simply disappeared under the shovel. "Our knowledge of the aquatic ecosystem is much more limited than anyone would like at this time," a 2006 federal Department of Fisheries and Oceans report states. "Our understanding of the importance of the river for resident and migrant fish is still poor, but it *appears* [author's emphasis] that there are fish of many species using the river year-round." The government has only limited knowledge of where fish spawn, where and when the major migratory movements occur, and what role the river flows play in the life cycles of various aquatic species. "The Athabasca River is larger and more ecologically complicated than any river studied to date for an IFN recommendation in Alberta," the report says.

Instream Flow Needs (IFNs) are the different amounts of water that various aquatic species need throughout their life cycle. The ideal IFN is the natural flow regime of a river—its year-round cycles of spring floods, summer depletions, winter freezes, etc. Any withdrawals from a river should attempt to mimic these cycles. A key element of any Instream Flow Need is what's called the Ecosystem Base Flow (EBF). This is a reference to the lowest natural flow rates of the river as well as to their duration and frequency. Scientists consider many aquatic species at greatest risk during these periods. The idea is to set an EBF flow rate that guarantees the river won't drop below these critical levels and that their duration and frequency will not vary from natural cycles. Unfortunately, with no IFN rate imposed on the oil companies, scientists are concerned that these base flow needs are frequently not being met.

The trouble is that nobody knows for sure since monitoring of the fish populations has been almost non-existent. Without adequate data, nobody really knows what's going on. The oil sands companies withdraw up to 20 percent of the water in the river during these low flow periods. One solution would be to store water, which would then be used during low flow periods. Unfortunately, the companies have very limited storage capacity; they can stockpile for thirty days at most. This means they cannot reduce their withdrawals during low flow periods without closing down their plants. "Meeting even a very low EBF will require significantly more than 30 days water storage," a federal report states. In order to meet a safe EBF, the Department of Fisheries and Oceans states that the oil sands companies will need enough storage capacity to last at least a winter and preferably up to two years. This would not be difficult to achieve; reservoirs in the south of Alberta have this capacity. Until the companies can construct these reservoirs, however, the DFO is allowing them to continue to breach the low flow needs until December 31, 2011. "It is important to point out that this decision is not based on science or biology, but on consideration for impacts to industry," the report states.

Until just thirty years ago, the Athabasca was the most natural-flowing, pristine river in the province. Since then, pulp mills and oil sands companies have changed all that. A proposal by Shell and Canadian Natural Resources in 2003 to build two new oil sands mines finally raised the issue of the river's long-term health. The question became how much water could be withdrawn from the river by the new projects without harming—or destroying—its aquatic life. With as many as eight new projects coming on stream over the next five years or so, this has become a pressing problem. It is the federal Department of Fisheries and Oceans' job to enforce the Fisheries Act, which in turn exists to protect the fisheries—the aquatic life of the nation's waterways. Alberta, however, while claiming to be mindful of the need to protect the river, has been pushing the boundaries in favour of industry. The result has been a typical clash of interests. The solution has been simply to hand over the responsibility to a so-called independent body.

In an astonishing act of surrender, the federal and provincial governments have assigned the critical task of setting flow rates in the lower Athabasca—the section downstream from the oil sands—to the industry-funded CEMA

CEMA is supposed to come up with river flow figures that would ensure oil sands water withdrawals do not harm life in the river. By the end of 2005, CEMA had missed its deadline to come up with the inflow rate recommendations. By the end of 2006, there were still no recommendations. In fact, important areas of the river, such as the delta, had not even been monitored. CEMA had no data sufficient to make an inflow stream rate recommendation. Because scientists have no direct scientific data upon which to base Athabasca flow rates, they are using as a model the flow rates imposed on the South Saskatchewan River basin. The success of these flow rates in the South Saskatchewan has never been fully monitored, according to a federal report; so nobody knows if they work for that river, never mind for the Athabasca.

Meanwhile, the government has continued to award long-term water withdrawal licences that pay little heed to the flow cycles of the river. The companies are generally permitted to remove the water they need throughout the year. Lack of scientific data wasn't the only reason industry-funded CEMA failed to set inflow stream needs. It was also because the companies refused to set any flow rates that would compromise their business. They "threatened legal action if their [water withdrawal] licences were changed," a 2006 DFO report said.

The Mikisew Cree have made it clear in writing to the minister of fisheries and oceans and to the minister of the environment in Alberta that they expect the river to be "fully protected" as per their treaty rights. The Cree want a "precautionary" rate set and have served notice that they are holding the DFO to its "responsibility for maintaining healthy and productive aquatic ecosystems and for sustaining fisheries and aquaculture."

Alberta is lobbying for a level that will not compromise the industry's water withdrawal licences while at the same time protecting the ecosystem as much as possible. DFO officials, who emphasize that "this is a very valuable fishery and deserves the highest level of protection," have stated that this will lead to a HADD—bureaucratic talk for "Harmful Alteration, Disruption or Destruction" of fish habitat. In other words, it might kill fish and even wipe out the fishery. The DFO has been reluctant to accept Alberta's position and as of February 2007 the two sides had still not come to a consensus. The DFO's main concern is the almost total lack of knowledge of the Athabasca fish population. It points out, however, that "oil sands development is proceeding at a record pace and DFO has to make regulatory decisions."

The pressure is on to react to industry demands. Given that the DFO presided over the almost total destruction of the east coast fishery and has done little to monitor the oil sands river basins, First Nations hunters and fishermen such as Joe Marcel have little faith in the federal government's commitment to protect the Athabasca River.

♦

Joe quickly lights a fire and I toss on some broken branches and before long I'm beginning to feel my feet and hands. With the engine silenced, the air is calm and still. The only noise is the crackling and steaming of the fire—and of course, the birds. The winter road from Fort McMurray to Fort Chipewyan goes through here, travelling over frozen land and water. Joe says that each year the season gets shorter and the road becomes more dangerous because the ice doesn't freeze as solid as it should. There are several daily flights between Fort McMurray and Fort Chipewyan, but the road is what everybody longs for. It's what sets them free.

It's also what gives them power. When the federal government decided in 2000 to extend the winter road north into the Northwest Territories to link up with a road to Fort Smith, the Cree sued, claiming they had not been consulted. The road in question was not very long—only 118 kilometres. But it gave rise to a pivotal legal case in the annals of the First Nations. That case, and the resulting judgment, is now of key importance to the continued growth of the oil sands.

The basis of the lawsuit went all the way back to 1899 and the signing of Treaty 8. This is the most important post-Confederation document for the region's First Nations as it lays out their traditional land rights. The treaty surrendered to the federal government 840,000 square kilometres of what is now northern Alberta south to Fort McMurray, northeastern British Columbia, northwestern Saskatchewan and the southern portion of the Northwest Territories. It's an area bigger than Alberta (661,185 square kilometres), Manitoba (650,087 square kilometres) or Saskatchewan (651,900 square kilometres). It was a heavy price to pay for the Crown's promise that the First Nations would retain hunting, trapping, and fishing rights in perpetuity. These rights were affirmed by the Constitution Act of 1982.

There was, however, one important rider. The treaty gave the government the right to exclude such "tracts as may be required or taken up from time to time for settlement, mining, lumbering, trading or other purposes." No one at the time could have imagined the oil sands and the extent to which their mining would compromise the First Nations' traditional hunting rights. If the First Nations could have foreseen such violent exploitation, one can only imagine whether or not they would have signed the treaty. This is not just idle speculation. Even though there is no written record from the treaty Indians that describes their thoughts or intentions at the time, the Supreme Court has said that judges have to evaluate the "common intentions at the time the treaty was made." And one of these "common intentions" was clearly to preserve the First Nations' hunter-gatherer lifestyle. Even so, the treaty recognized that when the white man chose to "take up" his right to settlement, mining, etc., a clash of civilizations would occur. Reconciliation would be a necessity.

A central principle in resolving Aboriginal claims is that the Crown must act honourably in its dealings with First Nations. The Supreme Court has stated:

> It is not as though the Treaty 8 First Nations did not pay dearly for their entitlement to honourable conduct on the part of the Crown; surrender of the aboriginal interest in an area larger than France is a hefty purchase price. The language of the treaty could not be clearer in foreshadowing change. Nevertheless the Crown was and is expected to manage the change honourably.

Which raises the question of whether the Crown acted honourably when it began in the 1960s allowing oil sands companies to bulldoze thousands of square kilometres of treaty lands without first consulting the First Nations.

The treaty was an attempt to reconcile the needs of a beef-and-wheat agrarian society with the ancient hunter-gatherer traditions of the region's First Nations—a lifestyle that knew nothing of private land ownership, a lifestyle to which men such as Joe Marcel still cling. The treaty recognized and encouraged the Indians' desire to continue to live off and move freely over their traditional lands. But it also recognized that this lifestyle would eventually conflict with the white settlements. Therefore, the treaty prescribed a process of consultation to "explain the relations" that would govern future interaction between these diametrically opposed lifestyles "and thus prevent any trouble."

This process can be triggered by the slightest impact to the Treaty 8 lands—in this case, a 118-kilometre winter road corridor that crossed over the traplines of fourteen Mikisew trappers and the hunting grounds of about a hundred hunters. This "may not seem very dramatic (unless you happen to be one of the trappers or hunters in question) but, in the context of a remote northern community of relatively few families, it is significant," the Supreme Court said. "Beyond that, however, the principle of consultation in advance of interference with existing treaty rights . . . goes to the heart of the relationship and concerns not only the Mikisew but other First Nations and non-aboriginal governments as well." In other words, the government had to consult with the First Nations before it built a road through Treaty 8 land. In this case, the federal government in 2000 notified the Cree of its intention to build the road, invited their comments at a public meeting and then went ahead and built the road. In 2005, the Supreme Court said that was not good enough. The court ruled that the government had to plan the road with the Cree, even to the point where the Cree could have a veto on its location. "The Crown must then attempt to deal with the Mikisew in good faith and with the intention of substantially addressing their concerns," the court said.

If such a relatively small issue as this winter road extension could trigger such extensive consultation, the obvious question was: what about the oil sands?

◆

When the fire dies down, Joe and I climb back into the boat. Joe pushes the throttle wide open. An hour later we suddenly emerge out of the narrow channels and into the broad expanse of Lake Athabasca with its big sky and limitless horizon. After spending hours in the confined waterways of the delta, it feels as if we've come up for air.

Joe continues east along the channel, which is marked by thin wooden poles stuck into sandbars as a warning of where the water level is so low we'd hit bottom. The lake stretches out on either side, but Joe won't leave the channel. He drives another kilometre or so into the lake before he turns his boat in a sweeping arc north and then west towards Fort Chipewyan. You can see the town on the distant shore with its pastel-coloured bungalows and white church steeples clinging to the granite rocks on the edge of the Canadian Shield. Joe steers the boat into the harbour and we tie up to the concrete pier near a small, rusting lake freighter sitting on blocks. Fort Chip is Alberta's oldest European settlement and first trading post, founded in 1778 at the confluence of the Athabasca, Peace and Slave Rivers. When rivers were the highways, this was the trading centre.

♦

The Hudson's Bay Company once ruled this town, bringing in men primarily from the remote Orkney Islands, off the northern coast of Scotland, to manage commerce with the Indians. Today the population is down to 1,200 Cree, Chipewyan (part of the Dene people), and Metis, with a few whites. Many still earn a subsistence living from hunting, trapping and fishing or from serving as guides in and around the delta. They don't have fond memories of the Hudson's Bay Company, which, they say, basically ripped them off at every opportunity. Nor do they recall with any warmth the American fishing companies that set up commercial fisheries on the lake. They often refused to pay the Indians for their walleye and whitefish, claiming a shipment had gone bad. The companies were so predatory that the federal government finally kicked them out in the 1960s. Before they left, they tried to fish out the spawning grounds.

Throughout this era, assimilation was federal policy. Each week Don Ehman, a psychologist from Edmonton, flies into Fort Chip to hold group therapy sessions with Aboriginals who were forced into residential schools. Members of the community still struggle with the psychological effects of being uprooted from their families and sent off to school to learn how to live as Caucasians. Ehman says about 90 percent of the residents who went to the schools suffered sexual and physical abuse. This is a community that has long and troubled memories.

The Alberta government and the oil sands companies are the most recent visitors wanting to "take up" Treaty 8 lands—in this case for mining, but also for logging. Until as recently as 2005, the Alberta government paid almost no attention to First Nations' rights as outlined in the treaty—and the Constitution—claiming this was a federal responsibility. But recent Supreme Court rulings—the 2005 winter road ruling being one of four important rulings about Native land rights since 1990—have changed all that. Suddenly both the government and energy companies are courting the local Native communities.

Every time an oil sands company has a new project, it flies executives to Fort Chipewyan on chartered aircraft to talk to the elders, many of whom don't speak English, about how the company is going to protect the environment. The oilmen bring their charts and videos and information sheets. They question the elders on their traditional land use of the area and then prepare land use studies for the EUB. The meetings are held in the community centre. To get there, the execs have to drive by the town's arena. In 2004 the roof fell in, and Wood Buffalo can't find the money to build a new arena. After the meetings, the company officials hand out to the elders envelopes of money and goodie bags filled with gifts such as camcorders and DVDs. "Years ago it was beads, booze and guns," Archie Waquan, a former Cree chief, says. "Now it's DVD players, cameras and $150."

The Mikisew Cree in Fort Chip stand alone. Much to their disappointment, other bands have settled. The Cree and Dene of Fort MacKay surrendered in 2006 after several decades of watching the oil sands companies wipe out their traditional lands. Now the community is pretty well surrounded by mines. The Cree and Dene agreed to accept $41.5 million in compensation and the transfer of twenty-three thousand acres of oil sands land to their reserve. They will have the right to royalties from that oil.

The Mikisew Cree say they don't want money. At least not yet. They want the oil sands expansion stopped. Then they want proper consultations as prescribed by Treaty 8 and upheld by the

Constitution and the Supreme Court, and only at that point do they want a settlement.

"In some cases the Supreme Court decisions state that it's possible the First Nations could have veto power [over the oil sands]," Jim Tanner, a consultant on First Nations rights, says. "They definitely in law have the ability to stop the oil sands."

◆

The residents of Fort Chip first felt the effects of the oil sands in 1982, when their fish began to taste like gasoline. "It smelt like burning rubber boots when you cooked them," John Rigney recalls. "I went back to the fisherman and says, 'Your fish taste like gasoline.' He gave me some fresh ones and they also tasted like gasoline."

A hundred and fifty kilometres upriver, Fort MacKay was having a similar experience. Chief Dorothy McDonald complained to the Alberta government, which refused to take any action. Finally she marched into the Fort McMurray courthouse and laid five complaints against Suncor, forcing the government's hand. It investigated the complaints and laid twenty-two charges against Suncor for polluting the river. But the trial stalled when the government's greenhorn lawyer, who was up against a phalanx of corporate pleaders, had a breakdown. The trial was delayed for a few months while the government assembled its own legal team. The trial showed that the government had been aware there had been an oil spill but had done nothing about it. Suncor was fined $38,000. The company quickly settled with the fishermen, paying them $42,000 to be divided equally among twenty fishermen. In return for the money, the fishermen agreed not to sue. The government closed down the Fort Chipewyan fishery for the next two years, which cost the fishermen more than $100,000 a year.

This spill, coupled with an earlier one from Syncrude, proved to the Indians that the Athabasca River, which they had relied on for thousands of years for fresh water, was now suspect.

The fish no longer tasted good and neither did the water they took from the lake. They also began to notice an increased incidence of cancers and other diseases they hadn't seen in their community before. It was Dr. John O'Connor who first brought their concerns to the government.

O'Connor, forty-nine, is a small Irish general practitioner who's not afraid to speak his mind. He has auburn hair with a touch of grey and a soft-spoken, thoughtful manner. He immigrated to Canada as a medical student and completed his training in Halifax. He came to Alberta in 1993 because he worried that being licensed to practice only in Nova Scotia might be too confining. He ended up in Fort McMurray. Two days each week he flies to Fort Chipewyan to treat patients at the community nursing station. Fort Chip residents call him Dr. O. When you speak to him, you can tell he's pleased by the close relationship he has built with the First Nations of Wood Buffalo. He knows most of the Native people personally and has a detailed knowledge of their family medical histories.

By 2003, he began to share the concerns of the Fort Chip community after he noticed an alarming number of rare cancer

Dr. John O'Connor

cases and autoimmune diseases, such as rheumatoid arthritis and lupus, developing among his Fort Chipewyan patients. "I discovered very close in time two cases of cholangiocarcinoma, cancer of the bile duct. Then there was a third. This is a rare cancer that's very aggressive, and it's very strange to have so many in such a small population." He says he also noticed an unusual number of thyroid problems. "At one point I had five or six patients in a row in the space of just a few months that we picked up with routine blood tests, and I sent them all down to the same endocrinologist in Edmonton. I think the third or fourth patient I sent down I had to get the endocrinologist on the phone, Dr. Andrea Opgennorth is her name, and she joked, 'What are you doing to those people in Fort Chip?!' 'Yeah,' I said, 'it is a little unusual.' She said, 'Yeah, it's very unusual for a population of that size.'"

Dr. O'Connor says he suspected that the diseases might be caused by pollution coming down the river from the pulp mills or the oil sands or from the old uranium mines on the east end of Lake Athabasca, or by a combination of all three. But he didn't know. Athough the community had become more sedentary and, like everywhere in Canada, there were issues of weight, he doubted the problem was lifestyle related because the local population was generally health conscious and most members of the community took care of themselves. He also knew that autoimmune diseases can be caused by arsenic and benzene as well as certain polycyclic aromatic hydrocarbons (PAHs) that include anthracene and chrysene, which are found in the oil sands.

Arsenic is found naturally in sediments around the oil sands and in some areas, such as the Cold Lake oil sands, in groundwater. Digging and drilling activities bring it to the surface, where it is released into surface water, increasing the overall arsenic concentration. (Alberta Health and Wellness supplies free kits for testing water wells in the area, but they don't include an analysis for arsenic.) This has become a particular problem with steam-assisted gravity drilling in the oil sands. Here they drill deep into sands that cannot be accessed with open-pit mines. Steam is pumped into the earth, reducing the viscosity of the oil, which is then pumped to the surface. (This technology was developed in Alberta with $55 million in federal funds.) Heavy metals are contained in the bitumen and in the drilling waste that is brought to the surface. High concentrations of arsenic—and a veritable junkyard of other toxic metals—are found in the mine tailings and coke. A 1998 study prepared for Suncor by Golder Associates of Calgary shows that arsenic and other metals in coke leach into groundwater "at concentrations exceeding regulatory guidelines." Arsenic is also a by-product of the bitumen extraction process. The Alberta government allows the oil sands companies to dump a limited amount of arsenic—about sixty kilograms each—into the Athabasca River every year.

Alarms were raised in the Fort McMurray area in the early 1990s as a result of studies done on the downstream effects of pollution from the pulp mills on the Athabasca River. Dr. David Schindler, who participated in these studies, said the PAH levels around the oil sands were the highest values he had ever seen in North America. His studies also noted that fish were showing serious signs of toxic stress, to the point where they were even changing sex, affecting their reproductive capabilities. He recommended continued monitoring of the river's toxicity, but this was never done. "That was when there were only two oil sands mines," he says. "Now the PAH levels could be much higher as [the number of mines increases] to eight or ten."

Benzene, PAHs and arsenic are all proven carcinogenic chemicals and can combine to disable the immune system. However, scientifically linking a single compound or any combination of compounds to specific health problems is like opening a can of worms, Schindler says. "And without any specific studies of exact data that are down there, it is almost impossible."

Still, Dr. O'Connor thought these pollutants were likely culprits. But first he had to find out if the number of strange diseases attacking his patients was in fact unusual. The problem here was that nobody had ever done a baseline study of the health of people living near the oil sands. So there was no historical data upon which to base statistical probabilities. All of which opened the field to deniers.

At the same time that Dr. O'Connor was noticing an increase in cancer cases, Shell and Canadian Natural Resources (CNR) were applying to the Alberta Energy and Utilities Board for permission to build two new open-pit oil sands mines. Dr. O'Connor and his boss, Dr. Michel Sauvé, who is chief of medicine for the Fort McMurray hospital, brought the concerns of the Fort Chipewyan community—concerns they shared—to the EUB. The EUB granted licences to both companies with the condition that they fund a baseline health study of the population of Fort Chipewyan. Dr. Sauvé suggested that patients with strange cancers or other diseases be tested for toxicity as part of the study; that would be a simple way of identifying a possible link between pollutants and the diseases. As of March 2007, the study had not even begun. "This is a failure of the regulatory process," Dr. Sauvé says. "If you look at the history of regulatory processes, they are actually designed largely by industry. What body would be looking at the overall effect of the oil sands industry on the water? CEMA. It has fifty members, and if you are ever going to design a committee to be completely impotent, then you are going to make sure it has so many voices it can never make a decision. It's a sham of oversight. It cannot succeed and needs to be revamped."

Dr. O'Connor also started lobbying Health Canada to do a study of diseases at Fort Chipewyan. Initially, Health Canada ignored him. But when he began talking to the local and national media about unusual numbers of rare cancers and other diseases in Fort Chipewyan, Health Canada suddenly changed its mind. In April 2006 Health Canada and Alberta's Health and Wellness department, which took a lead role, sent up a small team of investigators to check out Dr. O'Connor's claims that an abnormally high number of serious illnesses were killing and injuring the people of Fort Chipewyan.

"The first thing one of the Health Canada people did was go into the kitchen at the nursing station and fill a glass full of water and drink it down and say, 'You see, there's nothing wrong with the water in Fort Chip,'" Dr. O'Connor recalls. "Bad luck, genetics, pollution—we don't know what's causing these diseases, but we'd like the questions answered. But the first thing Health Canada did was come in and defend the water, which was very odd."

O'Connor suspected that this was not going to be a serious study.

The study team took away hospital records of deceased patients and promised to study records at hospitals in Fort McMurray as well as records of band members who no longer lived in the community of Fort Chip. The investigators predicted the study would not be completed until fall.

Meanwhile, Suncor was applying for approval of a new open-pit mine called the North Steepbank Extension, named after the Steepbank River, a navigable river that runs through the middle of the mine area. They also wanted to build a new upgrader called the Voyageur. The projects would more than double Suncor's crude oil output to 550,000 barrels a day. The footprints of the mine extension and new upgrader would total 9,600 acres, but the overall area affected would be 16,884 acres. The project would destroy a small river called Unnamed Creek. As compensation for the destruction of this fish habitat, Suncor promised to enhance the fish population of the Steepbank. (According to federal law, fish habitats cannot be destroyed unless there is a plan to enhance them in another area in the region. They call this "habitat compensation." Experts say that nobody ever really checks to see if this has been successful. Furthermore, it's difficult to enhance populations since nature sets its own levels. Everyone knows this, but it's part of the image-based politics of the environment.) The project will include an enormous disposal area to stockpile sulphur and coke. Suncor's hearing before the EUB began on July 5, 2006, in Fort McMurray.

Among the fourteen environmental impact assessments filed by Suncor was information about existing and potential chemical contamination in the water, soil, plants and wildlife in and around the Athabasca and Steepbank Rivers. (In 1997,

Suncor had declared it would spend $90 million on technical, social and environmental studies for its expansion projects.) Benzene, mercury and cadmium, which is also a carcinogenic compound, were labelled among the "chemicals of potential concern." Arsenic was not included in this group, but the reports noted that high levels of arsenic—considered to be above the "quality guidelines"—were found in the roots of cattail reeds around Fort McMurray as well as in the area of the mine extension and the Voyageur upgrader site, in the sediment of several lakes and creeks, and in parts of the Athabasca River near the Suncor site and all the way down to Embarras River in the delta. Here the maximum level was four hundred times the amount recommended in the water quality guidelines set by the U.S. Environmental Protection Agency. Arsenic in the sediment of the Athabasca River near Suncor's mine also exceeded the guidelines. The report concluded: "Total metal levels (including arsenic and mercury) in the Athabasca River have been above water quality guidelines, similar to other water bodies in the Oil Sands Region . . . Chronic toxicity has been observed when laboratory organisms are exposed to Athabasca River sediments."

But the real bombshell at the EUB hearings came in the form of a 2005 Golder report for Suncor which predicted that moose meat could have 453 times the acceptable levels of arsenic sometime in the future. This raised the obvious question of how much arsenic moose and other wildlife have in them now. Nobody knew. Hunters, however, had complained that moose meat did not taste normal and that they were finding cysts in the animals' organs. They also complained that muskrat meat was excessively red and they had been discovering muskrats dead in their burrows.

The Suncor arsenic reports became part of the EUB public record in July 2006. Fearing that these reports would raise concerns about the health of downstream Native communities, the government health investigators studying Fort Chipewyan's cancer problems suddenly showed up at the hearing and declared that their analysis of the town's medical records showed there was no evidence of increased cancer rates or any other abnormal rates of disease. In fact, they said they thought the community's over-all health was above average. (Their sudden haste even caught Health Canada spokesperson Jeannie Smith off guard. "I read [about the study] in the paper when I was at home. I couldn't believe it was already released. I just didn't think it was ready.")

A few days after their presentation to the EUB, the investigators showed up at Fort Chipewyan to present their report to the community. Community members, who had watched their friends and relatives die of cancers nobody had ever seen before in Fort Chipewyan, were unhappy that the investigators had not first presented the results to them. They were also surprised that the report was completed so quickly when they had been told not to expect any results until at least the fall. But more than any-thing, they were stunned by the results. "I have known a whole host of people who have had bowel cancer," John Rigney, who himself has had bowel cancer, says. "I could name ten. I don't know what the cause is, but it's not been seen here before."

Community members questioned the investigators about their methodology. The investigators admitted they had not traced band members who had left the reserve (they had never even requested a membership list from the council); they had not looked up records in Edmonton hospitals where Dr. O'Connor had sent his cancer and thyroid patients; they hadn't examined files at the hospital in Fort McMurray; and they hadn't looked at the active files in the Fort Chipewyan nurses' station. Furthermore, they had picked up four cases of bile duct cancer at the hospital in Fort McMurray—which they considered "not significant but provoca-tive"—but found only one case of this cancer at Fort Chipewyan. Dr. O'Connor was convinced that some of those cancer patients in Fort McMurray were actually from Fort Chipewyan. He believed they were patients he had sent to Fort McMurray for treatment, where they had died. He asked whether this was the case. "I never got an answer," he says.

"There were three absolutely positive cases of cholangio-carcinoma" at Fort Chipewyan that were confirmed by biopsies, and two other cases of patients who were too ill to have further treatment but where scans confirmed the diagnosis, he says. "So they had this half-assed report with a spokesperson from the cancer board admitting twice that we don't have complete data for 2004, 2005 and 2006. I think that it's completely irresponsible of them to state that there are no unusual health problems at Fort Chipewyan."

The study team did, however, raise one concern that wasn't in their report: arsenic. They warned people in the community that moose meat and marsh plants could have dangerous levels of the metalloid. Unaware of the Suncor reports about arsenic content, the Chipewyan residents thought this warning was odd and questioned the team as to why they had raised the issue. They got no answers. Then, four months later, the truth came out: the local *Fort McMurray Today* paper reported on the moose-arsenic prediction in the Suncor report. The Alberta Health and Wellness department immediately reacted by claiming that Suncor's study was suspect, bringing into question the supposed high arsenic level in moose. Instead of being 453 times the acceptable levels, health officials said they were "10 to 30 times higher than anything we had seen before." This still would make them dangerously high, and the question arose of why these government studies that revealed high levels of arsenic in moose had never been made public.

"It's always been like if we withhold the information from the people, we do not get them all alarmed, the whole bit," Archie Waquan says. "They withhold the information from us and I don't think it's completely fair. It's 453 times what humans should take. In wild creatures like moose, one thing about moose is it eats water plants. It also in the winter months eats willows. That's their diet . . . If it's in the moose, it'll be in everything we eat— rats [muskrats], cranberries and all that."

The report alarmed Fort Chipewyan residents, who didn't know whether they should continue to eat moose or, for that matter, any other game. Alberta Health responded to their concerns on November 27, 2006, by flying up their food expert,

Alex Mackenzie. He reassured the community that their moose meat was safe and claimed that the Suncor study was a "fabrication and just a wild guess" without giving any further explanation for this astonishing statement. But when members of the community asked if it was safe to eat deer, berries or muskrats, Mackenzie replied: "No, we can't tell you that it's safe." Mackenzie then asked the residents to collect moose meat samples for Alberta Health to examine. He handed out biohazard bags and instructed the residents to put two hundred grams of moose meat in each bag and send them to the department.

For Dr. O'Connor, Mackenzie's performance was unbelievable. He wondered why the government was so reluctant to take the health problems at Fort Chipewyan seriously. "There's no rigour about it. There's no protocol. They have no way of knowing if the samples haven't been contaminated. They have no way of knowing where the moose was killed. In many instances they won't know if it was frozen in a freezer for a few years or freshly hunted. These moose, they don't stand in one position—they migrate. They don't even know, actually, whether the meat they get is moose or not. So the whole way this is being handled is very slipshod, and again it looks as it did in July that they have probably no intention of taking this seriously."

The problem with the government's statistical analysis is that unless you come up with astronomical levels of disease, the numbers are meaningless. This is because the population base in Fort Chipewyan is simply too small for accurate short-term testing. A sudden increase in a cancer rate in a population of 1,200 can easily be explained away as a statistical anomaly. In the world of statistical probability, five cancers, while not normal, could simply be random chance. This was the case, for instance, with lupus: the government analysis showed that there was an elevated level of the disease in Fort Chipewyan and the rest of Wood Buffalo, but it dismissed this as not statistically significant. Both industry and governments are well aware that these small statistical studies are largely pointless. Scientists deal in probabilities; small sampling significantly reduces this factor. "I have always found that these small communities kind of play into industry's hands by wanting a health study," Dr. David Schindler, the water expert, says.

The commercial fishery of Fort Chipewyan is effectively dead. Residents had already been warned not to eat fish more than once a week because of mercury poisoning and other toxins. With this latest scare, it seemed that all of their staple foods were gradually being poisoned.

The EUB has since approved the Suncor expansion. The board members stated that they did not consider the arsenic issue serious enough to delay the project.

If the food supply for the First Nations of northern Alberta and possibly the Territories as well—since they are all part of the same watershed—is being irrevocably contaminated, this could give the First Nations a powerful claim that their traditional treaty rights have been seriously violated. You can't hunt, trap and fish a poisoned land. The cost of cleaning it up could be enormous. The compensation to the First Nations—if indeed you could even put a monetary figure on it—would have to be astronomical.

"You take away our land, you destroy it, we are a nobody," Archie says. "We have to make sure the land is healthy. That's what gives us our life." If you shoot a moose, you have enough protein to last a year. The land is their Safeway. "This thing [the oil sands] is going so fast that nobody has time to react to it. It allows the companies to control the agenda. We have a government right now that has no control over anything."

◆

Nothing prepares you for the sheer magnitude of the oil sands as seen from the air. When you are standing in the mining pit amid the shovel-and-truck hustle, it all seems normal, safe and right. It seems as if this is the way life has always been around here. But flying overhead at 3,500 feet, the picture is much more disturbing. The black open-pit mines butt up against the surrounding vegetation of the boreal forest with its lakes, streams and marshes. The contrast between a dead zone and a living ecosystem marks a clear and unmistakable catastrophe.

Rob Elford steers his single-engine Cessna west of the Athabasca River. Not long after we left Fort Chip and gained altitude, I could see the oil sand mines creeping out in all directions towards every horizon. The scar on the earth is grotesque but impressive. The mines hug the riverbanks. The sun glints off their huge tailing ponds. Their stacks flare gas and gush clouds of steam and CO_2s into the atmosphere. The boreal forest stands in silent surrender, waiting to be sacrificed, as is evidenced by the huge swaths of forest that have been cleared away in preparation for the drilling rigs, pipelines and extractors.

You can also see the expanding square hatching of the steam-assisted gravity drilling projects (called SAGD) that will soon cover most of northeastern Alberta. At first glance they don't look as violent or intrusive as the open-pit mines, but the effect on the boreal forest and the wildlife amounts to the same thing. Tens of thousands of acres are bulldozed and wildlife habitat is destroyed by a broadening patchwork of drilling platforms, upgrader plants and thousands of kilometres of roads and pipelines a hundred metres apart, slashing through the forest and tearing up the land. A Parks Canada official who testified about the 118-kilometre winter road extension north of Fort Chipewyan was asked whether such a small road really had any effect on the pattern of moose and other wildlife. "I would be foolish if I said [it] didn't," he replied. With the billions of dollars in tax subsidies and royalty holidays that this industry receives each year, Canadians are subsidizing the total destruction of this environment.

The First Nations have hunted these lands for about eight thousand years. The oil sands, of course, provide employment to hundreds of First Nations members from Fort McMurray and Fort MacKay, fewer from Fort Chipewyan. Some Indians have started businesses that do contract work for the oil companies. The work is there for any First Nations member who wants it.

But men like Joe Marcel, who have spent their lives hunting and fishing and working as guides to provide for their families, don't want to end their traditional hunter-gatherer lifestyle. The money is definitely alluring. But Joe wonders if spending your day cooped up in a truck or in a security guard station, as many Native people now do, is worth the price. Unfortunately, the way things are going, he may have no choice.

In June 1899, the Treaty 8 commissioners noted that "the white man is bound to come in and open up the country." However, they assured the Indians that "the same means of earning a livelihood would continue after the treaty as existed before it."

Joe Marcel wants to hold the government to that promise.

CHAPTER 13

THE LAST COWBOYS AND COWGIRLS

IN WHICH THREE WOMEN TAKE ON BIG OIL
AND BIG GOVERNMENT
AND WE DISCOVER WHOM NOT TO MESS WITH

JESSICA ERNST MOVED TO ALBERTA IN 1982 BECAUSE SHE FELL in love with the sky. It made her feel as though she could reach up and touch infinity.

She bought a fifty-acre ranch about an hour's drive east of Calgary on the soft edge of the badlands. "We have very sharp, steep coulees, dramatic terrain, some fantastic ecological features that are very rare where there are natural north-facing spruce groves right on the prairie on the steep banks of the coulees." On the ranch is a small bungalow, which she fixed up, and a couple of barns, as well as an old frontier homestead that she intends to renovate but never seems to get around to it what with all the work she does as an environmental consultant to the oil and gas industry.

Her land begins at the end of a narrow road about a two-minute walk outside the tiny hamlet of Rosebud. It's nestled at the bottom of a broad valley, a position that affords a degree of protection against the violent winds that sometimes blow across the treeless plains. Cattle graze on neighbouring lands. On the high plains topside of the coulee are endless fields of wheat and barley stretching as far as the eye can see, which around here is pretty far.

Rosebud, a quaint, cozy hamlet, is part of Alberta's Bible belt. It's an odd place for an independent, strong-minded woman such as Jessica to live. The local mission church operates a "Christian theatre and theatre school" called the Rosebud School of the Arts. "They tried quite hard to get me to go to the fundamentalist church when I first moved to Rosebud," Jessica says. "It was hard work to get the people to accept that I am too private a person to go to church. It took a few years." To some of the more extreme members of the church community, a godless woman living by herself on her own acreage didn't seem right. When gas companies began blanketing the area with coal bed methane (CBM) wells and Jessica openly opposed them, that feeling of distrust grew.

If you follow the valley about half a kilometre west towards the hamlet of Redland, you'll come across the Lauridsen ranch. It's run by Peter Lauridsen and his wife, Fiona. They have one girl and two boys, who are in high school. Peter's parents emigrated from Denmark after the Second World War and the Lauridsens have been operating a mixed farm in the area, rearing cows and growing various cash crops including wheat, barley and canola, ever since. In 2000, Peter and a relative in Denmark bought a 932-acre spread between Redland and Rosebud and called it Valhalla Farms Inc. The property came with a ranch house, corrals and a Quonset—a corrugated metal shelter for equipment—located at the bottom of the Rosebud River valley.

The most important aspect of the farm was its reliable water supply. It was a slow feed, but with a system of three wells and a holding cistern it was enough to supply both their cattle and the Lauridsen family with good clean water. In the dry, parched farmlands of southern Alberta, water is gold. Without a clean supply, no bank will loan you money and your house and stables will be basically worthless. The Lauridsens' wells were tied into the same aquifer that fed Jessica's acreage and also the village of Rosebud.

Farming was new to Fiona. She grew up in Glasgow, Scotland, where she studied chemistry in university, and then in 1981 immigrated to Canada. She quickly fell in love with the big-sky country. She also fell in love with Peter, and before she knew it she found herself running a mixed farm.

Farther down the valley, in the hamlet of Redland, Debbie Signer was also starting a new venture. Debbie is a native Albertan, born and bred on a 2,000-acre farm about seven kilometres northeast of Drumheller. She moved to Australia for a while, where she kept horses, and then returned to Alberta and decided to open a bed and breakfast that would cater to Rosebud theatregoers and people who just wanted a few days of restful country living. She bought a small plot of land in 1998 and dug a new well fifty-six metres deep that tapped into the same aquifer that fed Fiona's and Jessica's wells. It produced enough good clean water to allow her to get a mortgage, and by 2002 she had built her B&B and was open for business.

Her new home was in a copse of trees and bushes at the end of a country road. It's an oasis of tranquility, with horses and cattle grazing on surrounding pasture land that gradually rises out of the valley over rolling hills and up onto the plains. She planted domestic saskatoons—a native blueberry—in a field next to her house. When Debbie speaks about the world she's created, it's inevitably in wistful tones. "It's so beautiful around here that people just want to come here to be part of something special."

That's why she called her bed and breakfast Field of Dreams.

When EnCana Corporation approached the Lauridsens in 2003, offering them $13,000 for access to the field behind their farmhouse where they wanted to drill a gas well, Fiona and her husband thanked the Lord. A drought that had gripped southern Alberta for three years was close to putting their farm out of business. So when the Lauridsens got the call from EnCana, "we were singing hallelujah," Fiona recalls. "It was money. It meant being able to hang in for another year. It was good money per acre. You are not going to get $13,000 off that little square of land. So, yeah, it seemed like a really good deal."

Fiona and Peter quickly signed the lease and cashed the cheque. Soon, bulldozers were levelling a drilling pad about two hundred metres from their house. Night and day, heavy trucks and equipment kicked up dust and noise on the dirt road as the company began the drilling, incinerating and flaring process. It didn't take long. Within two weeks the well was in, the telltale orange steel cattle barrier set in place to protect the wellhead— or "Christmas tree," as workers like to call the above-ground valve-and-pipe assembly—and the surrounding land returned to pasture. The gas well seemed unobtrusive.

By March 2004, wellheads had sprung up all around the hamlet and across the high plains like some kind of alien growth. Gas wells have been drilled in Rosebud since the 1950s, but nobody had ever seen anything like the numbers companies including EnCana Corporation and Husky Energy were drilling around Rosebud and Redland. Farmers used to get maybe one well on a quarter section; now they were getting as many as three on a single pad. The high plains began to resemble one big gas farm.

The noise was deafening—not so much from the constant traffic of heavy machinery, but from the huge compressors built near the gas wells that blast like giant vacuum cleaners or jet engines. Jessica and a number of farmers complained to the companies and wrote letters to the government about the noise. The companies responded by building walls of hay bales around the compressors and installing soundproofing that killed the brute force of the roar. But you could still hear it. When you are accustomed to country life, that kind of industrial noise is a sleep barrier. But in the end, most people resigned themselves to the changes. Farmers and ranchers all over the region were benefiting. EnCana gave money to replace the roof at a local hockey arena and promised a donation to the theatre school. As Fiona says, these were hard times and the farming community was quick to lay down the red carpet.

Then suddenly their wells went bad.

The first sign of trouble came in the spring of 2005 when Jessica developed a skin rash and eye irritations. "My doctor thought I had been burned by industrial soap," she says. The rash, which covered her entire body except her neck and head, burned her skin. Her eyes also began to sting. She tried taking more and more baths, sometimes two or three a day, thinking the cool water would alleviate the pain of the rash. But it only got worse.

Then Fiona's family also got skin rashes. She recalls: "I thought it was the harvest dust because it was harvest time, September, October, and I would come in every night and run the shower water over my eyes to try and get all the dust out, and of course the next day my eyes were bad again. It took a while before I actually clued in that it was the water." Fiona's cattle refused to drink the well water—as did Jessica's two Jack Russell terriers— and Fiona began to hear gas popping in her taps. "The tap would be almost jumping because there was so much gas coming out, and the water would pour white. It looked like a glass of Alka-Seltzer." She also noticed that her sinks and toilet bowls were suddenly sparkling clean. Normally they had a slight rusty iron stain, which she would scrub off with a strong cleanser. As a chemist, it was clear to her that some kind of gas and chemical solvent had got into her water.

Down the valley, Debbie was experiencing identical problems. Her taps hissed like tea kettles and her toilets were gleaming white. Debbie got into the shower one day and immediately felt as if she were taking an acid bath. "The pain in my eyes was so intense. I tried to rinse them out and it got even worse."

Jessica began reading up on water well contamination and decided to conduct a simple experiment she read about on the Internet. She filled a large plastic pop bottle with tap water, capped it for a few seconds, allowing the gas to gather, flipped off the top and passed a flame over the opening. She jumped back when the gas lit up like a rocket, with a sharp blue flame shooting about a foot out of the bottle, partially melting the plastic. Amazed and slightly giddy at the sight of her water catching fire, Jessica knew that she had a big problem. It wasn't long before she found out that her neighbours had one too.

♦

Debbie Signer, Fiona Lauridsen and Jessica Ernst in front of a gas well on the Lauridsens' farm

Methane gas forms naturally in some water wells in Alberta. It can leach from coal seams or can be created by otherwise harmless bacteria in the well. Scientists with the Alberta Geological Survey recently discovered that the action of a water pump can prompt a certain kind of bacteria to create methane. It gives water a bubbly fizz. Ingestion of absorbed methane is not in itself considered a health hazard. The critical problem is that it's an odourless gas and can build up in enclosed areas. Wellhouses have been known suddenly to explode at the flick of an electrical switch. Fortunately, naturally formed methane in aquifers is fairly rare. According to Alberta Environment, of the approximately 500,000 water wells in the province, only about 906 have methane, even though about 26,000 wells are in aquifers that touch on coal seams. An Alberta Research Council report stated in 2003, "there have been very few cases where natural methane leakage has occurred." So it was unlikely that the methane which was appearing around the wells of Rosebud was occurring naturally.

But methane was only one problem facing the valley dwellers of Rosebud and Redland. Clearly, a powerful chemical that burned their bodies and efficiently cleaned their toilets had invaded their wells. Jessica, Debbie and Fiona were determined to find out what it was. Debbie phoned the Alberta environment department in Calgary and spoke to Darren Bourget, the district compliance manager. "I said I really think you should come out and look at this. My trust was immediately diminished when he said, 'You're not affected.'"

That statement puzzled her. What did he mean by "You're not affected"? She knew her neighbours were suffering the same water problems. But the environment official seemed to be imply-ing that there was some other issue affecting water in the area which Debbie didn't know about.

She decided to play along. "I said, 'How do you know I'm not affected if you won't even come out and test this water?' I forget his reply, but I ended up asking him, 'Who in the hell do you work for? What is this "I'm not affected" and you won't even come out?' Well, that started the fight."

Debbie and her neighbours didn't realize it, but they were essentially guinea pigs in an enormous gas drilling program that would soon cover most of the southern half of Alberta. They now believe they were paying the price for a government that had allowed drilling to go ahead without even basic monitoring to ensure its safety. Their quiet rural corner of Alberta had become part of a huge project, begun in 2001, to exploit coal bed methane (CBM).

◆

Conventional gas reserves were rapidly declining—primarily because of escalating sales to the United States—and Alberta desperately needed a replacement. But extracting for coal bed methane is a different process than drilling for conventional natural gas. (Natural gas is composed of 70 to 90 percent methane, with propane, ethane and butane making up most of the rest.) Conventional gas is generally found in dome-shaped reservoirs below impermeable rock formations deep underground. The hard part is finding the reservoir; the easy part is extracting the gas. Coal bed methane is just the opposite. Coal seams are relatively easy to locate particularly since the southern half of Alberta is basically underlayed with them. It's extracting the methane that's tricky.

Every miner knows that coal contains lots of methane. The more you drill a coal seam, the more methane is released. It's why coal miners are forever at risk of blowing themselves up. Miners usually just vent the gas into the atmosphere. But with high gas prices, the methane has become valuable. Methane literally clings to tiny pores in the coal through absorption. Like charcoal inserts in shoes, coal absorbs everything. The coal formations have to be fractured to free the gas and create pathways for it to travel to the borehole. To do this, companies drill into the coal seam, perforate the steel bore casing with small explosive charges, and then pressure-pump a recipe of "fracturing fluids," through the holes to force open or "fracture" the coal seams. In shallow coal seams the fractures tend to spread horizontally. In deeper seams, they are more verticle.

Around Rosebud, the coal seams are generally dry, what they call subsaturated, meaning they contain little or no water. They are also shallow, about 120 to 500 metres below the surface. The seams are narrow horizontal formations usually no more than a metre to three metres thick. They comprise layered and stacked small rectangular cubes separated by tiny fissures or cleats. The fracturing basically shakes up the coal seam like a box of sugar cubes. When the coal cubes settle back they never settle into their original positions, which means that the cracks are wider and the methane can escape. The well bore naturally reduces the pressure in the seam causing the methane to release from the coal. The gas then travels up the well bore, moving from a high pressure to a lower pressure zone.

The fluids pumped in to force open the coal seams vary from well to well. The content of the fracing (pronounced "fracking") recipe is usually proprietary and not disclosed to the public or to regulatory agencies. It can contain any number of combinations of substances including nitrogen, water, hydrochloric acids, chemical solvents and diesel fuel. Most of the chemicals and liquids are pumped out again, but inevitably some stay behind. Fracing companies will also pump in a propant to help keep the cracks open. Often this is sand or a plastic bead substitute, both of which are permeable allowing the gas to escape. To ensure the sand finds its way into all the cracks, it is lubricated with oil.

The coal seams around Rosebud are so dry that coal dust or "fines," which are created in the drilling and fracing process, can be a problem. The dust can clog up the pathways and slow or even stop production. Companies use chemical agents to bust the clogs and keep the pathways open. Again, the content of these agents is proprietary and the companies are not required to disclose it.

In Jessica's neck of the woods, companies like EnCana claim they use only pressurized nitrogen to frac the coals. "I don't know all the particulars of the technologies that are applied," EnCana spokesperson Alan Boras said. "Some of them are proprietary. But the depth and separation and mangagement of the well bore is designed to prevent interactions between where the well water would be and where we would seek gas out of the coal seams." All the gas and oil companies say this, but unfortunately for people such as Jessica and her neighbours the results don't always turn out that way.

◆

Fracing was first developed in 1949 when engineers from Halliburton Company of Houston, Texas, pressure-pumped gasoline, napalm, crude oil and sand into an Oklahoma oil well, hoping to enhance production by splitting the rock seams and freeing trapped oil and gas. It worked, and Halliburton has been a leader in the field ever since. The company claims that fracturing has increased global oil and gas production by up to 33 percent. The company's patented methods are a major money-maker for Halliburton, generating about US$1.5 billion a year, according to published reports.

Oil and gas companies have always maintained that, in drilling for conventional gas reserves, their wells are too deep for fracing to affect ground water and human health. CBM, however, involves shallow drilling and fracing. After drilling for CBM began in earnest in the U.S. in the late 1980s, it didn't take long before plenty of anecdotal evidence surfaced that CBM fracing was a problem. Complaints began to multiply of wells going bad in Wyoming, Colorado, New Mexico, Virginia and Alabama.

In spring 2001, Ballard Petroleum drilled four CBM wells on a pad in Colorado near the home of Laura Amos and her family. "Fracturing created or opened a hydrogeological connection between our water well and the gas well, sending the cap of our water well flying and blowing our water into the air like a geyser at Yellowstone," Laura said at the time. "Immediately our water turned grey, had a horrible smell, and bubbled like 7UP." Tests showed that her well had up to thirteen milligrams of methane per litre of water, which is dangerously high; methane is combustible at one milligram per litre. Isotopic tests showed the methane likely came from Ballard's gas well. Calgary's EnCana Corporation bought Ballard about six months after the well was drilled, so it inherited the problem. EnCana trucked water to the Amos home for three months.

In 2003, Laura had breathing problems while on holiday in Florida. At the age of forty she was diagnosed with a rare tumour in her adrenal gland. Doctors had to remove both the tumour and the gland. She says she believes the tumour was caused by the chemical 2-butoxyethanol (2-BE), commonly used as a solvent in dry cleaning, household products and paint thinners. It is also used as a fracing additive. In fairly high doses it can cause irritation to the eyes and skin, breathing problems, high blood pressure as well as adrenal gland disorders, according to the U.S. Agency for Toxic Substances and Disease Registry.

EnCana initially said it did not believe 2-BE was used in its fracing. But the Colorado Oil and Gas Conservation Commission investigated the drilling records of other wells in the area of Laura Amos's well and discovered that Ballard had used 2-BE on one well thirty-eight days after Laura's well blew up. The COGCC ruled in March 2006 that EnCana had contaminated her well and fined the company $99,400. EnCana agreed to pay the fine but denied any wrongdoing. Amos reached an out-of-court settlement with EnCana but cannot reveal the terms. She and her family have since moved. The state also ordered EnCana to continue supplying area residents with safe potable water.

This wasn't the first time EnCana had been fined. A year earlier, Colorado fined the company $371,200 after natural gas seeped from an EnCana well into the West Divide Creek, contaminating the waterway. The state is spending the money on a hydrogeological study of the area around the leaking well. It is also studying health problems raised by area residents, who say they have suffered burning and itching of the skin, headaches and vision loss, which they blame on the CBM wells.

Oil and gas companies have good reason to fear potential water problems linked to CBM. The contamination of groundwater reservoirs has the potential to bring CBM drilling to a grinding halt. Governments in Canada and the United States, which are desperate to restock dwindling natural gas reserves, understandably don't want that to happen. In the States, Halliburton and its supporters have lobbied heavily against any regulation of oil and gas well fracturing. It is the only industry in the United States that is allowed to inject hazardous chemicals and other dangerous fluids into and around fresh water aquifers without any regulation.

According to the *Los Angeles Times*, U.S. vice president Dick Cheney, who from 1995 to 2000 was Halliburton's chief executive and continued to receive payments from the company until 2005, personally attempted to insert into the U.S. National Energy Policy a clause exempting fracturing from regulation under the Safe Drinking Water Act. The Environmental Protection Agency (EPA) successfully opposed this clause. In the end, however, thanks to the appeal process, Cheney got his wish on the exemption.

In 2001, under orders from a federal appeals court, the EPA began investigating allegations that fracing could poison groundwater. The investigation was to assess whether the practice should be regulated under the Safe Drinking Water Act. The EPA report, published in June 2004, concluded that "fracturing fluids into coalbed methane wells poses little or no threat" to drinking water supplies. Consequently, the EPA ruled that the government shouldn't regulate fracing activities. But that was not the end of the issue.

Colorado is one of the largest CBM drilling areas in the United States. Immediately following the EPA report, three engineers in the EPA's Denver office complained that the report was "scientifically unsound." In a letter to the U.S. Congress, Weston Wilson, one of the dissident engineers, said the report was based on "limited" research and its conclusions were "unsupportable." Wilson noted that the EPA's own studies showed methane migrating into aquifers from exploited coal formations. In one county, methane seepage through the soil was so extensive that the CBM operator was forced to buy out three ranches whose wells had been contaminated. Wilson also noted that the EPA did not bother to investigate if methane could travel along CBM fractures. Furthermore, he noted that the EPA was unable to trace chemical contamination because the contents of fracing fluids are patented recipes and proprietary. Companies such as Halliburton refuse to disclose them. The EPA report itself stated that the "chemical composition of many fracturing fluids used by these service companies may be proprietary and EPA was unable to find complete chemical analyses of any fracturing fluids in the literature."

Wilson also noted that the EPA had not investigated incidents in Colorado where methane and fracing chemicals had migrated into water wells. Finally, he pointed out what he believed was an important conflict of interest: a seven-man panel of outside experts had reviewed the EPA report. Three of the members worked for energy companies, including Halliburton, while two others were former employees of energy companies. This panel had pressured the EPA (1) to remove references in earlier drafts to evidence that fracturing can pose a danger to water wells and (2) to exempt fracing from drinking water regulations. The EPA agreed to these changes. Earlier drafts had included the fact that fracing fluids contained high concentrations of dangerous chemicals, including benzene, phenanthrenes, naphthalene, fluorenes, aromatics, ethylene glycol and methanol. According to the Oil and Gas Accountability Project, a Washington think tank, references to these chemicals were removed from the final report at the request of the panel.

Despite what it said in its report, the EPA must have been concerned about the contamination of wells from CBM fracturing, because in 2003 three of the world's largest oil and gas well service companies—Halliburton Energy Services Inc., Schlumberger Technology Corporation and BJ Services Company—signed a voluntary agreement to eliminate diesel fuel from fracturing fluids. The agreement states that "while the companies do not necessarily agree that hydraulic fracturing fluids using diesel fuel endanger underground sources of drinking water when they are injected into CBM production wells, the companies are prepared to enter into this agreement in response to EPA's concerns and to reduce potential risks to the environment." The agreement allows the companies to resume the use of diesel fuel whenever they choose as long as they notify the EPA within thirty days.

Following Wilson's whistle-blowing, EPA inspector general Nikki Tinsley opened an investigation into the EPA report. Before she could complete her inquiry, however, she suddenly resigned in January 2006 in protest over new White House salary measures that she claimed would compromise her credibility as an independent investigator. The measures made her salary level contingent on a performance review from the White House. When she left, the investigation died.

◆

If you fly over eastern Alberta in the area of Lloydminster, you'll see hundreds of pear-shaped bare spots about five metres in diameter scattered throughout the wheat and canola fields. Scientists refer to them as "plumes." They are barren earth. Nothing grows there. This is because the gas wells in the area leak methane.

By the time Alberta began drilling for CBM, there was plenty of evidence in the government's own archives that methane gas from producing and dormant wells could migrate into aquifers and to the surface. In 1995, the Saskatchewan Research Council and the Alberta government studied methane gas leakage and migration from plugged oil and gas wells around Lloydminster. One of the researchers was Dr. Karlis Muehlenbachs, a geochemist in earth and atmospheric sciences at the University of Alberta. He found that a "large number" of well sites were leaking methane into groundwater aquifers and also up through the soil, killing vegetation around the wellhead (methane deprives roots of oxygen). Tests revealed that methane levels were up to fourteen milligrams per litre. Muehlenbachs is categorical: "There is no question that methane gas migrates into aquifers."

When companies abandon a non-producing well, they are required by law to plug it with mud and cement. This is supposed to stop harmful gases from migrating upwards and contaminating shallow aquifers and surface vegetation. But geologists admit that the cement plugs are seldom perfect. Gaps form between the casings and the borehole walls and sometimes channel into the cement itself. This is particularly critical in older wells where surface casings were designed to anchor drilling equipment in the event of a blowout rather than to protect groundwater. Over time, as the ground moves and borehole casings age and corrode, the gaps can become more pronounced. Studies done in Alberta and Saskatchewan show that about 57 percent of old wells leak methane and other gases into aquifers and the atmosphere. Nobody knows how much methane leaks each year from these oil and gas wells. Aggressive bacteria eat up a lot of methane before it enters the atmosphere, Dr. Muehlenbachs says. But estimates indicate that the amounts are still substantial. The U.S.

Environmental Protection Agency claims that methane leakage from oil and gas wells and pipelines makes up more than one-quarter of the total methane emissions to the atmosphere. Given the fact that there are more than 300,000 oil and gas wells in Alberta (of which about 142,500 still produce oil and gas), leakage of that magnitude can be harmful to the atmosphere. Methane is twenty-three times more powerful than carbon dioxide as a greenhouse gas. With more than 60,000 CBM wells planned in Alberta, the problem could be enormous.

"I see all kinds of very poor bond logs [acoustic readings that can show gaps in cement casings]," one veteran Alberta geologist, who didn't want his name used for fear he would lose business, says. "I have never seen a bond log that shows me absolute cement top to bottom."

Some companies don't even bother to plug non-producing wells, he says. Fixing leaks and plugging wells can cost hundreds of thousands of dollars per well. If a company doesn't officially abandon the well, they are not required to plug it. "Lots of wells are put on standby because it's easier and cheaper than if they try to abandon it," Muehlenbachs says. "And that is a really serious issue. They are usually leaking. And the only reason that they don't legally abandon them is because there is obviously something wrong with them. So the ones there's nothing wrong with they will legally abandon. So selectively you are left with the ones that have problems. And the big problem is that a lot of them have this gas migration. Gas leaks to the surface and into the aquifers and soils and stuff."

There have been numerous other examples of gas wells leaking into groundwater. In the Milk River gas fields in southeast Alberta and across the border into Saskatchewan, studies show that 80 percent of the gas wells leak into aquifers. This is blamed partially on the fact that the wells are in a valley and the depths are shallow—much like the wells around Jessica, Fiona and Debbie.

◆

Despite widespread evidence of water well contamination around CBM drilling, when companies such as EnCana and Husky began, in 2001, drilling more than 7,500 CBM wells in the Horseshoe Canyon formation east of Calgary, the Alberta government took no steps to protect area wells. It simply followed the EPA's lead in the States and accepted promises from the companies that fracing for CBM was not a danger to groundwater. Ignoring the experiences in Colorado and elsewhere, the Alberta Energy and Utilities Commission claimed there has never been an example of oil and gas activity contaminating water wells. Nor did the government make any effort to require that water wells close to CBM wells be tested for methane and chemical content before the CBM wells were drilled. This would have given them baseline data that would allow them to help trace any changes in the wells to CBM drilling and fracing activity. If people suddenly have problems with their wells in CBM drilling areas, the government claims it is because of bad well management or naturally forming swamp methane—not CBM. And because no baseline testing was done, the government and the companies are able to maintain a measure of deniability. That was the unpleasant reality that Jessica, Fiona and Debbie faced when they began complaining that CBM had contaminated their wells. Without baseline data, their accusations that CBM was responsible were difficult, if not impossible, to prove.

◆

In the fall of 2005, Fiona and Jessica began calling the Alberta environment department about their contaminated water wells. They got the same runaround as Debbie. "I wanted to find out how I go about the process of making a complaint and having my well tested," Fiona explains. "They basically said, 'There is no process. There's no problem. Your problem is bacteria.'"

Methane can be broken down into two categories. Thermogenetic methane is the kind found in a gas field, pumped out and pipelined to your home. Biogenic methane is created by bacteria fermentation, such as swamp gas. Scientists can tell the difference by examining the carbon isotopes of the gas—their atomic structure. The Alberta environment department claims that the methane found in water wells is biogenic and is therefore caused by bacteria. In other words, the government blames the property owners for not cleaning their dirty wells. And the government is right—to a degree. The gas in the Rosebud wells is biogenic. But, claims Muehlenbachs, so is the gas from the CBM wells. Coal seams can collect through absorption huge commercial amounts of biogenic gas, he says. "Right now Alberta Environment is really big on saying [the contaminated water wells are] biofouled. It's your own fault, bad well management. I just don't believe that."

It took Jessica, Fiona and Debbie more than a month just to convince Alberta Environment officials to test their wells for methane. "Alberta Environment told me I had to complain to the company," Fiona says. "That way the government has no record that there has ever been a complaint. They have actually said that." When Fiona filed a complaint with EnCana, they agreed to test her water. Fiona didn't trust the company to carry out an investigation on itself. "Of course they are going to come and say 'it wasn't us.'" She demanded that a representative from Alberta Environment be present when the tests were conducted, and that the government take samples of its own for testing. She also wanted a third set of samples she could take to a laboratory of her choice.

Finally, in December 2005, Alberta Environment officials and EnCana came and tested her water. The government tests showed that there was no bacteria in her well. They also showed that dissolved methane in her water was between 39 and 45 milligrams per litre, which is extremely high. EnCana tested for methane gas emitted from the water. Technicians trap the air in a bag and measure the methane content. These tests showed between 65 and 78 percent methane, which again is dangerously high. They also indicated that there was a large amount of ethane in her water. Ethane is the second-largest component of natural gas, and its presence suggested that the methane in Fiona's water likely was coming from a gas well and not from bacteria, as the Alberta environment department continued to claim despite the tests showing the contrary. Fiona's own independent laboratory test results also showed extremely high methane counts. Fiona sampled the well water as well as the fresh intakes from the aquifer. The results showed that the water fresh from the aquifer had a much higher methane count—66.3 milligrams per litre—than the well water, which was 42.8. This indicated that the contamination was coming from the aquifer and not from any bacterial action in the well.

Similar readings came out of both Jessica's and Debbie's wells.

Still, EnCana and the government insisted the three women were responsible for their own well contamination. Over time they came out with a host of often contradictory explanations describing why the women were to blame for their own well problems. One Alberta Environment inspector told Jessica that because she didn't run cattle, she didn't use her water well often enough, allowing bacteria to thrive. Another environment department official, a hydrologist, told the three women that they used their wells too much, forcing the methane to release from the coals.

Then EnCana claimed that a bacteria called pseudomonas had caused their skin and eye irritations. This is a bacteria that sometimes generates in hot tubs and, after a few days of exposure, can cause an itchy, spotty red rash on the skin. But pseudomonas is primarily an oleophilic bacteria. This means that pseudomonas love to feed off hydrocarbons, breaking them down into methanol, water and carbon dioxide. The oil industry sometimes injects pseudomonas bacteria into wells to dissolve the heavier waxy oils so crude can flow more freely. They are also used to break down hydrocarbon pollutants in refinery waste water and oil spills. The presence of pseudomonas in Rosebud wells therefore would be more an indication of hydrocarbons in the water than of bad well management. In other words, oil and gas well contaminants can create a situation where pseudomonas bacteria flourish. The rash it produces, however, is different from what Jessica and her neighbours had experienced. What's more, pseudomonas do not account for the immediate burning sensation to both the skin and the eyes. In any case, none of the tests to date has indicated the presence of pseudomonas bacteria in their water. But that didn't seem to matter to EnCana or the government. "It was tough to stay sane," Jessica says.

Jessica and Fiona took their fight on February 28, 2006, to the Alberta Legislative Assembly. This for them was dubious territory. After all, EnCana Corporation was the largest single contributor to the Progressive Conservatives' 2004 campaign fund and each year is one of the largest contributors to Tory Party coffers. Added to that was the women's firm belief that this government had basically sold out to the oil and gas industry. Perched in the visitors' gallery, they sat tight and listened.

Opposition members began pounding away at the government for its failure to protect one of life's fundamental ingredients—fresh water. Environment minister Guy Boutilier protested repeatedly that he was doing everything in his power to solve the problem and protect Alberta's fresh water supplies. "As Alberta Environment I will use every fibre of energy in my body to assist this family relative to safe drinking water now and into the future. I can assure you that we are working with them and we will continue to work with them because this is a very important issue to this family and to many other families that have been impacted . . . I'm using my energy to get these people safe drinking water. We will do everything in our power to get them that."

The three women waited another two months before the government agreed to truck water to their homes. Jessica had to spend five thousand dollars to put cisterns into her basement. At the demand of the government, EnCana began paying for water deliveries to Fiona's farm, while the Alberta government paid for deliveries for Jessica and Debbie as well as other residents of the area. Their fear of explosive gases subsided and they no longer had skin or eye irritations.

Then, four months later, Debbie Signer's water deliveries were stopped. She was stunned to receive a letter from the environment department blaming her for the well contamination, claiming it was a bacteria problem. Wells throughout her valley had suddenly gone bad after years of use and the government was isolating her brand new well and declaring it guilty.

Furious, Debbie whipped off a letter of protest to Premier Ralph Klein. That did the trick. Two weeks later she received a cheery letter from Boutilier—"Hi Debbie"—informing her the government had changed its mind and was reinstating her water deliveries. But he warned it was an "interim measure."

"We have been lied to and basically cheated by a government that is more interested in protecting the oil and gas industry than in the well-being of its citizens," Debbie says. "They keep insisting that my well was contaminated because of bad maintenance, that it's my own fault, despite all evidence to the contrary. We just don't trust them anymore. Any of them."

Soon local TV stations and newspapers were running stories on the Rosebud "firewater," with pictures of Jessica's water exploding in a blue flame. The government responded by doing more tests. The results were the same or worse, showing in some cases even higher methane content. Throughout it all, the government's and company's responses were the same: they blamed the people of Rosebud for "biofouling" their own wells.

Because of Muehlenbachs's work sampling leaking wells during the 1990s, Alberta Environment sent him samples of the gases coming from the Rosebud water for isotopic analysis. He found that the methane isotopic signature showed him very little. But when he found traces of ethane, butane and propane, which reflect all the characteristics of a natural gas well, he was convinced that the contamination was not caused by bacteria biofouling. The problem was likely from deeper gas migration, either from CBM wells or from older oil and gas wells. "If you look at the ethane in particular in some of these problem wells, it looks like they could very well be a mixture of some kind of deeper gas with the shallow gas." Lack of historical data on the condition of the wells before CBM came along makes it almost impossible to come up with a definitive ruling. "All I knew was that the water well today had ethane in it. I don't know if it had ethane last year. So I can't say for sure that these water wells are contaminated [by CBM], but I could say that they might be contaminated where the companies and the government are saying they are not contaminated." In other words, Muehlenbachs concludes that the Rosebud wells such as the Lauridsens' are definitely contaminated by migrating gases from drilling activity, but he has no idea whether it is old or new drilling activity. And without the historical data it will be practically impossible to prove one way or the other.

Strangely, even before Alberta's CBM pilot project began in 2001, the Alberta government listed "groundwater contamination" and "gas migration potential" as "key issues" posed by CBM. Yet when contamination surfaced in the aquifers of Rosebud and Redland, transforming water taps into potential blowtorches, wells into explosive devices and water into acidic chemical soup, the government denied that gas migration was a problem and blamed the landowners for poor well maintenance. And that was even before they tested the wells.

By February 2007, two years after Jessica, Fiona and Debbie began experiencing water problems, the government had still not changed its conclusions, despite Muehlenbachs's work and their own testing, which clearly pointed to a potential gas well problem. Muehlenbachs has no explanation for this, but he speculates that the government is reluctant to acknowledge the very real possibility of contamination because there could be a huge liability on both its part and the part of the companies. He sums it up this way: "This is a resource-based economy. You just extract it and say, 'What, me worry?'"

What was not widely known at the time was that in March 2004 EnCana fractured into the Rosebud aquifer at depths of 125 to 142 metres. The well flowed gas until June, when groundwater began gushing into the well through the perforations at a rate of 5.6 litres per minute. EnCana plugged the well with cement. Then, in August 2004, a local farmer named Sean Kenney, who lives in Redland not far from Debbie, returned home with his family after a few days away. "My water was no darn good when we came home," Kenney recalls. "It was full of dark black stuff, coal I guess you would call it, just like coal." Given that his well was fifty years old, he thought that maybe the casing had caved in. So he drilled a new well. "We didn't think anything of it to begin with. But then we couldn't get the new well to clean up. It came out black too."

Sean owned another house in the hamlet of Redland, which had a well that was dug in 2001. "I went and darn if I walked into the house and turned the tap on and it's full of black stuff. So that's what kind of started the whole thing, wondering what might be the problem there." He thought his problems might have something to do with one of the forty-six gas wells in his vicinity. He called the environment ministry and the next thing he knew, representatives from EnCana were at his doorstep wanting to investigate his water problems. The company hired a groundwater consulting firm to study his wells.

To Kenney's surprise, the tests showed a large amount of nitrogen in his well. EnCana uses nitrogen to frac all its CBM wells. Despite the fact that EnCana admitted it had fraced into the aquifer, its report blamed Kenney's problems on failed well casings in both his old and new wells. It didn't mention the well at Kenney's other house at all. As for the nitrogen, EnCana noted that a similar concentration of nitrogen was found in a water well about 260 kilometres north of Redland in a town called Calmar. Based on that one well, EnCana concluded that the nitrogen in Kenney's well was natural. "The sad thing is I can't say that they are right or wrong," Kenney says. "I don't have the pocketbook to spend the kind of money that they did on their report." His water has returned to normal.

When Jessica, Fiona and Debbie found out about Kenney's well and that EnCana had fraced into their aquifer, they were more convinced than ever that CBM drilling had caused the problem with their wells. But they had no proof, and without proof there was nothing they could do.

After the Kenney report came out, EnCana announced it would no longer fracture above 200 metres deep. Yet that is of little comfort to local residents who note that most of the CBM wells are drilled on the plains high above valley hamlets such as Rosebud. So 200 metres will potentially bring fractures level with valley aquifers. If companies want to tap into the seam, they might have to fracture into an aquifer.

On January 31, 2006, months after Jessica and her neighbours raised the alarm, the EUB rushed to issue Directive 027. It forbids fracturing within 200 metres of a water well if the depth of the fracture is within 25 metres of the depth of the water well. But while the EUB maintains in public a happy confidence in CBM, in private the agency's worries about water contamination are rising. Evidence of this can be seen in the EUB's CBM licensing permits, which are public but which almost nobody in the public ever reads. They are now replete with indications of concern over groundwater contamination. The agency began requiring that gas companies install monitoring wells in aquifers close to their CBM drilling to monitor any changes to the groundwater—a clear indication of concern over water well contamination. It also began insisting on improved well bore casing protection. "It is prudent for industry to carefully design and monitor fracturing operations shallower than 200 metres to ensure protection of water wells and shallow aquifers," the EUB states. Finally, it requires baseline testing of water wells within 600 metres of a CBM well. It is clear that fears of ground aquifer contamination both immediate and into the distant future are beginning to preoccupy the agency.

Both Alberta Environment and the EUB admit that they simply don't have the manpower to monitor the oil and gas industry. With all the cutbacks during the 1990s, Alberta Environment is left with about fifty compliance inspectors to oversee fresh water in the province. The EUB has about eighty inspectors to cover the entire oil and gas industry. Consequently, they leave it to the industry to monitor itself. Both organizations admit that even when a complaint is filed, their first step is to call the company and ask them to investigate.

"Water wells in Alberta have been and are being contaminated," Muehlenbachs says. "It's a public PR statement that there has never been an example of a contaminated well. This is a complete falsehood."

Why Jessica, Debbie and Fiona suffered skin and eye burns from the well water has still not been resolved. But in May 2007, Debbie obtained results from a chemical analysis of her water well that the Alberta Environment had commissioned in November 2006. Oxygen and water are the two basic elements of life. But it took Debbie six months to get the results of these tests. Eventually she was forced to file an access to information request. This sparked action and the next day an environment official delivered the results to her doorstep. "He told me, 'I was in the area so I thought I would hand them to you,'" she says.

The results were, in her own words, "stunning." They proved her well was a chemical soup of 58 petroleum pollutants, most of which can be found in fracing fluids such as diesel fuel. The soup includes pentane, propane, butane, pentene, octane, hexane, toluene, styrene, tetrachloroethylene and benzene. Some of these can cause severe burning to the skin and eyes. Benzene is a proven carcinogen and, among many other health effects, can damage the immune system. The results lay to rest any argument that the pollutants came from bacteria in a badly managed well and were therefore Debbie's own fault. After studying the results, she says, "it took a while for it to sink in that they hadn't told me anything about this."

When I called EnCana and asked about the test results, they said they were not aware of them, refused to comment and continued to maintain that the Rosebud wells were a biofouling problem. Fiona's and Jessica's wells had not been tested for chemicals.

Despite the fact that water wells in the Rosebud area were contaminated and in some cases still are as of this writing, the government has made no effort to curtail the drilling, perforating and continued fracing of CBM wells in the area. Blame fell on the landowners. By 2007, none of the contaminated private Rosebud wells had recovered. The methane count in Jessica's water well showed signs of increasing as drilling in the area increased. Jessica, Debbie and Fiona want to hook up to the hamlet's reservoir, but it too still showed signs of contamination.

EnCana declared in February 2007 recorded net earnings of $5.7 billion for 2006—among the largest ever reported by a Canadian company.

CBM drilling around Rosebud is only the beginning. Over the next five to ten years, gas companies are expected to sink tens of thousands of CBM wells into the coal formations of Alberta. Moving north and east, the coal seams run deeper than the relatively shallow seams around Rosebud. The coal tends also to contain large quantities of water. To coax the methane out of the wet coal, energy companies will have to pump out thousands of gallons of groundwater. This will inevitably deplete these valuable water reserves. Even though they contain higher levels of salinity than the shallow wells, they could still be critical during times of drought. "When you consider that 90 percent of rural Albertans are dependent on groundwater I think there may well be periods when we have to depend on these deeper resources," says Mary Griffiths, a senior environmental policy analyst for Calgary's Pembina Institute. "I think that it is really important to have those resources as uncontaminated as possible."

Equally worrisome is the fact that deeper coal bed drilling will require large amounts of fracing fluids to help open the seams. Because of the increased ground pressure, nitrogen will not be powerful enough to do the job. Water and a host of fracing chemicals will likely be used. This will increase the potential for contamination of the deeper aquifers.

Meanwhile, Alberta energy companies are also beginning to explore for slate gas. Slate underlies almost the entire province in fairly thick, continuous seams. It contains pockets of conventional gas as well as gas absorbed by the shale itself. Extracting it can require even more intensive fracturing and drilling than CBM.

Yet as the energy industry expands its drilling intensity the government is not monitoring groundwater aquifers. Griffiths notes that Alberta Environment has reduced by half the amount of groundwater monitoring wells it operates. In the 1990s it monitored four hundred wells. Now it monitors only two hundred despite the huge increase in drilling. This means that widespread depletion and devastation of underground aquifers could be occuring even today, but unless it affects operating water wells—as happened to Fiona's, Debbie's and Jessica's, to name only a few—nobody will know about it. In this sense, the contaminated wells of Rosebud could be the potential canary in the coal mine.

◆

"Why did you call it Happy Valley?" I ask Francis Gardner as we walk towards his truck.

"Because everybody was constantly feuding," he says, chuckling.

Francis has spent the last few days separating his calves from their mothers. They can still see their mothers in an adjacent field. Now the calves are bawling their eyes out and when they see Francis they all crowd towards the fence, hundreds of pitiful cow eyes following Francis to the truck, mooing in mournful unison, every last one of them accusing Francis of calf abuse. "They blame me and they know that I can make it right," he says.

Francis Gardner

We climb into the truck and slowly drive along a dirt track adjacent to the pasture. The herd of young cattle jostles to keep pace. Francis carefully gears down as we head up the side of what he calls Calving Hill because that's where the calves are kept in the spring. As we progress up the steep, grassy hillside, the valley begins to reveal itself—its broad expanse and the foothills that roll into it. It all seems clearer and better defined from up high. Clumps of pine and diamond willow trees, short, tangled cousins of the much taller eastern willow, cling to the hillsides. A hundred years ago these hills were bare of trees. Natural fires would have culled the saplings and helped preserve the native grasses. But they don't allow that to happen anymore. So the trees take hold and the grasses that are so valuable to grazing recede. "This country was designed to burn," Francis says.

In the distance, rising above the foothills, the snow-capped Rockies tower against the western sky, and the higher we climb on Calving Hill, the grander they become.

Francis wants to give me an aerial view of his 8,400-acre ranch and a clear idea of the unique and ancient natural cycle of life that he and his fellow ranchers in Happy Valley are desperately trying to preserve.

It is not unbroken rangeland. Every so often the truck has to avoid the rocky outcrop of vertical sandstone that cuts through the grassland. These are the rock formations that capture the rainwater and melting snows, making life possible in a region that verges on the semi-arid. These northwestern foothills are in part not only the source but also the natural purification plant for most of North America's major watersheds, including the Mississippi, Mackenzie, Bow, and North and South Saskatchewan Rivers as well as the massive Ogallala aquifer that stretches from North Dakota to Texas. "They are like great big blotters," Francis says of the sandstone formations. "Spectacular pure water comes out of those beds. I mean, it's just absolutely astonishing how wonderful it is."

Francis stops to open a gate. We enter a new pasture, edging through a herd of mature cattle that will soon be off to the butcher's. A few stubborn cows stand firm before suddenly bolting off the track, kicking up their rear hoofs as if warding off the truck. The engine grinds its way up the hillside.

Francis runs an organic ranch, meaning his cows fatten off the land. In truth, "fatten" is probably not the right word. Francis's cattle are not fat. They are lean, muscular machines. They don't spend their entire lives in feedlots, huddling cheek to cheek with tens of thousands of other cows in confined corrals, knee-deep in manure, jumped-up with antibiotics while speed-feeding on ground-up grain and God knows what else for weeks on end, never moving, just prepping for the butcher. I ask him if it costs more money to run an organic farm. "No, not in this country. Not at all. Because organic is one hundred percent compatible with the natural systems. That's why we went there. Everything we had here was basically organic. We just had to have the paperwork to say that it was." To make it work, Francis needs every one of his 8,400 acres. It comes down to about 24 acres per cow on open grassland and 64 acres on the foothills. His cattle need the full breadth of a rangeland.

From the top of Calving Hill, you can see Francis's Mount Sentinel Ranch spread out in the valley and foothills below. It extends about eight kilometres north to south and six kilometres east to west. It's late November, and the colours are dusty browns and light greens against a mountain ridge of brilliant white snow. In the spring and summer, the valley breaks out into a sea of purple, yellow and orange wildflowers. It's a magnificent, unique region of huge cattle ranches and protected parkland that can't be found anywhere else in Canada. Francis's ranch is among the smallest in the valley. About twenty families still ranch here, and some outfits are two or three times larger. In many ways the region represents the essence of Alberta, its magnified skies and sweeping landscapes populated by horses, cows, cougars, deer, wolves, bear, elk, gophers and cowboys.

Happy Valley is located in Alberta's southwest corner. It begins about 30 kilometres south of Calgary at the town of Longview and runs due south about 130 kilometres to the

Crowsnest Pass and Oldman River. Bisecting the valley is Highway 22. Some people call this two-lane paved road the Cowboy Trail. But not Francis. For him it's got nothing to do with cowboys. It cuts his land in half and brings down all the city people from Calgary with their recreational vehicles, not to mention the oil and gas rigs, bulldozers and pipeline trucks, and any number of other heavy mining and drilling vehicles that are beginning to skin the landscape and tear up the last remaining natural rangeland in Canada. Consequently, Happy Valley is far from happy. But this time it's got good reason.

◆

Francis's family has ranched these rangelands since 1898. His grandfather, who was in the British navy, discovered them while riding the CPR from Vancouver to Halifax. When the train emerged from the Kicking Horse Pass, through Banff and into the foothills, this wandering sailor found his home. He returned a few years later and bought the land where Francis and I are now standing.

The original rangeland and prairie that Francis's grandfather saw more than a century ago as he travelled across the Canadian West is gone. It has been replaced by a patchwork of square, rectangular and circular fields carved out of what was once one of the world's great grasslands. Irrigation machines now dictate the fields' geometry. Heavy shots of fossil fuel–based nitrogen fertilizer are required annually to restore the land's fertility. The prairie's once-black soil and protein-rich grasses naturally supported vast herds of wild buffalo over 255,000 square kilometres of prairie, from Winnipeg to the Rocky Mountains. Now those original grasslands, which contained up to two hundred species of self-generating, mostly fescue grasses, make up less than 5 percent of the prairies. They have disappeared under the plow and under the weight of oil and gas drilling. And nobody has found a way to reseed natural prairie grasses. Once they are gone, they are gone forever. A good part of what remains is right here in the foothills of Happy Valley.

The sun is warm, but the air is November cool. Francis is sixty-four and doesn't ride much anymore because of a hip problem, which is one reason we drove the truck up here. The other is that I can't ride a horse. Pointing to the thick grasses that top Calving Hill, he says, "This shows all the variety and diversity of what it should look like." He bends down and runs his big hands through the vegetation until he comes up with a fistful of thin, tangled brown grass. It looks silky and delicate, but it's rough to the touch. "This is what makes native grassland function," he says. I'm immediately reminded of Pete up at the Syncrude mine, reaching down to grab a handful of oil sands and telling me that this clump of tar is what it's all about.

What Francis has in his hand is rough fescue—one of the richest, most productive grasses nature has ever created. "It's a relic, a bit of functioning antiquity that hasn't been plowed under because the topography is too steep, the altitude is too high. We only have forty-four days frost free. That's what has saved it. Otherwise it would be all grain and farming." Rough fescue is the reason Francis's cows can still survive on this land year-round without much help from feed grain.

Rough fescue is in many ways the perfect grass. Its roots run about three metres into the soil, so it can tolerate all kinds of dry conditions as well as fire. Its thick, tangled stems catch the snow and rain and keep the wind off the soil. (The great dust bowls of the 1930s were caused by the fact that settlers had shaved off the native grasslands, allowing the powerful prairie winds to blow away the topsoil.) Its main asset is a high protein content, which it retains over the winter, allowing fall and winter grazing. It keeps animals alive in a harsh climate. In spring it returns carbon into the soil, replenishing its energy bank. Scientists claim it captures more carbon than a forest. In other words, it's self-fertilizing. "Rough fescue can handle whatever you can throw at it except overgrazing and people," Francis says. Wild buffalo were smart. They knew enough to move off to other pastures in the spring and summer, and feed off other natural species while allowing the fescue to regenerate. Cows are not so smart, and have to be rotated through the pastures. But the point is the same: rough fescue is a renewable energy source capable of sustaining vast herds of cattle through the winter. Francis's handful of fescue has more energy than Pete's handful of oil sand. And with each new year, that fescue energy is replenished and multiplies. And that's why, Francis says, his handful of rough fescue grass is really what it's all about.

Alberta's oil and gas industry started just north of here, in Turner Valley. Over the years Francis has watched and witnessed how destructive it can be. He says that when he was young he could read by the light of the gas flares. The oil industry thought gas had no value and flared off most of it to get at the oil. Now, because the well pressure disappeared with the gas, oil companies have to put enormous amounts of fresh water into the wells to float the oil and pump it out. That water disappears thousands of metres down a hole, is contaminated and lost forever.

Francis knows that the oil and gas industry is hard-wired to extract no matter the cost to the environment. And the industry will bring other development, including housing subdivisions, which are already encroaching on the northern part of the valley.

Happy Valley has seen its share of oil and gas development, but nothing like the coming invasion. Oil companies are poised to cover this valley with CBM and sour gas wells. And although the government has made noises about protecting the valley, Francis and the other ranchers are convinced that the politicians are "completely in the pocket of the oil industry" and that their only goal is the "orderly production of the resource"—although the way things are going in Alberta, it's not that orderly.

The ranchers believe that more oil and gas drilling will doom Happy Valley. In addition to tearing up the land, the gas crews will bring invasive species of weeds and less-nutritious grasses into the valley, which will spread across the rangeland and destroy what's left of the rough fescue. A century ago a lot of these less-hardy grasses would have been wiped out by drought and fire, leaving the fescue to prosper. But not today. In fact, you can see the changes already. Francis points out where an underground oil pipeline travels along the eastern section of the valley below. You can see the light-coloured grass, which is not native, following the pipeline all down the valley.

Francis has five pipelines going through his land, paying him $20,000 a year in rent. Oil companies have sprayed the herbicide 2,4,5-T to try to kill the weeds in a cockeyed attempt to stop their spread into the rangelands. The herbicide, which is one of the ingredients of the powerful defoliant Agent Orange, still shows up in Francis's water. In the past, the oil companies' drilling and blasting have literally rocked the water table, draining his well and filling dried-up ponds.

So when Shell came knocking in 2000, asking to put in a seismic line across the valley where they dynamite drill holes and take seismic readings, Francis said no. No more oil and gas companies on his land. "If you decide for whatever reason that you are not going to do it their way, then they will do everything in their power to intimidate you or run you off the land. They'll do whatever it takes. We had a face-to-face with Shell Oil and they wanted to go across this valley. I finally said, 'Eff you guys, let's fight. 'Cause you are not going to cross this valley. I'll be dead and buried before you go across this valley.' They phoned the Mounties in Turner Valley. I phoned the Mounties in Nanton, and the guy in Nanton, I explained what was going on. I said there's going to be a confrontation. 'Give him shit, boy,' he said. 'Just leave your gun in the house.' Which was pretty nice of him. The Mountie in Turner Valley phoned me up very businesslike: 'Mr. Gardner, we understand there has been a bit of a problem.' I said yes and then explained it. And when I was through explaining to him what happened, his voice was just trembling. He was furious. He said, 'Thank you, Mr. Gardner, you sound like a reasonable man trying to defend his family.' And so right away Shell Oil wanted to meet me. Rather than the confrontation, they wanted a meeting. So the way they'll meet with you if you are dumb enough to go see them alone, they put you in a hot seat, they'll put you in a hotel room and they'll have a chair sitting there and there will be about three or four of them and they'll get to hammering at you, they'll tag-team you and they beat you down. I said I'll meet with you, but I took about five neighbours with me. We walked in and they didn't know what to say. They had nowhere for us to sit. There's no ways you can deal with them otherwise. They are absolutely vicious. This is free enterprise."

◆

That evening I sit down to dinner with Francis, his wife, Bonnie, and three of his neighbouring ranchers and their wives. We eat at a restaurant in Longview and they talk about their conservation group, which they call the Pekisko Rangeland Group. They have banded together to try to educate Albertans on the importance of preserving this ancient self-sustaining ecosystem that is so much more powerful than any handful of oil sands. They are all well-heeled ranchers and have the money and knowledge to get their message across. But they are only a handful of about twenty families, and they are up against a province of city dwellers who see their destiny in oil. Still, the Pekisko Group is gearing up for a fight.

Any conversation with Albertan ranchers or farmers looking to challenge the oil patch sooner or later includes the mention of two men: Wayne Roberts and Wiebo Ludwig.

Wayne Roberts was the owner of Eagle Ridge Ranch, about eighty kilometres north of Calgary. On October 3, 1998, he shot oil executive Patrick Kent, forty-two, dead. The two men had been feuding over a leaking oil well, as well as any number of things that had to do with the oil company's lease and its contamination of Roberts's property. Kent had come to the ranch to check the well. The two men argued. Things got out of hand. Roberts went into his house, retrieved his pistol, came outside and pumped four shots point-blank into Kent. In just a few seconds of pent-up craziness, Kent lost his life and Roberts lost his freedom. He's now serving life in prison for murder.

Then there was Christian evangelist Wiebo Ludwig, the oil patch terrorist who believed sour gas wells were harming his family. He launched a bombing campaign to drive the companies off his land. He got a 28-month sentence.

Both events climaxed in 1998, and the trials had the effect of bringing the oil patch battles to the attention of Canadians who until then had viewed working pumpjacks as a sign of welcomed prosperity.

As we chat around the dining table, one of the ranchers quietly mentions Roberts and Ludwig, wondering if I've heard of them. Eyebrows are raised and everybody looks a bit sheepish and uncomfortable. Their reaction is not an awkward expression of admiration; it is an involuntary revelation of fear and helplessness. Fear that their world is crumbling—diminishing their lives and the lives of everyone around them. Knowing that unless there's a major turnaround in the way society thinks and functions, their rangeland will be sacrificed to oil and gas, as is happening in the Athabasca and east of here in Rosebud and in so many other places in Alberta. Battling a government they regard as deaf and an urban culture that seems disconnected and uninterested. But still not abandoning hope. Not resigned to the fact that, as things are going, they will indeed be the last cowboys.

◆

By May 2007, oil prices had crawled back up over sixty dollars a barrel and energy companies had announced record profits for 2006. Suncor alone reported net earnings had doubled to $3 billion. Syncrude's owners were celebrating similar hikes in profits and had announced first quarter 2007 profits up as much as 188 percent.

Foreign companies had continued their buyout of the sands, moving Canada one step closer to becoming a colonial corporate economy while our governments remain silent. Norway's state oil company, Statoil ASA, bought North American Oil Sands Corporation for $2.2 billion. Once the company gets its steam-assisted extraction projects up and running, Norwegians, whose North Sea oil reserves are declining, could be making more money out of the oil sands than Alberta's taxpayers—adding to Norway's huge $300-billion-plus national energy fund.

And the situation just gets crazier. Instead of a rise in royalties that would mirror the leap in oil sands profits, Alberta premier Ed Stelmach's first budget predicted a huge drop. Because of generous tax incentives, by 2010, oil sands royalties would fall to $1.2 billion, from $2.4 billion. They would not return to present levels of $2.4 billion until 2015. Meanwhile, the province predicted 2007 spending would rise 23 percent—its largest increase in history. Spiralling inflation and an overheated energy sector were eating up taxpayers's money.

The environment was faring no better. In his first throne speech, Stelmach promised a more eco-friendly government and a "made-in-Alberta" climate change strategy. But it didn't go much further than words. Part of his strategy is the suggestion of a pipeline—costing anywhere from $1.5-billion to $5 billion—that will take the province's huge carbon dioxide emissions and inject them into depleted oil and gas wells where they will be stored presumably forever. It's called carbon sequestration and the jury is still out on whether the stored CO_2 will leak back to the surface.

In fact, the world's largest carbon sequestration test project is already showing disturbing signs it might be leaking. EnCana is storing about one million metric tons of carbon dioxide a year in an oil field near Weyburn in southern Saskatchewan. EnCana calls it the "world's largest natural laboratory."

It's not strictly speaking an environmental project. EnCana buys the compressed carbon dioxide from a coal gasification plant in Beulah, North Dakota. The gas is liquefied and piped 320 kilometres to EnCana's Weyburn oil field where it is injected along with water 1,500 metres deep into any one of the 1,100 aging oil wells in the area. The injection increases well pressure and the CO_2 reduces viscosity of crude oil releasing oil from the rock pores and easing its flow towards the well bore. EnCana claims the CO_2 increases production as much as 60 percent. After the oil is pumped to the surface, the CO_2 is separated and reinjected into the well for permanent storage. EnCana plans to store 30 million tons of CO_2 in the Weyburn field, which it says is equivalent to taking 6.8 million cars off the road for a year. Governments like Alberta's hope it will prove to be a safe, leak-proof solution to carbon emissions. But on the south edge of the world's largest natural laboratory, there's a problem—and it's literally exploding out of the ground.

This is where Jane and Cameron Kerr live. Or at least used to live. Until 2005 they lived here amid their 1,400 acres of grain and rangeland. When EnCana's CO_2 project began in 2000, it never really occurred to them that they were basically lab rats in the world's biggest laboratory. But they got the message four years later when several small ponds in a new gravel pit near their home began to go bad. A thick greenish yellow algae covered the once pristine water. A silvery slick oozed from the soil and traced an oily film over the surface. The Kerrs soon began finding the dead bodies of frogs, toads, birds, a goat, a rabbit, a cat and several wild animals near the pond. Some had horrible hemorrhages. Mosquitoes and groundhogs disappeared from the area. It became a dead zone. Then the Kerrs' household well went bad and something corrosive ate away the galvanized coating on the pipes. If that wasn't enough, in the fall of 2005, the gravel pit began literally to explode with gases. The Kerrs could hear the bang of the exploding earth. "At that point we evacuated our home," Jane says.

They were forced to live in a motel for five months until they found a house to rent in Weyburn. Jane works as a nurse and they live off the rent of their land, cattle and annual leasing fees from the oil wells on their property. So far water tests show the presence of large amounts of arsenic, bromine, phenols and hydrocarbons plus naphthalene (with pseudomonas bacteria). There is also an indication of the presence of the highly toxic carcinogenic benzo(a)pyrene, which is found in crude oil.

Living in the world's largest natural laboratory doesn't impress the Kerrs. Whether this leakage has been caused by the enormous amounts of pressurized CO_2 that EnCana is injecting into area wells is a possibility that the Kerrs don't believe EnCana has taken seriously. The company has dismissed their complaints.

In the letter to the couple dated June 4, 2007, EnCana's lawyer maintained that there is "[no] evidence of shallow groundwater or surface water impact from EnCana's operations."

"EnCana told us that the toxins in our well water and gravel pit are naturally forming," Jane says.

Cameron, who at sixty-one years old had been farming his land for more than forty years with his father and then with his own family, adds: "We've had gravel pits around our place since the sixties and you could dig a hole in the gravel and wait for the water to gather and clear out and then cup it in your hands and drink it. I sure wouldn't want to try that today."

The Kerrs believe it is significant that the contamination is surfacing through the gravel pit, which is the most porous sediment in an area that otherwise has deep, almost impenetrable clay.

"The [oil] wells around here are all old and they leak," Cameron says. "They have put so many chemicals into the ground over the years. Now EnCana is injecting a new technology (CO_2) down antiquated wells and suddenly, after living there for thirty years, we had to abandon our home."

EnCana promises that in the next phase of the project it will "increase knowledge and assessment of risks associated with leakage from abandoned wells caused by material and cement degradation."

For Jane and Cameron Kerr, who believe they have "unearthed a nightmare below," EnCana should have been checking for leaks years ago.

Meanwhile, Prime Minister Harper released his made-in-the-U.S.A. climate change policy, which essentially gutted the Kyoto Protocol. At least until 2010, Harper's policy exempts the entire oil sands industry from having to make any emission reductions. The government was promising 20 percent reductions in greenhouse gas emissions based on 2006 levels by 2020. Climate change scientists say a minimum 80 percent reduction overall is needed if this world is going to save itself from catastrophe. Clearly, Harper isn't buying it. Or doesn't care.

◆

May brings more bad news.

About 190 kilometres north of Redland and Rosebud the same assortment of hydrocarbons that had turned up in Debbie Singer's well has been discovered in a well at the Wagon Trail ranch near Ponoka. Here, over rolling parkland, Shawn and his wife, Ronalie Campbell, run 250 head of cattle. Their household well, which they also use to water cattle, has been fouled by methane, ethane, propane, butane and pentane. The water burns their skin and smells so bad even the cattle are reluctant to drink it. Hydrologists have fingerprinted the pollutants as coming from oil and gas wells, of which they have 32 on their property plus hundreds more within a ten-kilometre radius. Several surround the contaminated well. They first noticed the contamination in early 2006. Since then it has worsened. In the last two years several calves have been born blind and a host of cattle have had deformed joints such as knees that bend backwards. "We've been ranching for thirty-five years and we have never seen this," Ronalie says. "This is becoming a contamination disaster that the government is overlooking." Neither the government nor the energy companies will let them test the nearby oil and gas wells for leaks. They're so mad they held a press conference May 2nd at the Alberta legislature to denounce the government and energy company's refusal to correct the problem and get them clean water. "We used to be able to drink this water right out of the well," Shawn says. "Now we're having second thoughts if we should even stay here."

It seems that the errant gases of Alberta's leaking oil and gas wells are creeping into aquifers and to the surface. I call Jessica and she quips that maybe Canada could meet its Kyoto emission commitments just by fixing its tens of thousands of leaking wells. She's off to Ottawa to testify before a House environment committee hearing on water contamination. She says that since Alberta won't listen to her, maybe the feds will.

◆

I call Dr. O'Connor to catch up on any developments with the health problems at Fort Chipewyan. To my surprise, I track him down in a small town on the southern tip of Nova Scotia called Barrington Passage. He is holding a week-long clinic. "I was never so happy for this to come along," he says. "It's so good to be by the sea." He says he and his wife intend to move there by September 2007. Then he adds that he can't talk to me. "Right now I'm muzzled."

"You're what?"

"The government has filed a complaint against me with the Alberta College of Physicians and Surgeons, claiming that I am unduly alarming the people of Fort Chipewyan and causing them to mistrust Health Canada."

Elders in the community of Fort Chipewyan had told me they admired Dr. O'Connor because he was a voice where they didn't have a voice. Now the government is trying to silence him and even take away his licence.

A call to Health Canada confirms that three of their staff doctors filed the complaint, but they won't send me a copy or reveal the names of the complaining physicians or comment further on the issue.

I phone Dr. Michel Sauvé at the Fort McMurray hospital. "There are actually five people who are signatories on this complaint," he says. "Three are federal Health Canada employees based in Edmonton and then an Alberta Environment bureaucrat and also a communications person. The complaint contains an analysis of about thirteen pages of everything he has said in the media. It's pretty clear that it's politically motivated."

I suggest that with all the health and pollution problems in Fort McMurray, it's hard to understand why the government would worry about Dr. O'Connor. Dr. Sauvé explains that the Alberta government had launched an advertising campaign in the Maritimes to attract workers. A labour shortage is probably the only thing that can slow the pace of growth at the sands, so they are doing their best to attract workers from poor provinces. Before Christmas, Dr. O'Connor sent a letter to the *Halifax Chronicle-Herald* announcing he was leaving Fort McMurray and essentially warning Maritimers not to come because of poor health care, scant and expensive housing, limited education facilities and no hope of improvement. The letter was widely debated in Nova Scotia. "Arguably with one letter John undid that whole campaign," Dr. Sauvé says. "They decided to shut him up or shut him down."

I can hear him chuckling over the phone. What amuses him is the lunacy of it all—the government chasing away a doctor from a region that's desperately in need of physicians simply for expressing the health care concerns of the community. Meanwhile it approves huge oil sands projects on the flimsiest of environmental and social impact studies. "If we approved drugs in Canada based on the way we approve these projects, we would let drug companies get away with murder. These megaprojects have as much impact as any given drug."

I ask him what exactly he means by that.

He says that recent estimates put illegal drug use at as high as 25 percent of Fort McMurray's population. "Crystal meth has turned out to be a rampant problem. The rehabilitation potential for that drug is in the 5 percent range. So it's highly, highly addictive. And we have a generation of youth that now has the highest rate in Canada for non-graduation from high schools. So it's short-term gain of employment at the expense of education. We are riding the crest of this boom with really no investment in the future."

I tell him it's Natland's atomic bomb. He doesn't understand. I explain that it was something that happened a long time ago, when the government had plans to nuke Alberta to get the oil out of the sands. There's a silence at the other end of the line, and I can almost hear him say, "Are you kidding?"

TO THE LAST DROP

IN WHICH CHARLIE FAIRBANK UNVEILS
THE FUTURE

As soon as you turn south past the village of Wyoming and onto the Oil Heritage Road, the powerful smell of petroleum kicks back your nostrils. Decades after the oil industry left Lambton County, the scent still lingers over this flat southwestern Ontario landscape.

Local heritage societies are preparing for celebrations in 2008 to mark the one hundred and fifth anniversary of the discovery of oil in Oil Springs. I mention to Charlie Fairbank that a lot has happened since then. He laughs at the understatement and then blurts out: "It's unbelievable what that little discovery has turned this world into."

Miraculously, Charlie and five other landowners in Oil Springs continue to operate some of the old wells, using the original wooden pumpjacks and jerker lines to coax the oil to the surface. Charlie has 320 producing wells, varying in depth from 116 to 122 metres. His neighbours operate another 180 working wells. Together they pump about 35,000 barrels of light crude oil a year, which will fuel about 1,000 cars for 12 months. That's not much oil by any standard. Most of what they bring up is water. The oil floats to the surface and is skimmed off. The water table in the area is totally contaminated by petroleum. Drinking water is pumped in from Lake Huron.

Charlie's work to keep the oil fields pumping started as more a hobby and labor of love than a desire to make money. Four generations have passed since his great-grandfather John Henry Fairbank discovered oil and helped turn the area into Canada's first oil boom town. Charlie, who is sixty-six years old, is just trying to keep that memory alive and attract tourists to a forgotten region where arguably the modern era began with a discovery that kick started the most brilliant, inventive and destructive age in the history of mankind. The age of energy.

Even Charlie was surprised at the way the oil markets have soared, turning his hobby into a good living. Once a week Imperial Oil, which abandoned these wells years ago, sends a truck to haul away his oil. He says his break-even point is an average of US$17 a barrel. Prices in the last few years have of course catapulted his business way over that mark. They eerily evoke the last, desperate days of whale oil production that preceded the Oil Springs discovery. At US$60 a barrel, he and his neighbours gross about US$2.1 million a year. Out of that he pays a tiny crew of roughnecks—Ontario's last oil men—to maintain the pumps. Two local machine shops use belt-driven laths to manufacture replacement parts. Charlie's best well produces no more than one barrel of oil a day. In other words, he's scavenging the last drops left behind by a bygone era.

Charlie pulls his pickup over to the side of a gravel road where his crew is pulling pipe out of an oil well. The well's disabled wooden pump jack stands idle, its walker beam resting against a post. Crew member Duncan Barnes has been working this well since early morning, cleaning the pipes and replacing the pump valve. It's a dirty job. He's caked in oil. From his grey hard hat to his coveralls to his knee-high rubber boots and monkey grip rubber gloves, oil is everywhere. The soil he's standing in is soaked in oil. The air is thick with it. The portable derrick—or pull machine—that rises above him like the mast of an old steel sailboat is covered in it. There's really nothing he can do to get away from it. It's the fabric of his life—and of Charlie's life too.

In a sense, Oil Springs was always ahead of the game. The first to find oil, refine it and turn it into big business. The first to boom and the first to bust. And now they are the first scavengers. Demand grows and reserves peak. The economics are frayed but good for his kind of work. It's not a conceit to imagine that in another generation or two we'll all be like Charlie: energy scavengers picking through what's left of our reserves, boiling the oil sands and pumping abandoned wells to the last drop.

A dinosaur of the oil sands

THE THING ABOUT CLIMATE CHANGE IS THAT IT PUTS INTO question everything we are and everything.we ever thought we'd be. Since the initial publication of *Stupid to the Last Drop*, many readers have written to me expressing their horror at the environmental destruction in Alberta and questioning the sanity of our stewardship over this vast territory. I wish I could say the book did the same for our politicians, but not a chance. The oil and gas industry is a juggernaut. According to Alberta Premier Ed Stelmach, there is "no touching the brake," and he means it.

Initially, we regarded the oil sands with greedy excitement and blind support. Now we are starting to recoil at the monster we have created. The sad truth is that however deep our sensibilities are to this huge man-made environmental catastrophe, we allow it to continue unabated. It's become part of the way we are. Production will increase sixfold as we hurtle our way towards Prime Minister Stephen Harper's vision of Canada as an "energy superpower." According to industry estimates, there's almost $1 trillion worth of oil to be extracted from the sands over the next two decades. So much of our national economy is now hitched to this beast that it seems there's no stopping it. Our governments continue to insist that it is possible to confront the challenges of chemical pollution and climate change and, at the same time, continue to expand our economy. This is an illusion for which we will pay dearly.

Our growth-bound economics was tolerable a century ago when the world's population was only about 1.5 billion people and the pace of destruction was slow. We're now at 6.6 billion. More than ever before the future of our species hinges on the careful stewardship of the earth. More value has to be placed on the preservation of a marshland or of a vast boreal forest than on the unfettered operation of an oil sands project. Our leaders either don't understand this concept or refuse to accept it because these values pose such a political risk in a mercantile society geared towards jobs at any cost.

The ties that bind government and industry in Alberta have tightened. Now big business has even assumed control of state planning with barely a whimper of protest from Albertans. In 2007, Stelmach appointed oil executive Heather Kennedy to head Alberta's new Oil Sands Sustainable Development Secretariat, with a mandate to plan the next 20 years of oil sands development. Technically, Kennedy is on leave from her job as a senior vice-president of Suncor. But while charting out Alberta's oil sands' future, she will remain on Suncor's payroll. The company has loaned her to the government to oversee this vital job and the government reimburses Suncor for her salary. In Alberta, there is no longer any pretense.

Canada's greenhouse gas emissions (GHGs) continue to rise at an alarming rate. Despite our Kyoto commitments to decrease emissions to 6 percent below 1990 levels by 2012, they have increased by 25 percent and are forecast to reach 32 percent by 2010. Almost all of this change is due to the oil sands. Given that exploitation of the sands is only beginning, what has been an alarming situation threatens to deteriorate rapidly into something that is truly frightening.

Neither the Alberta nor the federal government, both run by parties with neo-conservative ideological commitments to the free market, has made any substantive plans for immediate reductions in greenhouse gas emissions or chemical pollution. Their policies are the policies of deferral. Alberta has announced that it will do nothing to curb growth for the next 20 years. Meanwhile, global warming is accelerating each decade at a record rate of 0.6 degrees Celsius (even higher in the Arctic), according to climate change models at the NASA Goddard Institute for Space Studies. This may seem insignificant, but when we consider that the earth's average temperature has risen a mere 5 to 6 degrees Celsius since the peak of the last ice age 20,000 years ago, a 0.6 rate of increase each decade is huge. It will lead to an average increase this century of at least 2 degrees Celsius, according to climate model projections.

Both the Alberta and federal governments have committed to reducing emissions to 14 percent below 2005 levels by 2050. To achieve this reduction they are relying almost exclusively on the untested technology of capturing and storing GHGs in old oil and gas wells and underground geological formations. Ottawa will spend $125 million to develop this carbon capture technology. If Jane and Cameron Kerr's farm near Weyburn, Saskatchewan, is any example—where gases exploded out of the ground and hydrocarbons contaminated their gravel pit pond and household well—there could be serious flaws in this technology. What if it doesn't work?

The cheap sell-off of our non-renewable resources contin-ues. The Alberta government's November 2007 Natural Gas Royalty Prices and Allowances report confirmed my contention that the royalties from the oil and gas industry essentially amounted to a fire sale—mostly to foreigners—of the nation's most valuable resources. The report noted that Alberta's royalties were the lowest in the world.

The ensuing public outcry, which was long overdue, spurred a hesitant Alberta government, whose party treasury is fat with oil and gas industry contributions, to increase royalties by a mere 20 percent. Industry executives and commentators wailed and threatened to slash their investments. But consider how much of an impact this will have on their bottom line: Paying another $1.4 billion a year is chicken feed to an industry that will generate an estimated $885 billion in gross income over the next 20 years. It seems that the industry's objections were just a ruse to keep the increase low, which they succeeded in doing. Not surprisingly, six months later—and almost immediately after the provincial election—the government announced its intention to roll back some aspects of the royalty increase claiming it needed to encourage even more deep-well oil and gas drilling.

Alberta's Heritage Fund remains at a mere $16 billion. Most of the money it earns from royalties goes directly into its daily expenditures where a good chunk is eaten up by inflation. In the last two years, Norway's fund, which is much younger than Alberta's, has increased to more than $400 billion from $306 billion. Norway took control of its oil business at an early stage. It's an extraordinary success story that shames our country.

The same generosity that Alberta offers the oil and gas industry unfortunately does not extend to the people of Rosebud, the natives of Athabasca and people living in other wilderness and rural areas where wells and waterways have been contaminated by oil and gas pollutants. In March of this year, the government sent letters to families living in rural areas around Rosebud announcing that it would no longer pay for water transportation to their homes. The reason? The government could find no proof that the hydrocarbons and chemicals poisoning their wells came from local drilling. The government still claims the old sop of industry that the pollution is "naturally forming."

Downriver from the oil sands in Fort Chipewyan, the local health authority commissioned a study by Dr. Kevin Timoney that was released in November 2007. It confirmed my contentions that the oil sands are poisoning the river system as well as the Peace-Athabasca Delta. Dr. Timoney found unsafe levels of arsenic, mercury and polycyclic aromatic hydrocarbons in

Lake Athabasca's fish, water and wildlife as well as in the sediments in the delta. "Concentrations of these contaminants, already high, appear to be rising," Dr. Timoney wrote. Yet the government has taken few steps to curtail the daily dumping of chemicals into the Athabasca River. First Nations' claims that this chemical pollution is causing high rates of cancer in communities downstream from the sand are simply denied. As of this writing, Dr. John O'Connor, who rang the alarm bell about high cancer rates at Fort Chipewyan, is still being hounded by the Alberta government and Health Canada for "unprofessional conduct" for demanding a health study of the community.

Yet the people of Alberta, in their wisdom, re-elected the Tories. Apathy in the province is so profound that only 41 percent of eligible voters even bothered to cast a ballot. Thus a party that for the last 18 years has sold out the province's environment and its economic future to the energy industry won a record majority of seats. Given the vital issues the province faces, this is unforgivable. Jobs today, but what of tomorrow?

One of Canada's great contemporary artists, Peter Doig, stated recently that everything in this nation lives on the edge of wilderness. As we gaze towards the back country from our lonely highways, our isolated cities and our lakeside cabins, we gaze into our soul. This is what we are destroying.

How stupid is that?

William Marsden, 2008

ACKNOWLEDGMENTS

MY FIRST EXPOSURE TO MANLEY NATLAND WAS A BRIEF
reference to him in Paul Chastko's book *Developing Alberta's Oil
Sands*. This sparked my research into Natland's history, his writings and his wonderfully evocative but totally loony idea of nuking
Alberta's oil sands. Natland's family as well as colleagues who
worked on Project Oil Sands filled in some of the missing pieces
to this strange and willful story. Chastko's book also helped me fill
in some of the background to the story of Karl Clark and Sidney
Ells. The rest comes from Clark's letters, diaries and various
papers and memorials. Ells has a remarkable and diverse opus of
work that includes his scientific research, fiction and non-fiction
writings as well as poetry and some wonderful pencil sketches
depicting his adventures in the north. He was a scientist and
adventurer who has never been given due credit for his work on
the oil sands. Several experts in the oil and gas industry took me
into the gas fields to experience first-hand the process of drilling
and bringing a well to life. Others explained the various technical
and scientific processes involved in coalbed methane, seismic
techniques, CO_2 sequestration and fracturing. Still others shared
tales of how to make—or lose—money in the oil business. Most

of them spoke to me on a private basis and didn't want to be named, fearing that it might affect their business. Thanks to Dan Woynillowicz and Chris Severson-Baker of the Pembina Institute and Professor Gordon Laxer of the Parkland Institute who took the time to talk to me about their personal experiences as free thinkers in the largely anti-intellectual world of the Klein Conservatives. Thanks to the people at the Oil Springs Museum and the Museum of Campbell River and the ranchers of Happy Valley and Rosebud. Thanks also to my wife, Janet, and my daughters Caroline and Katharine, for reading the manuscript and offering critical comments. Finally, I want to thank the editors and designers at Knopf Canada, especially publisher Diane Martin and associate publisher Michael Schellenberg. It's always a pleasure working with you.

William Marsden
wmarsden@sympatico.ca